One Thing I Know

One Thing I Know

How the Blind Man of John 9 Leads
an Audience toward Belief

Britt Leslie

PICKWICK Publications · Eugene, Oregon

ONE THING I KNOW
How the Blind Man of John 9 Leads an Audience toward Belief

Copyright © 2015 Britt Leslie. All rights reserved. Except for brief quotations in critical publications or reviews, no part of this book may be reproduced in any manner without prior written permission from the publisher. Write: Permissions. Wipf and Stock Publishers, 199 W. 8th Ave., Suite 3, Eugene, OR 97401.

Pickwick Publications
An Imprint of Wipf and Stock Publishers
199 W. 8th Ave., Suite 3
Eugene, OR 97401

www.wipfandstock.com

ISBN 13: 978-1-4982-0970-0

Cataloguing-in-Publication data:

Leslie, Britt.

One thing I know : how the blind man of John 9 leads an audience toward belief / Britt Leslie.

xii + 208 p. ; 23 cm. Includes bibliographical references.

ISBN 13: 978-1-4982-0970-0

1. Bible. N.T.—John IX—Criticism, interpretation, etc. 2. Healing of the man born blind (Miracle). I. Title.

BS2615.2 L47 2015

Manufactured in the U.S.A.   04/15/2015

For Tracey, my βοηθός

Contents

List of Figures and Tables | viii
Acknowledgments | ix
Abbreviations | xi

1 Introduction | 1
2 Patterns and Structures in the Text of John 9 | 25
3 Narrative Analysis | 68
4 Social Science Analysis | 116
5 Irony, Humor, Sarcasm, and Wit | 154
6 Conclusions | 179

Bibliography | 197

Figures and Tables

Table 1.1   Pattern of Verses 4–5 | 18

Table 1.2   Pattern of Verses 3–4 | 18

Table 3.1   Contrast of the Healed Man with the Pharisees | 81

Figure 3.1 Widening of the Healed Man's Understanding of Jesus | 89

Table 3.2   Plot Tensions and Resolution in John 9 | 110

Table 5.1   How Humor Works | 156

Table 5.2   Shift from Proper to Improper | 157

Table 5.3   Reversal of Evaluation | 157

Table 5.4   Absurd, Abnormal, and Quirky Logic | 158

Table 5.5   Example of Irony using John 9:5 | 160

Table 5.6   Steps for Irony with example from John 9:5 | 161

Table 5.7   Irony, Giving Glory to God | 171

Table 5.8   Humor, Surely You Don't Want to Become His Disciples | 174

Table 5.9   Pun, Here is a Sight to See | 174

Table 6.1   Formatted Modern-Style Text | 182

Table 6.2   Unformatted, Ancient-Style Text | 182

Acknowledgments

I WISH TO PUBLICALLY thank the following, without whom, none of this would be possible. Dr. David Rhoads professor emeritus from Lutheran School of Theology at Chicago (LSTC) where I received my PhD, and Dr. Thomas Boomershine professor emeritus from United Theological Seminary (UTS) in Dayton, OH where I received both my MDiv and MA. As my dissertation advisor, Dr. Rhoads provided immense academic and personal support. As my MA thesis advisor Dr. Boomershine showed likewise academic and personal support and introduced me to the areas of study utilized in this work. He also introduced me to Dr. Rhoads who shares the same passion in these areas and cultivated mine. Of course I wish to thank the institutions LSTC and UTS themselves for providing the academically and spiritually nurturing environments in which I learned.

I wish to thank the members of my dissertation colloquy at LSTC who gave much needed advice and constructive criticism: Dr. Esther Menn, Dr. Barbara Rossing, and Dr. Raymond Pickett.

Additionally, Dr. Larry Welborn currently of Fordham University, professor at UTS at the time I was there, and Dr. Thomas Dozeman of UTS were both instrumental in nurturing my passion for exegesis. Thank you both.

I wish to thank Dr. K. C. Hanson my editor for valuable input and Wipf and Stock publishing for partnering with me in bringing my dissertation to print.

Finally, but certainly not least, I want to thank my beloved wife, the Rev. Tracey Leslie, for her undying love and support in so much more than my academic endeavors. Words fail where emotion runs deep.

Abbreviations

ABD	*The Anchor Bible Dictionary.* 6 vols. Edited by David Noel Freedman. New York: Doubleday, 1992.
Ann.	Tacitus, *Annals*
BDAG	W. Bauer, F. W. Danker, W. F. Arndt, and F. W. Gingrich. *A Greek-English Lexicon of the New Testament and Other Early Christian Literature.* 3rd ed. Chicago: University of Chicago Press, 2000
Brut.	Cicero, *Brutus*
EDNT	*Exegetical Dictionary of the New Testament.* 3 vols. Edited by Horst Balz and Gerhard Schneider. Grand Rapids, Michigan: Eerdmans, 1993
Inst.	Quintilian, *Institutes of Oratory*
L&N	J. P. Louw and E. A. Nida, eds. *Greek-English Lexicon of the New Testament Based on Semantic Domains.* New York: United Bible Societies, 1988
LSJ	H. G. Liddell, R. Scott, and H. S. Jones. *A Greek-English Lexicon.* Oxford: Clarendon, 1940
m.	Mishnah
NA27	Eberhard Nestle, Erwin Nestle, Barbara Aland, and Kurt Aland. *Novum Testamentum Graece.* 27th ed. Stuttgart: Deutsche Bibelgesellschaft, 2007
Nic. Eth.	Aristotle, *Nicomachean Ethics*

NIDB	*The New Interpreter's Dictionary of the Bible.* Edited by Katharine Doob Sakenfeld. Nashville: Abingdon, 2006–2009
Noc. Att.	Aulus Gellius, *Attic Nights*
NRSV	*The Holy Bible: Containing the Old and New Testaments with the Apocryphal/Deuterocanonical Books : New Revised Standard Version.* New York: Oxford University Press, 1989
Phdr.	Plato, *Phaedrus*
Phil.	Sophocles, *Philoctetes*
Plut.	Plutarch
TDNT	*Theological Dictionary of the New Testament.* 10 vols. Edited by G. Kittel and G. Friedrich. Translated by G. W. Bromiley. Grand Rapids: Erdmans, 1964–1976
TDNTA	*Theological Dictionary of the New Testament: Abridged in One Volume.* Translated by G. W. Bromiley. Grand Rapids: Eerdmans, 1985
Tim.	Plato, *Timaeus*
Hist.	Tacitus, *History*

1

Introduction

The Question for Investigation

It is my thesis that the episode[1] of the blind man in John 9 is designed to evoke in hearers[2] a relationship of trust in Jesus as light and an experience of Jesus as light of the world. Light is thought of in antiquity as both a source of life and evidence of life. This is explicit in John where we see Jesus described as both "light" and "life" (John 1:3–5). This thesis about chapter 9 is in line with the overall stated purpose of the gospel of John, namely that the gospel was written "so that" (ἵνα) you may come to believe that Jesus is the Messiah, the Son of God, and that through believing you may have life in his name" (John 20:31 NRSV).

I wish to investigate my thesis by use of a synthetic multidisciplinary approach. My hope is that in combining the disciplines of narrative criticism, social-science criticism, discourse studies, and performance criticism, an analytical and interpretive benefit will be yielded which exceeds that of simply adding the individually yielded insights of each discipline.

Thesis

The overall purpose of the Gospel of John is to *elicit in the hearer* trust (πιστεύω) in Jesus (John 20:31), a relationship that brings with it abundant life (ζωή) (John 10:10). Life in the Gospel of John is bound up with

---

1. In this work I will use "episode" to refer to a fully developed story within the larger gospel story. "Story" will refer to the gospel story as a whole.

2. I will refer to John's audience as "hearers" or "audience" rather than "readers" given the likelihood that most would have experienced the gospel as read *to* them by a "reader" or storyteller.

the concept of light (φῶς) (1:4). John 9, like the larger gospel narrative, seeks to elicit in the hearer, trust in Jesus and an experience of Jesus as light (= life) of the world. Specifically, John 9 accomplishes the characterization of Jesus by demonstrating (primarily showing rather than telling) the direct effects of this light on a man lacking inner light (blind) from birth. Such a person is the perfect subject to demonstrate Jesus's effect as light of the world. Because he was born blind, any light (light = sight) that he acquires must have come from Jesus his healer.[3]

I shall attempt to demonstrate how the episode of the man born blind functions rhetorically to kindle in the hearer light, that is, a relationship of trust (πιστεύω) with Jesus as light of the world. Note that I have chosen the English word "trust" here for the Greek verb πιστεύω rather than the usual translation of "believe" (as in the above quoted NRSV translation). I think that "trust" more fully captures the nuance of the Johannine use of πιστεύω, which is relational.[4] The modern English speaking Westerner, for the most part, can understand "believe" on the level of a purely mental exercise, where "trust," in addition to mental assent, implies more of a relational investment.

In summary there are two parts to the above thesis. First, it is my thesis that John 9 asserts and demonstrates a statement about Jesus: *Jesus is the light of the world who brings life.* Second, it is my thesis that through John 9 the author attempts to *elicit in the hearer trust in Jesus as light.* The second part of this thesis goes a step beyond the first part from an *assertion about* Jesus to an attempt to *elicit a response*, namely a relationship of trust, between the hearer of John's Gospel and Jesus.

In fact, John 9 seems to almost provide a template for the incorporation of a member of the Johannine community. It is the story of a person who receives his sight, both physical and spiritual, is then cast out from his own people for witnessing that his healer is from God. He is sought out by his healer, trusts and worships. The central figure of the Johannine community then pronounces that the representatives of the broader (expelling) community abide in sin.

John 9, and particularly the climactic scene vv. 35–39, functions within the rest of the gospel to accomplish that expressed goal of trust

---

3. This statement makes more sense when one remembers that vision in antiquity is conceived of by the majority of people as one's inner light shining forth from one's heart *out of* one's eyes in order to touch objects beheld. This will be discussed in chapter 3.

4. Even though in my title I retain the more traditional translation.

in Jesus in two ways. First, it removes the negative cultural consequences which come from trust, namely expulsion from the synagogue (9:22; 12:42; 16:2) and being removed from one's community. This is demonstrated when Jesus seeks out and elicits the trust of the healed man after his expulsion. Second, this initiation into the new community of Jesus the Good Shepherd (cf. 10:3–4) happens specifically through trust (cf. 9:35, 38) in Jesus. Furthermore, this is an initiation into a community where one will never be "cast out" (ἐκβάλλω, 6:37 cf. 934). The members of the synagogue community may well be "cast out" (ἐκβάλλω, 9:34) by their leaders, but those who are part of the community that Jesus establishes (John 6:37; cf. 1:12) will *never* be "cast out" (6:37) by their leader.

Previous Investigations

Historical Critical/Purpose of the Gospel

Martyn

In *History and Theology in the Fourth Gospel*,[5] Louis J. Martyn attempts to link the Fourth Gospel with the history and experiences of a particular community, the Johannine Community. Essentially Martyn sees John 9 as a kind of narrative autobiography of the Johannine Community. They are made to see who Jesus really is, come to belief, and are expelled from the synagogue because of their witness. He essentially sees three phases of the community's development. 1) Prior to the 80s CE, those who believed in Jesus as Messiah continued living life as a Jew and engaging in synagogue worship. 2) Sometime after the 80s a middle period existed within the community where they were viewed with suspicion over the community's claims about Jesus and eventually were expelled from the synagogue (9:33; 12:42; 16:2). The *Brikat ha-minim* was used as an instrument to enforce this. This is acted out in John 9 as an autobiographical drama. 3) The expelled community, gradually forming an identity apart from the synagogue and Judaism, began to address the Christian Jews who remained in the synagogue. They argued that there could be no middle road and one had to be a part of the Johannine community openly (cf. 12:42–43).

---

5. Martyn, *History and Theology*.

Brown

Raymond Brown traces out his theory in his Anchor Bible commentary on John, his book *The Community of the Beloved Disciple*, and also his Anchor Bible commentary on the Johannine Epistles (which contains much of *Community*).[6] His reconstruction of the history of the community is more complex than Martyn's. He sees four phases in the life of the community.

1) Prior to the writing of the Gospel, the community begins with the Beloved Disciple, an historical figure and ex-disciple of John the Baptist. He is a follower of Jesus from the beginning, but not one of the twelve. The Beloved Disciple links the historical Jesus with the Johannine community.

2) As the Gospel was being written, the community began to be in conflict with various groups: Jews, Jewish Christians with a lower Christology, followers of John the Baptist, and "crypto-Christians." The conflict with the Jews may have been from the admittance of Samaritans into the community. An increasingly higher Christology developed and those who did not share this Christology were also considered to be in conflict with the community. The "crypto-Christians," or Jews who believed in Jesus but did not confess openly, were considered to be in conflict with the community as well (cf. 12:42–43). We get the picture of a community with a high Christology that sees itself as not of this world and in conflict with "the world." The community then takes a closed stance against outsiders.

It is during this phase that expulsion of Johannine Christians from the synagogue takes place. This has the effect of sharpening the isolation of the community. The community is therefore understandably very critical (12:42; cf. 9:22–23; 19:38) of those who believe, but because they do not confess Jesus as Christ, remain in synagogue life and community.

3) When the epistles were being written by a different author than the Gospel, there were internal divisions and splits. These grew from differing interpretations within the community of the Fourth Gospel itself. Brown sees the orthodox community[7] now moving in the direction of the larger church and the secessionist (cf. 1 John 2:19) moving toward what would be known as docetism.

---

6. Brown, *John I–XII*; Brown, *Community*; Brown, *Epistles*; and also, Brown, *Introduction to John*.

7. Simply those of the viewpoint represented by the epistles.

4) After the letters were written the orthodox community eventually merges with the larger church which has accepted the high Christology. Brown points to the writings of Ignatious of Antioch (around 110 CE) as evidence for this merge. The secessionists eventually become Gnostics. As specific as all this sounds (even more so in *The Community of the Beloved Disciple*), Brown himself acknowledges the highly tentative nature of the endeavor by saying that "perhaps" should be placed before each assertion.[8]

Others

While Brown and Martyn theorize that various parts of the Gospel can be attributed to various circumstances in the life of one group (the Johannine Community), *George Richter*[9] theorizes that the work of various groups is reflected within the Gospel, there is the influence of several different groups that built progressively on the work of the other. *Cullman*[10] theorizes that there were two groups of followers of Jesus, the twelve disciples from the Galilee in the North and those associated with the Beloved Disciple from the South in Judea. *Langbrandtner*[11] argued that the Gospel was originally written by someone with a Gnostic outlook and was reworked by an anti-Gnostic redactor. These two perspectives represented a major struggle within the Johannine Community for about 40 years.

The common thread in all of the above authors is that in one way or another, each seeks to use historical-critical analysis of the Gospel (and perhaps epistles) to discern a particular geographically located community or communities and then discern the circumstances of that community or communities in the working out (writing, redacting etc.) of the Fourth Gospel.

---

8. Brown, *Introduction to the New Testament*, 374.
9. Richter, "Eschatologie."
10. Cullmann, *Johannine*.
11. Langbrandtner, *Weltferner Gott oder Gott der Liebe*.

Sectarian understanding of the Johannine Community

Meeks[12] takes a sociological approach and analyzes the ascent/descent motif in John. He concludes that the Johannine community is "sectarian"[13] and isolated. Of John he states, "If one 'believes' what is said in this book, he is quite literally taken out of the ordinary world of social reality. Contrariwise, this can hardly happen unless one stands already within the counter-cultural group or at least in some ambivalent relationship between it and the larger society."[14] Although not all scholars would use the word "sectarian" or "sect" to describe Johannine Christianity, Meeks's conclusions of an isolationist society have greatly influenced theories of the Johannine community.[15] This influenced Neyrey's conclusions about the Johannine community as well.

Neyrey[16] argues that the high Christology in John indicates a revolt against prevailing views. He uses Mary Douglas's group/grid model to argue that the community revolted against the prevailing social system. The dualism found in John is used to create boundary markers that cordon off the community from other social groups.

Malina and Rohrbaugh both[17] argue from the perspective of anti-language that the evangelist is writing to and for an "anti-society," a society that exists outside the usual social constructs, is isolationist and close knit. anti-language serves to reinforce the value system and ideology of the anti-society.

Nonsectarian understanding of the Johannine Community

In opposition to the idea that the Johannine Community is sectarian (or at least wrought with isolationist tendencies) stands the work of Carson and Köstenberger. Carson argues that John 20:31 should be understood to mean, 'that you may believe that the Christ, the Son of God, is Jesus.' This is meant in the sense of coming to belief rather than continuing

---

12. Meeks, "Man from Heaven," 44–72.
13. Ibid., 71.
14. Ibid.
15. Kysar, "Whence and Whither," 69.
16. Neyrey, *Ideology of Revolt*.
17. Malina, "Maverick"; Rohrbaugh, "Gospel of John," 257–63; Malina and Rohrbaugh, *Social-Science Commentary on John*.

in belief as most would see it.[18] Under the direction of Carson, Köstenberger[19] argues in his dissertation that Jesus has been sent by the Father to accomplish a threefold mission: 1) To perfectly do his Father's will, 2) to come from and return to the Father through obedience to death on the cross and resurrection, 3) to be shepherd/teacher who calls his followers to bear fruit (cf. John 15). He sees the disciples' mission of the as similar but different. As Jesus is sent to do the will of the Father, so the disciples are sent to do the will of Jesus. This is done by demonstrating love and unity. He argues the Gospel's primary purpose is evangelical because the disciples are commissioned by Jesus and sent into the world (20:19–23). He also argues that the Fourth Gospel is primarily concerned with the nature of Jesus and is therefore a missionary document.

Comparing the Philo community, the Qumran community, and the Johannine community, Fuglseth[20] concludes that the Johannine community is more of a cult than sectarian or part of the mainstream body of Christianity. He studies the Philo community and determines that it represents the kind of writing found in a parent body. The Qumran community, he concludes, is mort representative of an isolated or sectarian group. The Johannine community falls in between. Not totally or even mostly isolationist, but also not part of the mainstream of Christianity at the end of the first century. The proper understanding of the community, he argues, is that of a cult. This is a group that claims to have a special kind of revelation but is also not entirely cut off from the main group nor closed off to the inflow of new members.

Ling[21] rejects the idea of sectarianism in favor of what he calls "virtuoso religion." He says, "the defining character of virtuoso religion is its ability to maintain alternative structures that present a reversed image of society whilst remaining within its ideological and institutional structures"[22]—a kind of "in the world not of the world" approach. He sees in the Fourth Gospel a very real concern for, and mission to, the poor in Judea. He notes, among other passages, John 9 as evidence of Jesus's ministry to the poor and also 12:1–8 as evidence of a common fund kept at Bethany (house of the poor) for the poor.

---

18. Carson, "Purpose"; Carson, "Syntactical."
19. Köstenberger, *Missions*.
20. Fuglseth, *Johannine Sectarianism*.
21. Ling, *The Judean Poor*.
22. Ibid., 205.

Bauckham/Klink

Bauckham and his doctoral advisee Klink hold that the Gospels were written for a much larger audience than one particular community.[23] Since B. H. Streeter,[24] the predominate assumption in scholarship has been that the gospels were written for and by a member or members of self-contained and geographically specific groups of Christians with each group having a geographical and sociological distance from the other that accounts for the differences among the gospels. Bauckham challenges that assumption. He argues that written communication is for the purpose of communicating across distances and that stories by and for particular communities would prefer oral communication. He also argues that early Christian leaders were, according to Paul's letters and Acts, highly mobile, thus making geographical separation between communities much less of an issue. He sees the gospels (including John) as ancient biography. As such they are designed to appeal to a wider, rather than a narrower, audience.

Klink adds to Bauckham by arguing for a relational model of community for the Gospel of John rather than a geographically localized one. In other words, the intended audience of the Fourth Gospel may exist in many geographical locations. Based on an examination of the kind of audience that the Fourth Gospel suggests, he argues that the audience was more like much of early Christianity and less like an isolated or sectarian community. As evidence he points to things like the word "messiah" being translated, the beloved disciple needing to be introduced to the audience, and the need for some geographical references to be explained.

Summary: open, evangelical and reinforcing

While I agree with Brown's statement that "perhaps" should be inserted in every sentence of the above reviewed historical reconstructions of the Johannine Community, I also think the same "perhaps" should be inserted in the various theories that reject a single localized community. Klink has much to offer, however, in his redefinition of community as relational over against geographical. The presence of relational communities does not necessarily exclude geographical ones as well. For example, John may

---

23. Bauckham, *Gospels for All Christians*; Bauckham, *Testimony*; Klink, *Sheep*.

24. Streeter, *Four Gospels*.

well be suited (as Klink and Bauckham argue) for a more general audience in a multiplicity of locations. I would cite statements such as "all who come to me," "whoever trusts in . . . ," "if anyone . . . ," etc., as evidence of this (see John 1:12; 3:15, 33, 36; 6:35, 47, 51, 57; 5:24; 6:35, 37, 40; 7:17, 37; 8:12, 51–52; 10:9; 11:25–26; 12:26, 44–45; 13:20; 14:9, 24; 15:6, 23). However, specific references to being cast out of the synagogue and fearing the Jewish authorities, as well as the highly polemical speeches against "the Jews" and the Pharisees and even the antagonistic relationship with "the world," also seem to imply some very specific historical circumstances of conflict with outsiders. I would argue that John's Gospel contains too many invitations to trust and has too many examples of those who come to trust to be understood as entirely closed off or sectarian (cf. 1:39, 46; 4:23, 29, 53; 6:26–29; 35–40; 66–68; 7:37–39; 10:38; 11:42). At the same time this does not rule out specific conflict with one or more synagogue communities. One must also notice the abundant references to "remaining/abiding/dwelling in . . ." and "being in," particularly in John 14–17 (cf. 8:31). These references would seem to indicate that the Gospel is intended for an audience who already trusts, written for the purpose of strengthening or at least maintaining that trust. The two options are not mutually exclusive. It makes sense, to use a Johannine metaphor, that a story designed to bring a sheep into the fold would also be designed to prevent that sheep from immediately wandering off![25] I believe that the Fourth Gospel is both evangelical (seeks to elicit belief) and reinforcing (seeks to maintain existing belief). Also, while it is most likely the product of real historical issues of persecution and expulsion, the community is open (not sectarian or isolated). This will be the premise from which I operate in the remainder of the dissertation. I will seek to answer: how does John 9 work within the whole gospel story to elicit (not mutually exclusive with maintaining) belief?

Narrative

There have been several undertakings that are either full narrative-critical investigations of the Gospel of John, or works that investigate a particular aspect of narrative criticism. I will outline ones that have significance for my investigation of John 9.

---

25. Carson, "Purpose," 649, also notes this.

In 1970 David Wead authored *The Literary Devices in John's Gospel* wherein he proceeds to investigate a number of literary devices that the author of John uses in order to fulfill his expressed purpose of trust (20:31). While this is not a full narrative-critical analysis, it contains many aspects of narrative-critical study that will be helpful to any investigation of John in general and John 9 in particular.

Wead begins the study with an analysis of the *point of view* that the narrator takes. This point of view is described as that of a "post resurrection" point of view. In other words, the narrator begins telling the story already knowing the end and knowing the implications of that end. This allows the author to break into the story at various points to explain the significance of an event in light of the end of the story. Because the narrator can share this point of view with the audience, it allows the author to paint the antagonists in the story in a undesirable way. These antagonists are those who fail to understand who Jesus is and where he is from. The origins of Jesus play a significant role in John 9 (being from God vs. not being from God, cf. 16, 30, 33).

Wead moves on from point of view to analyze the use of the sign in John. He investigates both the background of σημεῖον and the specific Johannine use. The use of *signs* by the author points to the legitimacy of Jesus as one from God and as the revealer of God to the world. This issue is also of significance for John 9 (cf. 16).

In his investigation of *irony* in John, Wead did not yet have the benefit of Wayne Booth's seminal work in 1974, *A Rhetoric of Irony*.[26] Even so, Wead makes a strong analysis beginning with irony in antiquity and moving on to evaluate specific themes where irony is used in John. He identifies five such themes: King of the Jews; Origin of the Christ; Jesus superior to the Patriarchs; the Destruction of the Temple; and Issues of Discipleship. In John 9, the issue of Jesus's *origin* is crucial. In addition, the theme of Jesus's *superiority to Moses* and the issue of *discipleship* also play a role.

Finally, Wead investigates the Johannine use of *metaphor*. To this end he identifies and discusses four Johannine metaphorical discourses: Jesus as the bread of life, the water of life, the door and the good shepherd (actually door and good shepherd are two metaphors within the same discourse), and the true vine. What he does not investigate is Jesus as light of the world. This metaphor for Jesus is significant in chapters 8 and

---

26. Booth, *Rhetoric*.

9 and is foreshadowed in the prologue. I will investigate this metaphor in the course of this dissertation.

Of course *Anatomy of the Fourth Gospel: A Study in Literary Design* (1983) by R. Alan Culpepper is the first full and complete narrative-critical analysis of the Gospel of John. Soon after this work and building off of it, Jeffrey Lloyd Staley wrote *The Print's First Kiss: A Rhetorical Investigation of the Implied Reader in the Fourth Gospel* (1988).

Culpepper divides and organizes his analysis of John into narrative-critical categories: narrator and point of view, narrative time, plot, characters, implicit commentary (where such things as misunderstanding, double meanings, irony and symbolism are used to provide comment and guidance toward properly understanding the rhetoric of the narrative), and the implied audience.[27] All of these categories of analysis that Culpepper applies to the Gospel as a whole can be applied to specific stories with the Gospel as well. Culpepper's aim was to analyze the rhetoric of John by analyzing each of its parts. He concludes that the most significant or compelling way in which the author communicates the narrative values is by the use of implicit commentary. Because implicit commentary is subtle, it carries greater rhetorical force. For example, as any given Johannine misunderstanding is exposed, the author has in one act both *warned* against the dangers of misunderstanding, *corrected* a misunderstanding, and *presented* a correct doctrine about Jesus. It will be my goal to analyze John 9 both as it stands on its own (its own internal rhetoric) and as it stands as part of the Gospel (what role in the Gospel's rhetoric does it play). In addition, the subtleties involved in implicit commentary seem to depend on phenomenon which may be culturally sensitive such as humor, irony, and shared cultural values. Specifically, I wish to explore how an ancient Eastern culture (embedded kinship, honor/shame, etc.) might perceive the story. One thing I would like to add to the narrative method spearheaded by Culpepper is an extra dimension of interpretation based on an understanding of the culture. In theory this is not a novel idea. Mark A. Powell points out that the social setting is part of the overall setting, along with spatial setting and temporal setting.[28]

Staley's work mentioned above builds on Culpepper's but focuses more on the effect that the narration of the story has on the "implied reader" (what I will be calling the implied audience). His premise is that

---

27. He uses the narrative critical term *implied reader* about which see n2 above.
28. Powell, *Narrative Criticism*, 70 and 74.

the narrator is not always reliable and sometimes sets the audience up for a fall, trick or trap of some sort. Although I do not necessarily agree with that premise, the idea and task of gauging reader (audience) response is an important one. It is also a task (I believe) which cannot fully be investigated without a thorough attempt to understand how the audience might interpret something from its *particular cultural perspective.*

Another work which must not be ignored is *Revelation in the Fourth Gospel* (1986) by Gail O'Day. In this work she focuses on the use of irony as a tool to reveal theological truth in the Fourth Gospel and proceeds with an analysis of John 4:4–42. Near the end of her analysis O'Day concludes that one must enter into the full imagery of the text in order to be fully affected by its values and its revelatory power. She states that, "the locus of revelation lies in the Gospel text and in the world created by the words of that text."[29] I agree, but what I would hope to add to the discipline of narrative analysis is a thorough investigation into the way that "world" would have been understood by the people of its original culture and time.

Stibbe of course has gained much ground on the narrative front in Johannine studies.[30] In addition to adapting elements of narrative study in his interpretations, he uses other disciplines as well, integrating them into the narrative approach. For example, in *John as Storyteller* he integrates social and historical methods into his analysis.

Finally, Craig Koester's work with symbolism should also be instructive.[31] (Although not a purely narrative approach, I will discuss it here.) It is Koester's conclusion that the variety of symbols in the Gospel leads the audience, who are from below, to know and trust the one who is from above. Only through symbol and metaphor can one from below begin to understand and trust the one from above. The symbols of light and blindness both play a part in revealing Jesus the light of the world in John 9. Powell notes that symbols often need to be understood through the lens of the culture.[32] This is particularly true for John's Gospel in relation to light, darkness, sight, and blindness. They were thought of quite differently in the first century Mediterranean than we think of them today.

---

29. O'Day, *Revelation*, 114.
30. Stibbe, *John as Storyteller*; Stibbe, *John's Gospel*; Stibbe, *John as Literature*.
31. Koester, *Symbolism*. This is a significantly revised edition since the 1995 edition.
32. Powell, *Narrative Criticism*, 29.

Social World

In examining the social-science aspect, I hope to build upon several works. First there is the general social-science commentary on the Gospel of John by Malina and Rohrbaugh.[33] There are a number of "reading scenarios" that Malina and Rohrbaugh identify as pertinent to John 9. First is the aspect of *sin*, which is defined as a breach of interpersonal relations. In the social world of John 9, all suffering and illness was thought to have personal causes (as opposed to our modern assumptions of genetic or microbiological causes). Malina and Rohrbaugh place Jesus in the category of a *folk healer* who treated the afflicted as "out patients" and accepted the descriptions of their various afflictions at face value. Folk healers were acknowledged by the community to be capable of restoring health. This brought Jesus into conflict with the Pharisees who were concerned with the Torah as spelled out in the Great Tradition of their scribal elders—a tradition that heavily emphasized issues of *purity and defilement*.

More specifically with respect to health and healthcare are the works of John Pilch, *Healing in the New Testament*, and Dawson, *Healing, Weakness and Power*.[34] Both examine the concept of sickness from the sociological standpoint of the New Testament world and contrast it with our modern and Western perspective. Pilch places the concept of sickness in the context of the ancient eastern personality and he attempts to provide an understanding of how such a personality would experience both illness and healing.

As part of the ancient personality, Malina, Rohrbaugh, and Pilch all speak of the three zones of interaction with the world, or a *three zoned personality*. This system consists of three interrelated aspects of personality. These are the zone of *emotion-fused thought*, which is symbolized by the eyes (organs of perception) and the heart (organ of thought and understanding); the zone of *self-expressive speech*, which is symbolized by the ears and mouth; and the zone of *purposeful action*, which is symbolized by the hands and feet. Each describes a part of the human being and a way in which the human being interacts with the world. An affliction affecting any one of these zones would have held certain significance with respect to how the afflicted person was understood to be limited.

Next there are the concepts of honor and shame. Since honor is a primary value to the ancient Easterner, and since all public interaction

---

33. Malina and Rohrbaugh, *Social-Science Commentary on John*.
34. Pilch, *Healing*; Dawson, *Healing, Weakness and Power*.

was an exercise in winning or losing honor, the interaction between the characters in John 9 is significant. Jesus and his disciples interact,[35] Jesus and the man born blind interact, the man and the townspeople interact, the man and the Pharisees interact twice, the Pharisees and the man's parents interact, and Jesus and the Pharisees interact. In each interaction, honor is won and lost. This will prove significant with respect to the characterization of the various characters.

Purity is another issue in this episode. The Pharisees wished to maintain a pure and undefiled nation by the observance of Torah and the Great Tradition. The conflict and tension of this story centers around a Sabbath day healing and the possible performance of creative work. If purity is to be maintained, the actions of Jesus and the results of those actions (a healed man) must be dealt with. In terms of purity and defilement, the continued presence of God with the nation was the issue at stake!

Finally, I will examine the concepts of light and blindness in antiquity. The concept of light is closely associated with life in the ancient Greco-Roman culture. This is also reflected in John 1:4 and 8:12. Jesus as light of the world not only restores sight to the man born blind but life as well. The act of seeing is thought of by most in Jesus's time as extramission. Light comes forth from ones heart and through the lamp of the eyes. A man *born* blind would be thought of as having darkness in ones heart. Jesus, the light of the world, replaces the darkness with his own light—a narrative working out of John 1:5.

Each of the above social-science issues identified play a role in the author's attempt to present Jesus as light of the world. I will build off the work of the above authors in each of these areas and present an overall sociological picture of the events in this story. In so doing, I hope to present a fuller understanding of the "world" in which the story takes place.

Performance Criticism

David Rhoads describes performance criticism as an emerging discipline that draws upon a number of New Testament methodologies.[36] This approach works with the understanding that all New Testament texts are

---

35. One might argue this is not really a public interaction yet, while it is an in-group interaction, there is no indication that it is indoors. They are "walking along" (Καὶ παράγων). However, although honor is not won or lost within an in-group, Jesus must still respond publically to the disciples question.

36. Rhoads, "Performance Part I"; Rhoads, "Performance Part II."

either written records of a performance or were written in order to be performed. The essential goal of performance criticism is to analyze a biblical text by studying it with the performance event in mind. By both studying a text for clues about how it might be preformed and by analyzing actual contemporary performances, Rhoads argues that one gains fresh insights into the original experience of the New Testament literature. He then goes on to suggest ways in which one might proceed to analyze a text using various categories of performance. I hope to build on Rhoads's work by attempting to assess what the rhetorical impact might be for a performance of John 9—how an original audience might have experienced it. Note that this is different than reader response criticism in that the categories for analysis are based on oral performances experienced by a group of hearers. One might more appropriately call this method hearer response criticism.

Prior to Rhoads's article, Shiner published a work on the performance of Mark.[37] In it he describes the fact that ancient speeches and stories were performed, and defends the premise that a first century gospel (Mark specifically) would have been performed. He then goes on to describe the various types of ancient performance, such as private and public readings, storytelling, or drama. Next he looks at various components of ancient performance, such as emotion, delivery, gestures and movement, applause lines, and the ancient audience.

As Rhoads has noted, performance criticism benefits from a number of different methodologies or biblical criticisms.[38] Each methodology— such as social-science criticism, narrative criticism, discourse analysis, historical criticism—helps to inform an understanding of an ancient performance. Understanding the performance helps us to understand the impact such a performance would have had on an ancient audience. This impact is precisely what I hope to understand for John 9. Based on multiple disciplines (discourse, narrative, social science, and irony) I want to answer how John 9 would have been performed and how would such a performance lead an audience toward trust.

---

37. Shiner, *Proclaiming*.
38. Rhoads, "Performance Part II," 165.

Course of This Investigation

Narrative

It is my plan to proceed with an analysis of John 9 with narrative criticism being the overarching discipline. Narrative criticism of course seeks to enter into, analyze, and understand the narrative world presented by the text. What I hope to accomplish is to add a social-science analysis of the events and characters described in the narrative in order to present an even fuller understanding of the narrative world presented by the text. Further, I will analyze the way in which that story is told. In other words, I will do an analysis of the patterns and verbal connections that may be present in the telling of the narrative. While narrative analysis has been present as a discipline since the early 1980s and is no longer "new," I hope to expand its horizons by incorporating both social science and an analysis of linguistic patterns into the workings of narrative criticism.

There are at least two interpretive areas I will address in the investigation of the man born blind. These are *language* and *cultural distance* (i.e. the distance from which a modern western interpreter is removed from the cultural assumptions and understandings of an ancient eastern audience). While this can be said of any biblical text, I will outline in the next two sections how each might impact an interpretation of John 9. This chapter will come after an investigation of the language and syntax.

Language

With respect to language, not only the lexical nuances, grammatical issues and syntactical structures should be analyzed, but the whole overarching pattern and flow of the language of the story should be taken into consideration. Therefore I will be looking at three things with respect to the area of language: the meaning of the Greek words themselves; patterns of words and phrases; and syntax. Because such a study is foundational in determining both what is being said and how it is being said, this chapter will precede the narrative analysis.

I will not only investigate lexical meaning in general, but I hope also to answer how various words are repeated throughout the gospel and how they are used within the Gospel. Do the meanings of these words change or alter as the gospel story progresses? Note that when I say "story" I mean the gospel story as a whole. I will call an *episode* a unit of text *within* the Gospel that contains a relatively complete story (in the generic sense), such as the "story" of the woman at the well or the "story" of the raising of Lazarus or, in this case, the "story" of the man born blind. So, a (Gospel) *story* contains episodes, *episodes* contain scenes, *scenes* contain sentences, *sentences* contain phrases or cola, *phrases* contain words, *words* contain syllables, and *syllables* contain *letters*. And each level has a pattern that makes some kind of sense.[39] I will be looking at how the meanings of certain words are changed and redefined by the episode and what meaning they carry with them into the episode based on how they have been used previously.

Let me say at this point that I think this is different than simply identifying John's special theological language. What I hope to do is look at the way in which the author uses stories and episodes within stories to add or to nuance or to change the meaning which that word (or perhaps group of words) carries with it into the next episode. An example of this might be the way in which the author uses the concept of the glorification of the Son or the lifting up of the Son in such a way as to convey that the death of Jesus is actually glory and not dishonor.

An example of word accretion from John 9 is seen in the word "work" (ἔργον). The word first appears in relation to Jesus's works in 4:34 where Jesus describes his "food" as doing God's will and completing God's "work." Later in chapter 5, when the paralyzed man is healed on the Sabbath, we see a deeper dimension of what this "work" involves when Jesus defends his Sabbath day healing by relating what he has done to the same kind of "work" that his Father is doing (cf. 5:17, 20, 36). Works not only define Jesus's purpose or goal (4:34), but also "testify" (μαρτυρέω, another important concept) about Jesus's origins. So in 5:36 the "works" testify that he is "sent" (ἀποστέλλω) by the Father. When we get to chapter 9, the entire episode of the man born blind is framed in the perspective of Jesus doing the work of the Father who "sent" him (πέμπω in 9:4, but πέμπω and ἀποστέλλω seem to be synonyms in John). The effect is that the entire episode can be understood as an episode that witnesses to who Jesus is and where he is from (cf. 9:29–33).

Also with respect to language, I wish to look at how patterns within the episode carry meaning from scene to scene within the episode, as well as how patterns act to define a word or a concept. So for example:

---

39. The general idea asserted here is from Black, *Linguistics*, 6-10.

John 9:4 and 5 relate Jesus as light of the world. Jesus's function as light is related to "working the works" of the "one who sent" him.

Table 1.1: Pattern of Verses 4–5

4 It is necessary for us	
(ἐργάζεσθαι) to work the works of him who sent me	A
while day it is.	B
Comes night	B'
when no one is able to work (ἐργάζεσθαι).	A'
5 While in the world I am,	A
Light	B
I am of the world."	A'

There are points of connection with vv. 1–3.

Table 1.2.: Pattern of Verses 3–4

3ᵇ but that might be revealed	A
the works (τὰ ἔργα) of God in him.	B
4 It is necessary for us to work	C
the works (τὰ ἔργα) of him who sent me	B'
while day it is.	A'

"The works of God" (τὰ ἔργα τοῦ θεοῦ) and "the works of the one who sent me" (τὰ ἔργα τοῦ πέμψαντός με) define one another. The "works of God" are "revealed" in the blind man (3b), the "works of the one who sent" are "worked" while it is day (4a).

Just as the works of God are revealed *in* the blind man (ἐν αὐτῷ, 3b), so also Jesus is *in* the world (ἐν τῷ κόσμῳ, 5a). As the works of God are revealed in the blind man, and as Jesus accomplishes (works) the works of God who sent him, then Jesus as light of the world is indirectly *in* the blind man. The fullness of this "work" is seen at the climax of the episode when trust is placed in Jesus by the man born blind.

Rhetorically, this scene functions to prepare the listener to understand the character of Jesus and the character of the man born blind. Jesus is the "light of the world," who is "sent" (πέμψαντός) to accomplish ("work," ἐργάζεσθαι) specific tasks ("works," ἔργα). The man born blind is the one in whom "God's works" will be "revealed." This is a foreshadowing of the man's function later in the episode. The short phrase φῶς εἰμι τοῦ κόσμου (I am the light of the world) moves the episode to the next level: a demonstration of what the light of the world does.

Social World/Social Science

The fourth chapter will involve a social-science analysis. The discipline of social-science criticism attempts to overcome the hurdle of *cultural distance*. There are at least three issues to address: first, the ancient understanding of *illness*; second, and related to the preceding, is the idea of *purity*; and third, the need to understand public encounters as framed in the ongoing challenge and riposte interaction of *honor and shame*.

First, with respect to the understanding of illness, we see at the very start of the episode an obvious issue—namely, the assumption that illness has some sort of personal cause ("who sinned . . .") as opposed to our modern understanding of disease, which has some sort of biological or bacteriological cause. Presumably the healing is also seen as an expression of personal causation. I want to investigate what it meant that Jesus was able to restore sight to a man born blind. Culturally what would that have told an ancient audience about Jesus? Investigation along this avenue will add insight to the narrative-critical task of character analysis.

Second, I will investigate how the specific disorder of blindness would have been understood with respect to how the ancients understood themselves to be comprised. Here I am thinking of the three basic zones of being: Eyes-Heart: emotion fused thought; Ears-Mouth: self revelation; and Hands-Feet: purposeful action. What impact does it have on the rhetoric of the text that a man once blind (zone of emotion fused thought responsible for the activities of perceiving, thinking, and understanding) is acting as a spokesperson about the nature of Christ in the presence of the "teachers of Israel" (cf. John 3:10)?

Third, with respect to the concept of purity, how would a man born blind (deformed) have been perceived? How can we better understand the perspective of the religious leaders if we think of them as the guardians of the purity of the nation? How does the episode itself change the concepts of purity? If the purpose of maintaining purity was to make the nation suitable for the presence of God amongst them, then what should we understand with respect to the presence of Jesus "the light of the world" and "word made flesh" "tabernacling" among his own who ironically do not receive him.

A further example might be the issue of saliva (9:6). Smith has noted that certain bodily fluids that would normally make one impure or contaminate, have the reverse effect if the origin is from an especially perfect specimen. An example of this might be the blood of a perfect sacrificial animal. There is an interesting parallel where Vespasian heals a blind man by moistening the afflicted man's eyes with his spittle (Tacitus, *The History* 4.81).

Fourth, the episode is replete with honor/shame challenge and riposte interactions. An ancient Mediterranean audience would be particularly tuned into the challenge/riposte dialogues present in the episode. Each time the man born blind successfully resolves a battery of questions by the religious leaders his honor rating increases slightly in the mind of the audience while that of the leaders slip. This is pertinent with respect to how credibly the religious leaders are characterized.

With respect to the characterization of the religious leaders, the presence of irony further helps to determine their characterization as those who do not know or understand Jesus's origins from above. For example, in 9:29 in their angry reply to the healed man, the Pharisees unintentionally betray their own lack of insight (eyes/heart, emotion-fused thought) and say of Jesus, "but this one, we do not know from where he comes." The Pharisees do not know from where Jesus comes, but the audience does know, thanks to the omniscient prologue. The deeper meaning is that disciples of Moses (cf. 9:28) do not know from where Jesus comes. Therefore they act inappropriately given the circumstance and foreshadow the final outcome of the episode—their own blindness.

A further irony is present with respect to the social location of the characters within this episode. The main characters within this episode are Jesus, the man born blind, and the Jewish religious authorities (referred to either as "the Jews" or "Pharisees"). In terms of social location, it would have been quite unusual and even ridiculous for one of higher social standing to compete for honor with one of lower social standing via the challenge-riposte interaction. Simply the idea of a theological debate between Pharisees and a beggar of that period would have appeared foolish. The fact that the beggar was deformed adds a further level of folly to the interaction. And (as was mentioned) a deformity in the zone of emotion-fused thought would have made the whole interaction that much more absurd.

As Malina has noted,[40] honor challenges take place only between social equals. To make an honor challenge is a claim to enter the social space of another. One acts in a dishonorable way and is a "bully" if one enters into a challenge/riposte with one of lower standing. One who challenges another of higher social standing is a pretender. The moment the Pharisees ask the blind man's opinion about Jesus in v. 17 an honor challenge is put forth. In v. 17, the Pharisees have either bullied the man or elevated him to their level. Ultimately we see it was simply bullying. Again, Malina notes that honor challenges received by those of greater social status by those of lesser are either ignored (resulting in dishonor for the receiver) or obliterated. In John 9, we have a case where one of higher standing challenges one of lower standing and yet the challengers proceed to obliterate their opponent anyway (v. 34; cf. 22).

Irony, Wit, and Humor

The analysis of irony, wit, and humor in an episode or narrative is properly under the domain of narrative criticism. Even so, this chapter will be separate and come fourth for two reasons. First, our episode is replete with irony, so much so that it deserves its own chapter. Second, irony, wit, and humor tend to be highly culturally contextualized. This is somewhat self evident when many jokes fail to cross the barriers of language and/or culture. An investigation of irony, wit, and humor therefore will benefit from the findings in the previous social-science chapter.

Performance Criticism

In the concluding chapter, I will synthesize the information from the preceding chapters in order to inform a performance critical analysis. As was mentioned above, the emerging method of Performance Criticism begins with the understanding that very little if any first century writings were composed without thought to principles of orality. To go a step further, one could say that all of the New Testament writings were

---

40. Malina, *New Testament World*, 34–35.

composed for the purpose of a performance to a gathered audience in some kind of setting. In the case of letters to particular congregations and even circular letters, the setting of the performance seems clear. They were to be performed in front of the worshiping community. The setting of a gospel performance is less clear.

My belief is that the Gospel of John was performed for those already trusting who are part of what has been called the Johannine community *as well as* for those not part of the in-group or believing community. Sections of the gospel lend themselves well to either setting. The initial chapters of the gospel, which contain invitations to "come and see" or lines describing how "many trusted in him" following a sign or long speech by Jesus for example, would work well with a narrator addressing a gathering crowd encouraging those on the outskirts to gather in closer and hear the rest of the narrative. On the other hand, sections of the farewell discourse seem geared to in-group believers. It is possible that the gospel was composed with two different audiences and two different settings in mind.

With respect to John 9, once again my belief is that its focus is primarily geared toward those who do not already trust, with the goal that they might come to trust. First, chapter 9 is still in a section of the gospel that does not assume the audience has trust in Jesus (this seems to change after chapter 12). Second, the protagonist of the episode is a man blind who comes to see, witness, and trust. This courageous (he was put out of the synagogue yet wins all of the honor challenges) journey from blindness to trust can be a model for any in the audience who do not yet trust.

I will proceed to analyze the performance aspects of John 9 with the following performance setting as my basic framework: John 9 is performed to a mixed audience of those who do and do not yet trust in Jesus as the Christ (cf. 20:31). The goal of the performance is that, like the man born blind, those who do not yet believe will come to trust (and will faithfully remain present in the audience as the narrator continues to the next episode in the gospel narrative).

The obvious (methodological?) problem with this is that we do not have at our disposal the ancient performance. We have only the written record of, or perhaps more accurately the script for, such an event. Even so, I will analyze based on the cues and clues contained in the text and also the information gleaned from all the preceding chapters in an attempt to fill in gaps according to our knowledge of the time and culture.

The goal of this analysis is to ascertain the rhetorical impact the performance would have on an audience. Or more pointedly, what was the author's rhetorical goal when composing this episode for performance? As I have already stated, I believe that the author's goal was that as a result of the performance those who do not yet trust in Jesus would experience Jesus as light of the world and be moved to trust. It is the *experience* of Jesus as light of the world *through the experience of the performance* which is crucial here. Although I may not be able to show that this happened in a particular historical place and time, I do hope to prove that this is what the author *intended* to accomplish.

Course of the Argument

To summarize, in the *second chapter* I will begin with an analysis of the linguistic patterns and structures in John 9. This analysis and accompanying translation will act as a base for the narrative, social science, and irony/humor/wit analyses that follow. In *chapter three* I will proceed along a narrative-critical pathway. I will begin by laying out an analysis of plot, then characters and then setting. As I proceed through each of these narrative elements I will apply analysis from chapter two by looking at patterns and structures to demonstrate how these rhetorically add to the narrative. In *chapter four* I will add data gleaned from analysis of the various social-science issues (illness, zones, purity, and honor/shame). In *chapter five* I will analyze the irony, humor, and wit contained in the episode. While social setting and the elements of irony, humor, and wit are rightfully a part of narrative analysis, they each play such a prominent part in the episode that they deserve their own chapter. Throughout I will also highlight clues from the text that indicate the author's intention with respect to the performance of the episode. My goal is to show the points at which information from all of the disciplines intersect to form the rhetorical pull of the text. Much like in the old days of transparencies and overhead projectors, as each transparency is laid on top of the last, a more complete picture arises. In the same way, as each chapter analyses a different aspect of the episode, it is my hope and goal that the findings from each might be synthesized into a more complete picture. The concluding chapter shall be my attempt at this. In addition to this "overlay" of transparencies, in the conclusion I shall also offer insights, based on the various chapters, about how a performance of the episode would proceed.

For example: with respect to characterization it is one thing to be *told* that Jesus is the light of the world (1:4–9; 8:12; 9:5). It is quite another thing to be *shown* this by the example of the light that Jesus gives shining anew out of the eyes of one born blind, one who never had light shining out of his eyes to begin with! This is a point of characterization that might be lost without the social and cultural data of chapter four. The man born blind would thus be performed with increasing courage as his conflict with the religious leaders intensifies and as the light kindled within him burns brighter. This conclusion is borne out by data discovered in chapter five. The author of the Fourth Gospel places all the best "zingers" on the lips of the man born blind. Sarcasm, irony, humor, and wordplay fill the man's speech to the Pharisees in the second interview (9:24–34). These are hardly lines that could be spoken in meekness.

2

Patterns and Structures in the Text of John 9

Introduction

IN THIS CHAPTER I will analyze the various patterns and structures in John 9. As mentioned in the introduction (p. 17), language is a layering of patterns arranged in a meaningful way in order to provide meaningful communication. A *story* contains *episodes* that contain *scenes* that contain *sentences* that contain *cola*.[1] In this chapter I will be looking at the patterns within the eight scenes (identified below) of this episode.

The flexibility of the Greek language—an inflected language, with minimal dependence on word order—makes for many possibilities of oral/aural patterning. Patterns can function in a number of ways. They can function to draw special attention to certain portions of the episode, they can function as memory aids for a storyteller, and they can serve to move the story or episode forward or to draw it out. Last, but not the least important, patterns can help to define or redefine word meanings. All of these functions will be seen in one form or another in the analysis of John 9.

Of course the Gospel of John would have been most likely experienced, like the majority of all other ancient literature of its time, *read aloud* by a performer (or "reader") *and heard* by an audience, most

---

1. Snyman, "Discourse Perspective," 356, defines a colon: "A colon is a syntactic unit, which has a central matrix consisting of a nominal element (subject) and a verbal element (predicate), each having the possibility of extended features. As long as all these features can be grouped under one N plus V, it forms one colon. A colon constitutes the smallest semantic unit." This is also the description given in Black, *Linguistics*, 139.

likely a group. The translation and analysis of various connections, verbal threads, and patterns are laid out visually for the purposes of this work. However, it is important to keep in mind that what *my audience* sees on the pages to follow, *John's audience* would have heard!

The analysis of such patterns and structures helps one to discover and to decipher the way in which the author argues for the following:

- Jesus is revealed by his actions as one *sent* from God.

- Traditional cultural understandings about sin are reversed: the man born blind is characterized with increasing sympathy while the Pharisees are characterized with decreasing sympathy.

- Traditional understanding of knowledge, insight, and understanding are reversed: the man born blind is one who (ironically) knows who Jesus is, while the Pharisees are progressively hardened to the evidence.

- Trust (πιστεύω) in Jesus, even in the face of persecution, is posited as a value in the narrative.

- The rhetoric of the discourse argues for:
  - the audience to choose courageous trust in Jesus even in the midst of potentially dire consequences.
  - the audience to feel safe and secure from the threat of social isolation (9:22; 12:42; 16:2) knowing that Jesus the good shepherd will take in all who are thrown out (ἐκβάλλω, 10:4 cf. 9:34–35).

Translation

The translation offered below is an attempt to preserve in English, the patterns and word order of the Greek. Of course when the preservation of the Greek patterns and word order diminishes the sense and intelligibility of the English, the syntax of common English is used. The line divisions, for the most part, reflect cola. The translation that follows is set out in a table with English on the left and Greek on the right. I have formatted this so that scenes are not broken across pages when possible.

John 9	NA27 John 9
Scene 1	
1 And passing by, he saw a man blind from birth.	1 Καὶ παράγων εἶδεν ἄνθρωπον τυφλὸν ἐκ γενετῆς.
2 And his disciples asked him, saying, "Teacher, who sinned, this one or his parents, that he was born blind?"	2 καὶ ἠρώτησαν αὐτὸν οἱ μαθηταὶ αὐτοῦ λέγοντες· ῥαββί, τίς ἥμαρτεν, οὗτος ἢ οἱ γονεῖς αὐτοῦ, ἵνα τυφλὸς γεννηθῇ;
3 Jesus answered, "Neither this one sinned nor his parents, but that the works of God might be revealed in him.	3 ἀπεκρίθη Ἰησοῦς· οὔτε οὗτος ἥμαρτεν οὔτε οἱ γονεῖς αὐτοῦ, ἀλλ' ἵνα φανερωθῇ τὰ ἔργα τοῦ θεοῦ ἐν αὐτῷ.
4 It is necessary for us to work the works of him who sent me while it is day. Night is coming when no one is able to work.	4 ἡμᾶς δεῖ ἐργάζεσθαι τὰ ἔργα τοῦ πέμψαντός με ἕως ἡμέρα ἐστίν· ἔρχεται νὺξ ὅτε οὐδεὶς δύναται ἐργάζεσθαι.
5 While I am in the world, I am *the* light of the world."	5 ὅταν ἐν τῷ κόσμῳ ὦ, φῶς εἰμι τοῦ κόσμου.

John 9	NA27 John 9

Scene 2

6 After saying these things,
   he spat on the ground
   and made clay from the saliva,
   and rubbed clay on his eyes.

6 ταῦτα εἰπὼν
ἔπτυσεν χαμαὶ
καὶ ἐποίησεν πηλὸν ἐκ τοῦ πτύσματος
καὶ ἐπέχρισεν αὐτοῦ τὸν πηλὸν ἐπὶ τοὺς ὀφθαλμοὺς

7 And he said to him,
   "go, wash in the pool of Siloam

   (which is translated "sent").
Then he went
and he washed,
and he came seeing.

7 καὶ εἶπεν αὐτῷ·
ὕπαγε νίψαι εἰς τὴν κολυμβήθραν τοῦ Σιλωάμ
(ὃ ἑρμηνεύεται ἀπεσταλμένος).
ἀπῆλθεν οὖν
καὶ ἐνίψατο
καὶ ἦλθεν βλέπων.

Scene 3

8 Then the neighbors and those
   seeing him before, that he was a beggar,
   began to say, "Isn't this fellow the one who was sitting and begging?"

8 Οἱ οὖν γείτονες καὶ οἱ θεωροῦντες αὐτὸν τὸ πρότερον ὅτι προσαίτης ἦν
ἔλεγον· οὐχ οὗτός ἐστιν ὁ καθήμενος καὶ προσαιτῶν;

9 Some were saying, "This is he,"
   and others were saying, "no, but he is like him."
He was saying, "I am he."

9 ἄλλοι ἔλεγον ὅτι οὗτός ἐστιν,
ἄλλοι ἔλεγον· οὐχί, ἀλλὰ ὅμοιος αὐτῷ ἐστιν.
ἐκεῖνος ἔλεγεν ὅτι ἐγώ εἰμι.

10 Then they were saying to him, "How were your eyes opened?"

10 ἔλεγον οὖν αὐτῷ· πῶς [οὖν] ἠνεῴχθησάν σου οἱ ὀφθαλμοί;

11 He answered, "That man who is called Jesus made clay
and spread it on my eyes,
and told me, 'Go into the pool of Siloam and wash.'
Therefore going and washing I gained my sight."

11 ἀπεκρίθη ἐκεῖνος· ὁ ἄνθρωπος ὁ λεγόμενος Ἰησοῦς πηλὸν ἐποίησεν
καὶ ἐπέχρισέν μου τοὺς ὀφθαλμοὺς
καὶ εἶπέν μοι ὅτι ὕπαγε εἰς τὸν Σιλωὰμ καὶ νίψαι·
ἀπελθὼν οὖν καὶ νιψάμενος ἀνέβλεψα.

12 Then they said to him, "Where is that fellow?"
He said, "I don't know."

12 καὶ εἶπαν αὐτῷ· ποῦ ἐστιν ἐκεῖνος;
λέγει· οὐκ οἶδα.

John 9	NA27 John 9

Scene 4

13 They bring him to the Pharisees, the one formerly blind.

13 Ἄγουσιν αὐτὸν πρὸς τοὺς Φαρισαίους
τόν ποτε τυφλόν.

14 Now it was a sabbath day when Jesus made the clay
and opened his eyes.

14 ἦν δὲ σάββατον ἐν ᾗ ἡμέρᾳ τὸν πηλὸν ἐποίησεν ὁ Ἰησοῦς
καὶ ἀνέῳξεν αὐτοῦ τοὺς ὀφθαλμούς.

15 So even the Pharisees were questioning him
how he gained his sight.
And he told them,
"He put clay on my eyes,
and I washed,
and I see."

15 πάλιν οὖν ἠρώτων αὐτὸν καὶ οἱ Φαρισαῖοι
πῶς ἀνέβλεψεν.
ὁ δὲ εἶπεν αὐτοῖς·
πηλὸν ἐπέθηκέν μου ἐπὶ τοὺς ὀφθαλμοὺς
καὶ ἐνιψάμην
καὶ βλέπω.

16 Then some of the Pharisees were saying,
"This fellow is not from God, because he does not keep the sabbath."
Others were saying,
"How can a sinful man do such signs?"
And there was a division among them.

16 ἔλεγον οὖν ἐκ τῶν Φαρισαίων τινές·
οὐκ ἔστιν οὗτος παρὰ θεοῦ ὁ ἄνθρωπος,
ὅτι τὸ σάββατον οὐ τηρεῖ.
ἄλλοι [δὲ] ἔλεγον·
πῶς δύναται ἄνθρωπος ἁμαρτωλὸς τοιαῦτα σημεῖα ποιεῖν;
καὶ σχίσμα ἦν ἐν αὐτοῖς.

17 So they say to the blind one again,
What do you say about him,
since he opened your eyes?
And he said, "He is a prophet."

17 λέγουσιν οὖν τῷ τυφλῷ πάλιν·
τί σὺ λέγεις περὶ αὐτοῦ,
ὅτι ἠνέῳξέν σου τοὺς ὀφθαλμούς;
ὁ δὲ εἶπεν ὅτι προφήτης ἐστίν.

John 9   NA27 John 9

Scene 5

18 Then the Jews did not believe about him,
that he was blind and got his sight,
until they summoned the parents of the one who got his sight.

19 And they asked them,
"Is this your son,
About whom you claim he was born blind?
Then how does he see now?

20 Then his parents answered them and said,
"We know that this is our son,
and that he was born blind.

21 But how he now sees, we don't know;
or who opened his eyes, we especially don't know.
Ask him, he's of age. He'll speak for himself.

22 His parents said these things because they were afraid of the Jews;
for the Jews had already agreed that if anyone should confess him as Christ,
he would be expelled from the synagogue.

23 Because of this, his parents said, "He's of age, ask him."

18 Οὐκ ἐπίστευσαν οὖν οἱ Ἰουδαῖοι περὶ αὐτοῦ
ὅτι ἦν τυφλὸς καὶ ἀνέβλεψεν
ἕως ὅτου ἐφώνησαν τοὺς γονεῖς αὐτοῦ τοῦ ἀναβλέψαντος

19 καὶ ἠρώτησαν αὐτοὺς λέγοντες·
οὗτός ἐστιν ὁ υἱὸς ὑμῶν,
ὃν ὑμεῖς λέγετε ὅτι τυφλὸς ἐγεννήθη;
πῶς οὖν βλέπει ἄρτι;

20 ἀπεκρίθησαν οὖν οἱ γονεῖς αὐτοῦ καὶ εἶπαν·
οἴδαμεν ὅτι οὗτός ἐστιν ὁ υἱὸς ἡμῶν
καὶ ὅτι τυφλὸς ἐγεννήθη·

21 πῶς δὲ νῦν βλέπει οὐκ οἴδαμεν,
ἢ τίς ἤνοιξεν αὐτοῦ τοὺς ὀφθαλμοὺς ἡμεῖς οὐκ οἴδαμεν·
αὐτὸν ἐρωτήσατε, ἡλικίαν ἔχει,
αὐτὸς περὶ ἑαυτοῦ λαλήσει.

22 ταῦτα εἶπαν οἱ γονεῖς αὐτοῦ ὅτι ἐφοβοῦντο τοὺς Ἰουδαίους·
ἤδη γὰρ συνετέθειντο οἱ Ἰουδαῖοι ἵνα ἐάν τις αὐτὸν ὁμολογήσῃ χριστόν,
ἀποσυνάγωγος γένηται.

23 διὰ τοῦτο οἱ γονεῖς αὐτοῦ εἶπαν ὅτι ἡλικίαν ἔχει, αὐτὸν ἐπερωτήσατε.

John 9	NA27 John 9

Scene 6
Conversation 1

24 Then a second time they summoned the man who was blind, and *they* said to him, Give glory to God. We know that this man is a sinner.	24 Ἐφώνησαν οὖν τὸν ἄνθρωπον ἐκ δευτέρου ὃς ἦν τυφλὸς καὶ εἶπαν αὐτῷ· δὸς δόξαν τῷ θεῷ· ἡμεῖς οἴδαμεν ὅτι οὗτος ὁ ἄνθρωπος ἁμαρτωλός ἐστιν.

Conversation 2

25 Then he answered, "Whether he is a sinner, I do not know. One *thing* I know; that I was blind and now I see."	25 ἀπεκρίθη οὖν ἐκεῖνος· εἰ ἁμαρτωλός ἐστιν οὐκ οἶδα· ἓν οἶδα ὅτι τυφλὸς ὢν ἄρτι βλέπω.
26 And they said to him, "What did he do to you? How did he open your eyes?"	26 εἶπον οὖν αὐτῷ· τί ἐποίησέν σοι; πῶς ἤνοιξέν σου τοὺς ὀφθαλμούς;
27 He answered them, "I told you already, and you did not listen. Why do you want to hear again? Surely you don't want to become his disciples?"	27 ἀπεκρίθη αὐτοῖς· εἶπον ὑμῖν ἤδη καὶ οὐκ ἠκούσατε· τί πάλιν θέλετε ἀκούειν; μὴ καὶ ὑμεῖς θέλετε αὐτοῦ μαθηταὶ γενέσθαι;

Conversation 3

28 Then they reviled him and said, "You are a disciple of that fellow, but we are disciples of Moses.	28 καὶ ἐλοιδόρησαν αὐτὸν καὶ εἶπον· σὺ μαθητὴς εἶ ἐκείνου, ἡμεῖς δὲ τοῦ Μωϋσέως ἐσμὲν μαθηταί· ς
29 We know that God has spoken by Moses, but this fellow, we do not know where he is from."	29 ἡμεῖς οἴδαμεν ὅτι Μωϋσεῖ λελάληκεν ὁ θεός, τοῦτον δὲ οὐκ οἴδαμεν πόθεν ἐστίν.

John 9	NA27 John 9
30 The man answered and said to them, "Now this is quite the sight, that you don't know where he is from, and he opened my eyes.	30 ἀπεκρίθη ὁ ἄνθρωπος καὶ εἶπεν αὐτοῖς· ἐν τούτῳ γὰρ τὸ θαυμαστόν ἐστιν, ὅτι ὑμεῖς οὐκ οἴδατε πόθεν ἐστίν, καὶ ἤνοιξέν μου τοὺς ὀφθαλμούς.
31 We know that God does not listen to sinners, but if anyone is God fearing, and does his will, he hears that fellow.	31 οἴδαμεν ὅτι ἁμαρτωλῶν ὁ θεὸς οὐκ ἀκούει, ἀλλ' ἐάν τις θεοσεβὴς ᾖ καὶ τὸ θέλημα αὐτοῦ ποιῇ τούτου ἀκούει.
32 From *the beginning of* the age it was never reported that anyone opened the eyes of one born blind.	32 ἐκ τοῦ αἰῶνος οὐκ ἠκούσθη ὅτι ἠνέῳξέν τις ὀφθαλμοὺς τυφλοῦ γεγεννημένου·
33 If this man were not from God, he could do nothing."	33 εἰ μὴ ἦν οὗτος παρὰ θεοῦ, οὐκ ἠδύνατο ποιεῖν οὐδέν.

Expulsion:

34 They answered and said to him, You were born completely in sins, and you teach us? And they threw him out.	34 ἀπεκρίθησαν καὶ εἶπαν αὐτῷ· ἐν ἁμαρτίαις σὺ ἐγεννήθης ὅλος καὶ σὺ διδάσκεις ἡμᾶς; καὶ ἐξέβαλον αὐτὸν ἔξω.

Scene 7

35 Jesus heard that they had thrown him out, and finding him, he said, "Do you trust in the son of man?	35 Ἤκουσεν Ἰησοῦς ὅτι ἐξέβαλον αὐτὸν ἔξω καὶ εὑρὼν αὐτὸν εἶπεν· σὺ πιστεύεις εἰς τὸν υἱὸν τοῦ ἀνθρώπου;
36 That one answered and said, "And who is he, Lord, so that I might trust in him?	36 ἀπεκρίθη ἐκεῖνος καὶ εἶπεν· καὶ τίς ἐστιν, κύριε, ἵνα πιστεύσω εἰς αὐτόν;
37 And Jesus said to him, "You have seen him, and he is the one talking to you."	37 εἶπεν αὐτῷ ὁ Ἰησοῦς· καὶ ἑώρακας αὐτὸν καὶ ὁ λαλῶν μετὰ σοῦ ἐκεῖνός ἐστιν.

John 9	NA27 John 9
38 And he said, "I trust, Lord!" And he bowed before him.	38 ὁ δὲ ἔφη· πιστεύω, κύριε· καὶ προσεκύνησεν αὐτῷ.

Scene 8

39 And Jesus said, "I came into this world for judgment, so that those who don't see might see, and those who see might become blind."	39 Καὶ εἶπεν ὁ Ἰησοῦς· εἰς κρίμα ἐγὼ εἰς τὸν κόσμον τοῦτον ἦλθον, ἵνα οἱ μὴ βλέποντες βλέπωσιν καὶ οἱ βλέποντες τυφλοὶ γένωνται.
40 And some of the Pharisees who were with him heard these things, and they said to him, "Surely *we* are not blind?"	40 ἤκουσαν ἐκ τῶν Φαρισαίων ταῦτα οἱ μετ' αὐτοῦ ὄντες καὶ εἶπον αὐτῷ· μὴ καὶ ἡμεῖς τυφλοί ἐσμεν;
41 Jesus said to them, "If you were blind, you would have no sin. But now that you say, 'We see,' your sin remains."	41 εἶπεν αὐτοῖς ὁ Ἰησοῦς· εἰ τυφλοὶ ἦτε, οὐκ ἂν εἴχετε ἁμαρτίαν· νῦν δὲ λέγετε ὅτι βλέπομεν, ἡ ἁμαρτία ὑμῶν μένει.

Analysis[2]

The chapter can be divided into eight scenes of unequal length. In each scene, exactly two of the total of six characters/character groups (Jesus, disciples, man born blind, man's neighbors, Pharisees and the man's parents) interact with one another.[3] The plot reaches its greatest tension in scene six where the man born blind is expelled from the synagogue.[4] The

---

2. My thanks to Margret Lee for providing an initial Sound Map.

3. Martyn, *History and Theology*, 37; Holleran, "Seeing the Light," 18.

4. Given that expulsion from the synagogue factors so importantly into the Fourth Gospel in general and this episode in particular I should take time at this point to define that issue. By this I mean a type of social ostracization that comes from being publicly cast out in shame. This loss of face, in a society where one's face (honor) is one's credit rating, would result in social isolation and perhaps even difficulty in attaining or the inability to attain access to goods for daily living. I will explain this more fully in the social-science chapter when dealing with issues of dyadic or collectivist personality.

climax occurs in scene seven where the man born blind is received by Jesus.[5]

Scene 1: Jesus and the Disciples, 1–5

John 9	NA27 John 9
1 And passing by, He saw a man blind from birth.	1 Καὶ παράγων εἶδεν ἄνθρωπον τυφλὸν ἐκ γενετῆς.
2 And his disciples asked him, saying,	2 καὶ ἠρώτησαν αὐτὸν οἱ μαθηταὶ αὐτοῦ λέγοντες·
"Teacher, who sinned, this one or his parents, that he was born blind?"	ῥαββί, τίς ἥμαρτεν, οὗτος ἢ οἱ γονεῖς αὐτοῦ, ἵνα τυφλὸς γεννηθῇ;
3 Jesus answered, "Neither this one sinned nor his parents, but that the works of God might be revealed in him.	3 ἀπεκρίθη Ἰησοῦς· οὔτε οὗτος ἥμαρτεν οὔτε οἱ γονεῖς αὐτοῦ, ἀλλ' ἵνα φανερωθῇ τὰ ἔργα τοῦ θεοῦ ἐν αὐτῷ.
4 It is necessary for us to work the works of him who sent me while it is day. Night comes when no one is able to work.	4 ἡμᾶς δεῖ ἐργάζεσθαι τὰ ἔργα τοῦ πέμψαντός με ἕως ἡμέρα ἐστίν· ἔρχεται νὺξ ὅτε οὐδεὶς δύναται ἐργάζεσθαι.
5 While I am in the world, I am *the* light of the world."	5 ὅταν ἐν τῷ κόσμῳ ᾦ, φῶς εἰμι τοῦ κόσμου.

The episode begins as Jesus and his disciples "walk along" and encounter a man born blind. Immediately the tension of sin is introduced into the plot. The disciples establish Jesus's expertise on the matter of sin by addressing him as "Rabbi." The question that they ask assumes that the man is blind as a result of sin, more specifically, either his own sin or his parents' sin. From Exodus 34:7 there comes the idea that children are punished for their parents' sin and portions of the book of Job express the view that sickness is seen as a punishment for sin. This understanding was present in Jesus's day as well. However, a negative evaluation of the blind man is rejected by Jesus. Jesus says that *neither* the blind man *nor* his parents sinned. In the middle of the episode, Jesus is the object of accusations of sin leveled by the Pharisees. This is rejected in turn by the

---

5. Holleran, "Seeing the Light," 14.

man born blind. The plot tension of who is sinful is a mystery to be solved much later in the episode, but with a twist.

Contrast: sin vs. God's works, 1–3

1	And passing by, He saw a man blind from birth.	
2	And his disciples asked him, saying,	A
	"Teacher, who sinned, this one, or his parents,	B
	that	*hina* (with the *result* that)
	he was born blind?"	C
3	Jesus answered,	A'
	"Neither this one sinned nor his parents,	B'
	but that	*all'hina* (*in order* that)
	might be revealed the works of God in him.	C'

And his disciples asked him, saying, "Teacher, who sinned, this one, or his parents,	But	Jesus answered, "Neither this one sinned nor his parents,
in order that blind he was born?"		in order that might be revealed the works of God in him.

In the layout above C and C' ironically match "born blind" with "be revealed." The word φανερόω carries the sense of "cause to be seen" but can metaphorically mean "to cause something to be fully known by revealing clearly and in some detail."[6] A sort of word play is involved here in that the man is *blind* so that God's works may be *seen*, made evident, demonstrated, or manifested. "Reveal," as used here, is not revealing information *about* something but God's works being demonstrated or made manifest *in* the man born blind. As one looks at the man's character development in the story, one sees the works of God. Those who cannot see this, such as the Pharisees, are the ones who are truly blind (9:40–41).

The strong adversative ἀλλά (*but* or *rather*) contrasts the assumption of the disciples with the purpose of God. The phrase ἵνα τυφλὸς γεννηθῇ;

---

6. φανερόω, in L&N, 1:337–38.

connects with ἵνα φανερωθῇ τὰ ἔργα τοῦ θεοῦ ἐν αὐτω, with the strong adversative conjunction ἀλλά. The conjunction ἵνα with a subjunctive is used to express *purpose* or sometimes *result*.[7] In this scene it is assumed by the disciples that sin *results* in the man being born blind. Jesus states that the real reason is for the *purpose* of "revealing" God's work.

The idea of "(to) work" (ἐργάζομαι) and "works" (ἔργον) in the Gospel are important.[8] Jesus's works *reveal* who Jesus is and *testify* to who Jesus is (5:36; 10:25; 10:37). It is Jesus's work which proves that he and the Father are mutually "in" one another (10:38; 14:10–11). Jesus's works are parallel with the works of the Father in such a way that the Father is actually "showing" (δείκνυμι)[9] Jesus the works (5:20).

This opening scene sets the stage on two fronts, "sin" and "revelation." The character development of the man born blind demonstrates the "works of God" being "revealed" as he gradually comes to trust in Jesus (the one sent). The character development of the Pharisees gradually demonstrates the concept of "sin" in John as they progressively become more hostile and reject the testimony of the man born blind. Sin in John is a matter of *not trusting* in the one whom the Father has sent (John 8:24; 10:25, 37, 38; 16:9). This episode helps to define sin in this way. At the end, the sin of the Pharisees who do not trust, "abides/remains/dwells" (μένω) in them.

The idea of "sin" as expressed in the verb ἁμαρτάνω and its relatives weaves its way through this episode. It is important with respect to the *credibility* of the man born blind and with respect to the *origin* of his controversial healer Jesus.

Jesus is light of the world, 4–5

Verses 4 and 5 define Jesus as light of the world. Jesus's function as light is related to "working the works" of the "one who sent" him.

---

7. ἵνα, BDAG, s.v. 3.

8. Also, Carter, *John and Empire*, 277.

9. In same semantic domain as φανερόω and can be defined as "to make known the character or significance of something by visual, auditory, gestural, or linguistic means" (L&N, 1:339).

PATTERNS AND STRUCTURES IN THE TEXT OF JOHN 9   37

4 It is necessary for us	
(ἐργάζεσθαι) to work the works of him who sent me	A
while day it is.	B
Comes night	B'
when no one is able to work (ἐργάζεσθαι).	A'

It is necessary for us

(ἐργάζεσθαι) to work the works of him who sent me	while day it is.
Comes night	when no one is able to work (ἐργάζεσθαι).

5 While in the world I am,	A
Light	B
I am of the world."	A'

While in the world		I am,
	Light	
I am		of the world.

Light is given a place of central importance at the center of the chiastic structure in v. 5. "Light" in v. 5 connects thematically with "day" (ἡμέρα) in v. 4. While Jesus is in the world it is day; so also while Jesus is in the world he does the works of the one who sent him. According to Genesis, both darkness and light exist as entities in their own right (Gen 1:2–3). In contrast to our modern understanding of light, which must have a source, light in Genesis existed *before* any source for it existed. The sun, moon and stars were created on the fourth day (Gen 1:14–19). Day (ἡμέρα) and night (νύξ) are the ordered structure of time in which light and darkness exist respectively (Gen 1:5). While the light (Jesus) is active in the world, the work of the one who sent the light must be done. There will be a time in John's Gospel when "night" (νύξ) comes (13:30) and no one will work. Time is reframed in terms of day and night. From the perspective of the "light" that is the "life of all people" and that "shines in the darkness" (John 1:4–5), is this a Sabbath healing or simply a daytime healing?

Also, there are points of connection with vv. 1–3.

3b but that might be revealed	A
the works (τὰ ἔργα) of God in him.	B
4 It is necessary for us to work	C
the works (τὰ ἔργα) of him who sent me	B'
while day it is.	A'

"The works of God" (τὰ ἔργα τοῦ θεοῦ) and "the works of him who sent me" (τὰ ἔργα τοῦ πέμψαντός με) define one another. The "works of God" are "revealed" in the blind man (3b), the "works of him who" sent are "worked" while it is day (4a).

Just as the works of God are revealed *in* the blind man (ἐν αὐτῷ) (3b), so also Jesus is *in* the world (ἐν τῷ κόσμῳ) (5a). As the works of God are revealed in the blind man and as Jesus accomplishes (works) the works of God who sent him, then Jesus as light of the world is indirectly *in* the blind man. The fullness of this "work" is seen at the climax of the episode when trust is placed in Jesus by the man born blind.

Rhetorically, this scene functions to prepare the listener to understand the characters of Jesus and the man born blind in specific ways. Jesus is the "light of the world," who is "sent" (πέμψαντός) to accomplish ("work" ἐργάζεσθαι) specific tasks ("works" ἔργα). The man born blind is the one in whom "God's works" will be "revealed." This is a foreshadowing of the man's function later in the episode. The short colon "φῶς εἰμι τοῦ κόσμου" (I am the light of the world) moves the episode to the next level: a demonstration of what the light of the world does.

Scene 2: Jesus heals the man born blind, 6–7

6 After saying these things, he spat on the ground and made clay from the saliva, and rubbed clay on the eyes of him.	6 ταῦτα εἰπὼν ἔπτυσεν χαμαὶ καὶ ἐποίησεν πηλὸν ἐκ τοῦ πτύσματος καὶ ἐπέχρισεν αὐτοῦ τὸν πηλὸν ἐπὶ τοὺς ὀφθαλμοὺς
7 And he said to him, "Go, wash in the pool of Siloam (which is translated "having been sent)." Then he went and washed, and came seeing.	7 καὶ εἶπεν αὐτῷ· ὕπαγε νίψαι εἰς τὴν κολυμβήθραν τοῦ Σιλωάμ (ὃ ἑρμηνεύεται ἀπεσταλμένος). ἀπῆλθεν οὖν καὶ ἐνίψατο καὶ ἦλθεν βλέπων.

Patterns in this scene can be laid out as follows:

6	After saying these things,	A	saying
	he spat on the ground	B	Indic. Aorist
	and made clay from the saliva,	C	Indic. Aorist
	and rubbed clay on the eyes of him.	D	Indic. Aorist
7	And he said to him,	A'	said
	"go, wash in the pool of Siloam	X	"go" Imperative.
	(which is translated "having been sent").	X	"sent" Perf. Part.
	Then he went	B'	Indic. Aorist
	and washed,	C'	Indic. Aorist
	and came seeing.	D'	Indic. Aorist

6	After saying (εἰπὼν) these things,	"go, wash in the pool of Siloam (which is translated "having been sent")."	7	And he said to him,
	he spat on the ground and made clay from the saliva, and rubbed clay on the eyes of him.			Then he went and washed, and came seeing (βλέπων).

The three indicative aorist verbs describing Jesus's action (ἔπτυσεν, ἐποίησεν, ἐπέχρισεν) match the three indicative aorist verbs that describe the action of the man (ἀπῆλθεν, ἐνίψατο, ἦλθεν). The participle εἰπὼν (saying) in v. 6 matches aurally and grammatically the participle βλέπων (seeing), forming an inclusio around these two verses.

At the center of vv. 6–7 stands an imperative phrase "Go wash in the pool of Siloam" with a relative clause that defines the meaning of "Siloam." The imperative phrase ὕπαγε νίψαι is one of only three imperatives in this episode. The other two are "ask" ἐρωτήσατε (21, 23) and "give" δὸς (24). As the various characters perform each imperative, the episode moves to a new scene. After the blind man "goes" he comes back able to see and we move into vv. 8ff. After the parents tell the Pharisees to "ask him" since he is of age, we move into vv 24ff. which contain the next imperative. Upon being commanded to "give glory to God" and admit that Jesus is a sinner, the blind man in fact does give glory to God but does not call Jesus a sinner. This results in his expulsion from the synagogue (foreshadowed in the "ask him" scene) and the climax of the episode in vv. 35ff.

Additionally, there are parallels between Jesus's imperatives in v. 7 and the indicative aorist responses by the man born blind:

7	And he said to him,		
	"go,	A	Imperative
	wash in the pool of Siloam	B	Imperative
	(which is translated "having been sent")."	C	Participle
	Then he went	A'	Indic. Aorist
	and washed,	B'	Indic. Aorist
	and came seeing.	C'	Indic. Aorist + Participle

The terms A and B (go, wash) obviously match the terms A' and B' (went and washed). This leaves open the possibility that "came seeing" (ἦλθεν βλέπων) helps define "having been sent" (ἀπεσταλμένος).

The word ἀπεσταλμένος (having been sent) in 9:7 or forms of its root appear only once in this discourse. However, it connects the discourse to other important statements about Jesus *throughout* the Gospel of John. With the exception of 1:6, 19, 24 the forms of this root are used exclusively to describe Jesus as the one who has been sent by the Father with a special mission.[10] Jesus, who is himself "sent"[11] by the Father, sends the man to a pool which means "sent." This connects the healing and its aftermath with the special purpose for which Jesus has been sent. Namely he has been sent to save and not condemn (3:17), to bring life (6:57; 17:3), and, in this passage, to bring sight. To bring sight is to bring light to the man so that his eyes can see. This particular understanding of vision will be discussed in the social-science chapter.

Rhetorically, the function of this scene adds to the characterization of Jesus as the one sent to do God's works. Specifically, in this case, that involves the restoring of sight to a man born blind. The end of this scene is punctuated by three staccato cola: "Then he went, and washed, and came seeing." These move the episode to the next scene, which describes the effect of the healing upon the bystanders.

Scene 3: Neighbors question the man, 8–12

8 Then the neighbors and those seeing him before, that he was a beggar, began to say, "Isn't this fellow the one who was sitting and begging?"	8 Οἱ οὖν γείτονες καὶ οἱ θεωροῦντες αὐτὸν τὸ πρότερον ὅτι προσαίτης ἦν ἔλεγον· οὐχ οὗτός ἐστιν ὁ καθήμενος καὶ προσαιτῶν;

---

10. See John 1:6, 19, 24; 3:17, 28, 34; 4:38; 5:33, 36, 38; 6:29, 57; 7:29, 32; 8:42; 9:7; 10:36; 11:3, 42; 13:16; 17:3, 8, 18, 21, 23, 25; 18:24; 20:21.

11. While πέμπω is used to describe Jesus in this episode (9:4) as I have already mentioned ἀποστέλλω is also used throughout John. Indeed, the two seem to be used interchangeably (5:23 π., 24 π., 30π., 36α., 37 π., 38 α.; 6:29 α., 38 π., 39 π., 44 π., 57 α.; 7:16 π., 18 π., 28 π., 29 α.; particularly 5:36-38). This is contra Neyrey, *Perspective*, 465-6 who sees πέμπω more in relation to specific tasks Jesus is "sent" to do and ἀποστέλλω more in relation to Jesus status as an "agent/ambassador." Even so, Neyrey presents an excellent analysis of the ways in which Jesus is "sent."

9 Some were saying, "This is he," and others were saying, "not, but he is like him." He was saying, "I am he."	9 ἄλλοι ἔλεγον ὅτι οὗτός ἐστιν, ἄλλοι ἔλεγον· οὐχί, ἀλλὰ ὅμοιος αὐτῷ ἐστιν. ἐκεῖνος ἔλεγεν ὅτι ἐγώ εἰμι.
10 Then they were saying to him, "How were your eyes opened?"	10 ἔλεγον οὖν αὐτῷ· πῶς [οὖν] ἠνεῴχθησάν σου οἱ ὀφθαλμοί;
11 He answered, "That man who is called Jesus made clay and spread it on my eyes, and told me, 'Go into the pool of Siloam and wash.' Therefore going and washing I gained my sight."	11 ἀπεκρίθη ἐκεῖνος· ὁ ἄνθρωπος ὁ λεγόμενος Ἰησοῦς πηλὸν ἐποίησεν καὶ ἐπέχρισέν μου τοὺς ὀφθαλμοὺς καὶ εἶπέν μοι ὅτι ὕπαγε εἰς τὸν Σιλωὰμ καὶ νίψαι· ἀπελθὼν οὖν καὶ νιψάμενος ἀνέβλεψα.
12 Then they said to him, "Where is that fellow?" He said, "I don't know."	12 καὶ εἶπαν αὐτῷ· ποῦ ἐστιν ἐκεῖνος; λέγει· οὐκ οἶδα.

This scene is organized into three conversations with the neighbors.

- Establishing his identity as the same man as the man formerly blind
- Establishing the means by which the healing took place
- Establishing (unsuccessfully) the whereabouts of Jesus

The use of the imperfect ἔλεγον in vv. 8–10 contrasts with the use of the aorist ἀπεκρίθη in v. 11. The conversation was an ongoing one (imperfect, incompleted action) until the healed man "answered" them (aorist, simple past).

The word ἀνοίγω (to open) used in vv. 10, 14, 17, 21, 26, 30, 32, is also used in 10:3 (of a gate opening) and 10:21 (referring to this episode). The only other two uses of ἀνοίγω in the whole Gospel are in 11:37 (referring back to this episode) and in 1:51 (Jesus's conversation with Nathanael) where Jesus tells Nathanael that he will see heaven "opened" and the angels ascending and descending upon the son of man. This use of ἀνοίγω connects the discourse of the man born blind with the discourse of the good shepherd (10:1–21) and brackets much of the intervening material as an inclusio. I believe the good shepherd discourse is actually part of a final conversation that Jesus has with the Pharisees (9:40—10:21).

The metaphor of the good shepherd is introduced in 10:1. However, the entire section of 9:40–10:21 is in answer to the question posed by the Pharisees in 9:40, "Surely we are not blind, are we?" Careful attention to the flow of the text, ignoring modern section titles, shows no break in conversation or narrative setting between 9:41 and 10:1–18. The metaphor of the good shepherd is a "figure of speech" (παροιμία, 10:6) which Jesus uses with the Pharisees directly after stating that their "sin remains/abides/dwells" (9:41). In this extended metaphor, Jesus casts himself as the only one who truly cares for the sheep (God's people who are part of the community of believers in Jesus), so much so that he lays down his life for them (10:15b). This care is in contrast to the "thief" (10:1) who does not enter by the gate, and who comes to "kill, steal, and destroy" (10:10). It is also in contrast to the hired hand, who does not "care" (μέλει, 10:13) for the sheep. So then, the sin of the Pharisees is their failure to "enter through the gate (Jesus) into the sheepfold" (10:1). They are not part of the community of believers. Also, they do not truly "care" (10:13) for the sheep.

The scene ends with the neighbors questioning the healed man about Jesus's location. It should be noted here that the man born blind has yet to actually see Jesus. His sight was restored *after* going away from Jesus to the Pool of Siloam and *after* washing. This is why the man does not recognize Jesus in v. 36. The man's response is a short colon: οὐκ οἶδα (I don't know). The first appearance of the word οἶδα (to know or to perceive) raises the issue of knowing in a very mundane way. This will be revisited as a major theme in vv. 24ff. For now the narrative moves to a new level. Without knowing the whereabouts of "the man called Jesus" the healed man is brought to the Pharisees for further examination.

Scene 4: Pharisees question the man 13–17

13 They bring him to the Pharisees, the one formerly blind.	13 Ἄγουσιν αὐτὸν πρὸς τοὺς Φαρισαίους τόν ποτε τυφλόν.
14 Now it was a sabbath day when Jesus made the clay and opened his eyes.	14 ἦν δὲ σάββατον ἐν ᾗ ἡμέρᾳ τὸν πηλὸν ἐποίησεν ὁ Ἰησοῦς καὶ ἀνέῳξεν αὐτοῦ τοὺς ὀφθαλμούς.
15 So even the Pharisees were questioning him how he gained his sight. And he told them, "He put clay on my eyes, and I washed, and I see."	15 πάλιν οὖν ἠρώτων αὐτὸν καὶ οἱ Φαρισαῖοι πῶς ἀνέβλεψεν. ὁ δὲ εἶπεν αὐτοῖς· πηλὸν ἐπέθηκέν μου ἐπὶ τοὺς ὀφθαλμοὺς καὶ ἐνιψάμην καὶ βλέπω.
16 Then some of the Pharisees were saying, "This fellow is not from God, because he does not keep the sabbath." Others were saying, "How can a sinful man do such signs?" And there was a division among them.	16 ἔλεγον οὖν ἐκ τῶν Φαρισαίων τινές· οὐκ ἔστιν οὗτος παρὰ θεοῦ ὁ ἄνθρωπος, ὅτι τὸ σάββατον οὐ τηρεῖ. ἄλλοι [δὲ] ἔλεγον· πῶς δύναται ἄνθρωπος ἁμαρτωλὸς τοιαῦτα σημεῖα ποιεῖν; καὶ σχίσμα ἦν ἐν αὐτοῖς.
17 So they say to the blind one again, What do you say about him, since he opened your eyes? And he said, "He is a prophet."	17 λέγουσιν οὖν τῷ τυφλῷ πάλιν· τί σὺ λέγεις περὶ αὐτοῦ, ὅτι ἠνέῳξέν σου τοὺς ὀφθαλμούς; ὁ δὲ εἶπεν ὅτι προφήτης ἐστίν.

This scene can be divided into four sections: a setting followed by three dialogues each introduced by the conjunction οὖν (then):

- Setting: Sabbath day
- Questioning: What did he do? (v. 15)
- Internal debate: Not from God ↔ Can a sinner do such signs? Division. (v. 16)
- Questioning: What do you say about him? (v. 17)

Verses 13–14: Setting

The setting is established in 13 and 14. Place is established in v. 13. The man is before the Pharisees for questioning. One can infer that they are in a synagogue but this is not necessarily the case. Time is established in v. 14. It is a Sabbath day. The phrase "now it was (ἦν δὲ) a Sabbath" is withheld from the audience until now. It heightens the drama of the episode.[12] The placing of this information is critical in relation to the response of the Pharisees. The verb "εἰμί" is in the imperfect. "It was and still is (imperfect) the Sabbath," would be a possible force of an imperfect. Even so, one mustn't force such an understanding given the lack of an aorist for εἰμί. Even so, the lack of any other time markers in the episode indicates it still is the Sabbath. The setting of a Sabbath day establishes the setting for the entire episode of the man born blind. It recalls the Sabbath day healing controversy described in 5:9–10, 16, 18; 7:22–23. The audience would already know this to be a hot button issue for the Pharisees as characterized in John's Gospel.

It is important to note here that irony of hypocrisy by the Pharisees is considerable. They interrogate on the Sabbath, they deliberate, they call witnesses and compel testimony, and they expel on the Sabbath. The information about the Sabbath is withheld until just now in the episode, when the Pharisees begin to interrogate.

Verse 15: What did he do?

The use of πάλιν οὖν . . . καὶ . . . working together give emphasis to the fact that it is the Pharisees who are now questioning the man. This emphasis coupled with the Sabbath day setting, increases the tension of the episode.

Verse 16: Not from God—Can a sinner do such signs?

16 Then some of the Pharisees were saying,	A
This man is not from God,	B
because the Sabbath he does not keep.	C
Others were saying,	A'
How can a sinful man, do such signs?	B'
And there was a division among them.	C'

---

12. Staley, "Stumbling, Reaching," 66.

As laid out above, B and B' describe the basic tension of the entire episode with respect to the origin of Jesus. This overarching tension is the "from God" or "not from God" controversy. A "man not from God" (B) = a "sinful man" (B'). But the question of signs is added at the end of B', which results in division over the sabbath issue (C and C').

The concept of "signs" is instrumental in the argument. The signs are a demonstration of the works of God for John. This demonstration was foreshadowed in the beginning of the episode at v. 3b, ἀλλ' ἵνα φανερωθῇ τὰ ἔργα τοῦ θεοῦ ἐν αὐτῷ (but that the works of God might be revealed in him) and v. 5b, φῶς εἰμι τοῦ κόσμου (I am *the* light of the world).

Because of the inconsistency between their concept of Jesus as sinner and the apparent miraculous sign, there is division among the Pharisees. More specifically, the division is related to the proper interpretation of the sign. The issue of sin blocks the authorities from understanding the sign at face value. The concept of sin has now become a major factor in the authorities' ability to understand "the man called Jesus."

The Pharisees cannot understand or see the sign because they do not have "opened" (v. 17) eyes (cf. 39ff.). They must ask the healed man to interpret in v. 17. The use of the imperfect ἔλεγον (were saying) gives the impression of an ongoing discussion about the meaning of the sign. This is also matched by the imperfect ἦν of σχίσμα ἦν (there was division). Not only is the discussion ongoing but the division is ongoing. The fact of division is highlighted by the word order σχίσμα ἦν (division there was) placing "division" in the foreground.

Verse 17: What do you say about him?

17 Then they say to the blind one *again*,
   What do you say about him,
   since He opened your eyes?
   And he said, "He is a prophet."

The re-inquisition of the man born blind is connected to the initial questioning with the adverb πάλιν (again). The Pharisees are unable to reach a decision about the origin of Jesus (from God vs. not from God) and must turn to the healed man for an answer about Jesus. By the Pharisees own admission the healed man is characterized as an authoritative witness to the person of Jesus "since" (ὅτι)[13] Jesus "opened" his eyes. This is the first

---

13. A marker of cause or reason based on an evident fact, "because, since, for, in

statement which the man makes about the person of Jesus. Up to this point in the episode the questions posed to the man have been purely circumstantial: "how were you healed" (chain of events) and "where is he" (location of healer).

The inability of the Pharisees, religious experts, to interpret the "sign," and their subsequent division about the origin and therefore identity of Jesus in v. 16, move the episode to a new level: determining the origin of Jesus. At this point the audience must struggle with the question of Jesus's origin and identity. Of course they have already been told in v. 4 who "sent" Jesus, but now the audience must see for themselves as the episode plays out. The answer from the healed man is simply, "he is a prophet." This short colon, προφήτης ἐστίν, punctuates the end of this scene while answering the question of origin. The audience would know that prophets are "from God."

The healed man is probably using prophet here as a general way of referring to Jesus as one who is from God (cf. 4:19). Brown notes that "the only prophets who worked notable healing miracles were Elijah and Elisha."[14] Scholars have however noted the similarity of Elisha instructing Naaman to wash in the Jordan to accomplish his healing (2 Kgs 5:10–14).[15] Jesus's status as "prophet" and from the perspective of the Pharisees a false prophet will be explored in more detail in the narrative chapter.

---

view of the fact that," L&N, 1:780.

14. Brown, *John*, 1:373. Barrett, *John*, 360.

15. Brown, *John*, 1:373; Barrett, *John*, 358; Beasley-Murray, *John*, 155.

Scene 5: Pharisees question the man's parents

18 Then the Jews did not believe about him, that he was blind and got his sight, until they summoned the parents of the one who got his sight.	18 Οὐκ ἐπίστευσαν οὖν οἱ Ἰουδαῖοι περὶ αὐτοῦ ὅτι ἦν τυφλὸς καὶ ἀνέβλεψεν ἕως ὅτου ἐφώνησαν τοὺς γονεῖς αὐτοῦ τοῦ ἀναβλέψαντος
19 And they asked them, "Is this your son, About whom you claim he was born blind? Then how does he see now?	19 καὶ ἠρώτησαν αὐτοὺς λέγοντες· οὗτός ἐστιν ὁ υἱὸς ὑμῶν, ὃν ὑμεῖς λέγετε ὅτι τυφλὸς ἐγεννήθη; πῶς οὖν βλέπει ἄρτι;
20 Then his parents answered them and said, "We know that this is our son, and that he was born blind.	20 ἀπεκρίθησαν οὖν οἱ γονεῖς αὐτοῦ καὶ εἶπαν· οἴδαμεν ὅτι οὗτός ἐστιν ὁ υἱὸς ἡμῶν καὶ ὅτι τυφλὸς ἐγεννήθη·
21 But how he now sees, we don't know; or who opened his eyes, we especially don't know. Ask him, he's of age. He'll speak for himself.	21 πῶς δὲ νῦν βλέπει οὐκ οἴδαμεν, ἢ τίς ἤνοιξεν αὐτοῦ τοὺς ὀφθαλμοὺς ἡμεῖς οὐκ οἴδαμεν· αὐτὸν ἐρωτήσατε, ἡλικίαν ἔχει, αὐτὸς περὶ ἑαυτοῦ λαλήσει.
22 His parents said these things because they were afraid of the Jews; for the Jews had already agreed that if anyone should confess him Christ, he would be expelled from the synagogue.	22 ταῦτα εἶπαν οἱ γονεῖς αὐτοῦ ὅτι ἐφοβοῦντο τοὺς Ἰουδαίους· ἤδη γὰρ συνετέθειντο οἱ Ἰουδαῖοι ἵνα ἐάν τις αὐτὸν ὁμολογήσῃ χριστόν, ἀποσυνάγωγος γένηται.
23 Because of this, his parents said, "He's of age, ask him."	23 διὰ τοῦτο οἱ γονεῖς αὐτοῦ εἶπαν ὅτι ἡλικίαν ἔχει, αὐτὸν ἐπερωτήσατε.

Verses 18–21: Was the man really born blind?

The thrust of 18 is important for this new direction of the narrative. The question posed to the healed man in v. 17, "what do you say about him," was premised on his experience with Jesus as healer "*since he opened your eyes.*" If this fact is undermined then his answer "he is a prophet" can be dismissed.

18 Then the Jews did not believe concerning him,
   that he was blind and saw again,
   until they called the parents of him seeing anew.
19 And they asked them, saying,   A
   Is this your son,   B
   whom you say that he was born blind?   C
   Then how does he see now?   D
20 Then his parents answered them and said,   A'
   We know that this is our son,   B'
   and that he was born blind.   C'
21 But how he now sees, *we* do not know;   D'
   or who opened his eyes, we especially do not know.   E
   Ask him, he is of age. He will speak about himself.

And they asked them, saying	Then his parents answered them and said
	We know
is this your son	that he is our son
	and [we know]
whom you say that he was born blind	that he was born blind
	but
how does he see now	how he sees
	we do not know
	who opened his eyes
	we especially do not know

As laid out above, in E, the parents add an extra dimension to their answer to the Pharisees. The Pharisees do not ask "who opened his eyes" but only "how does he see now?" The additional element of "who" redirects the episode to the central issue of the origin and nature of "the man called Jesus." In the phrase ἡμεῖς οὐκ οἴδαμεν, the ἡμεῖς is redundant since the second person plural pronoun is already present in the pronominal ending of οἴδαμεν. Such a redundancy adds emphasis to the statement.[16]

---

16. Black, *New Testament Greek*, 67–68, §65.3; Nunn, *Short Syntax*, 50, §2.50. Note the lack of ἡμεῖς in their two prior instances of "οἴδαμεν" (9:20–21a).

21 But how he now sees,	A
we do not know;	B
or who opened his eyes,	A'
we do not know.	B'
Ask him, he is of age.	A"
He will speak about himself.	B"

In v. 21 the pattern sets up the healed man as one who knows. "He will speak about himself" (B") implies he "knows" in contrast to what the parents "do not know" (B and B')

Asking	Knowing
21 But how he now sees,	we do not know;
or who opened his eyes,	we do not know.
Ask him, he is of age.	He will speak about himself.

Verses 22–23: Decision to expel confessors of Jesus

22 His parents said *these things* A	A
because *they feared* B the Jews;	B
for already the *Jews had agreed* C	C
that if anyone should confess him *as* Christ,	X
he *would be expelled from the synagogue.* C'	C'
23 for *this reason*, B' his parents said,	B'
"*He is of age, ask him*." A'	A'

In A and A', the movement is from general "these things" to the specific in A' which states what his parents said, "he is of age, ask him." In B and B' each begin with a word (ὅτι) and phrase (διὰ τοῦτο) which indicate cause or reason. They indicate the reason for the parents' speech. Again, in C and C', a general statement in C that "the Jews had agreed" is delineated with the more specific statement in C' that "he would be expelled from the synagogue." At the center of the two verse structure is the subordinate conditional clause "that if anyone should confess him as Christ."

Ironically the Pharisees "had already agreed together" (συνετέθειντο v. 22) to expel any confessing Jesus as Christ but were "divided" (σχίσμα

v. 16) about the sign and about whether or not he was "from God" (παρὰ θεοῦ v. 16).

A ↓	His parents said these things	"He is of age, ask him."	A'
B ↓	because they feared the Jews;	for this reason, his parents said,	B' ↑
C →	for already the Jews had agreed together	he would be expelled from the synagogue.	C' ↑

These verses are a digression that adds needed information to the entire episode. The Jews "had already agreed together" (συνετέθειντο pluperfect of συντίθημι meaning to agree together) to expel confessors of Jesus as Christ. The pluperfect is an unusual tense that draws much attention to itself.[17] It occurs only 34 times out of the Fourth Gospel's 3,620[18] verbal appearances. This agreement, although told late in the episode, should be seen as overshadowing the whole episode. The lateness of its presentation has the effect of heightening the tension even more. This is not simply about a sabbath controversy but rather about one's security within ones community. The seriousness of this shift in community, which accompanies a shift in trust and confession, will be explored in the social-science chapter in relation to the collectivist personality of an ancient Mediterranean person.

In the middle of the ABCCBA pattern is the conditional purpose clause, "that if any should confess him as Christ . . ." The attitudes and beliefs of "someone" or "anyone" (τὶς) about Jesus in relation to messiahship are given central importance. This highlights a potential clue about the origin and nature of "the man called Jesus."

17. Westfall, "Prominence," 79. She defines prominence as, "the use of devices that languages have which enable a speaker to highlight material and make some part of the text stand out in some way." P. 1. In her section on Markedness and Aspect/Tense she describes how different tenses increase prominence, drawing attention, in relation to each other.

aorist	unmarked	default tense
imperfect	↓	distant, indefinite action
present	↓	close, indefinite action
perfect	↓	definite, contoured
pluperfect	marked	Rare, definite, contoured

18. This is a search of the NA27 and includes participles. Without participles the count is 3,132. To contextualize the rarity, the aorist appears 1,187 times and the present 1,245 times (both not including participles).

Scene 6: Pharisees expel the man verses 24–34

Verses 24–25: First conversation, the man "gives glory" to God

24 Then a second time they summoned the man who was blind, and *they said* to him, Give glory to God. We know that this man is a sinner.	24 Ἐφώνησαν οὖν τὸν ἄνθρωπον ἐκ δευτέρου ὃς ἦν τυφλὸς καὶ εἶπαν αὐτῷ· δὸς δόξαν τῷ θεῷ· ἡμεῖς οἴδαμεν ὅτι οὗτος ὁ ἄνθρωπος ἁμαρτωλός ἐστιν.
25 Then he answered, "Whether he is a sinner, I do not know. One *thing* I know; that I was blind and now I see."	25 ἀπεκρίθη οὖν ἐκεῖνος· εἰ ἁμαρτωλός ἐστιν οὐκ οἶδα· ἓν οἶδα ὅτι τυφλὸς ὢν ἄρτι βλέπω.

24 Then a second time they called the man who was blind,
   and *they said* to him,   A
   Give glory to God.   B
   We *know* that this man is a *sinner*.   C
25 Then he answered and *said*,   A'
   Whether he is a *sinner*, I do not *know*.   C'
   One *thing* I know: that being blind, now I see.   B'

A	B	C
They said		
	Give glory to God	
		We *know* that this man is a *sinner*.
He said		
		Whether he is a *sinner*, I do not *know*.
	One thing I know: that being blind, now I see.	

The ABCACB semi-chiastic pattern accomplishes two things. It contrasts the man's knowledge with the Pharisee's knowledge. It also equates "being blind now I see" with "give glory to God." In C, the Pharisees' "knowledge" of Jesus as a sinner is matched by C', where the man denies knowing whether Jesus is a sinner or not. In B, glory to God is called for; and in B', glory to God is provided in the man's proclamation of his healing. In highlighting the results of Jesus having worked (or accomplished) the "the works of God" (v. 4), the healed man ironically obeys the command of the Pharisees to "give glory to God," but not to the effect the Pharisees had hoped.

Verses 26–27: Second conversation, Pharisees do not hear

26 And they said to him,	26 εἶπον οὖν αὐτῷ·
What did he do to you?	τί ἐποίησέν σοι;
How did he open your eyes?	πῶς ἤνοιξέν σου τοὺς ὀφθαλμούς;
27 He answered them,	27 ἀπεκρίθη αὐτοῖς·
"I told you already, and you did not listen.	εἶπον ὑμῖν ἤδη καὶ οὐκ ἠκούσατε·
Why do you want to hear again?	τί πάλιν θέλετε ἀκούειν;
Surely you don't want to become his disciples?"	μὴ καὶ ὑμεῖς θέλετε αὐτοῦ μαθηταὶ γενέσθαι;

26 And they said to him,	A
What did he do to you?	B
How did he open your eyes?	C
27 He answered them,	A
I spoke to you already, and you did not *listen*.	B'
Why again do you wish to *hear*?	C'
Surely you don't wish to become his disciples?	D

In the BC phrases, the Pharisees *again* question the man in the same way as in v. 15. These are matched by a two part statement about listening/hearing (ἀκούω) in B'C'. I have translated the first instance of ἀκούω in v. 27 as "listen," since "listen" implies understanding and response. The Pharisees are unable or unwilling to "listen to" the answers to their own questions! It is therefore ironic that they make the claim to "know" that Jesus is a sinner (v. 24). A third term is added to the pattern, D. Sarcasm is used to highlight the motive of the Pharisees' question. The healed man poses the question "why do you wish (θέλετε) to hear?" and answers it sarcastically with a question expecting a negative answer, "surely (καὶ) you don't (μὴ) wish (θέλετε) to become his disciples?"

Why again do you wish to hear?	A B
Surely you don't wish to become his disciples?	A B'

This structure defines disciples of Jesus as ones who "listen." By implication, Pharisees, who are not disciples of Jesus, are not able to "listen." This interpretation depends upon the wordplay of ἀκούω. In addition to simple sensory perception, ἀκούω can mean "to understand" and also "to obey."[19] The Pharisees do not truly wish to "listen" (understand) what happened to the man, since once before they "heard" (sensory perception) and ignored the man's answer, questioning his parents in an attempt to impeach his credibility (vv. 17–18). What good will it do for them to "hear" (sensory perception) again (v. 27).

Verses 28–33: Third conversation, man demonstrates that Jesus is "from God"

28 Then they reviled him and said, "You are a disciple of that fellow, but we are disciples of Moses.	28 καὶ ἐλοιδόρησαν αὐτὸν καὶ εἶπον· σὺ μαθητὴς εἶ ἐκείνου, ἡμεῖς δὲ τοῦ Μωϋσέως ἐσμὲν μαθηταί· ς
29 We know that God has spoken by Moses, but this fellow, we do not know where he is from."	29 ἡμεῖς οἴδαμεν ὅτι Μωϋσεῖ λελάληκεν ὁ θεός, τοῦτον δὲ οὐκ οἴδαμεν πόθεν ἐστίν.
30 The man answered and said to them, "Now this is quite the sight, that you don't know where he is from, and he opened my eyes.	30 ἀπεκρίθη ὁ ἄνθρωπος καὶ εἶπεν αὐτοῖς· ἐν τούτῳ γὰρ τὸ θαυμαστόν ἐστιν, ὅτι ὑμεῖς οὐκ οἴδατε πόθεν ἐστίν, καὶ ἤνοιξέν μου τοὺς ὀφθαλμούς.

---

19. L&N, 2:8.

31 We know that God does not listen to sinners, but if anyone is God fearing, and does his will, he hears that one.	31 οἴδαμεν ὅτι ἁμαρτωλῶν ὁ θεὸς οὐκ ἀκούει, ἀλλ' ἐάν τις θεοσεβὴς ᾖ καὶ τὸ θέλημα αὐτοῦ ποιῇ τούτου ἀκούει.
32 From *the beginning of* the age it was never reported that anyone opened the eyes of one born blind.	32 ἐκ τοῦ αἰῶνος οὐκ ἠκούσθη ὅτι ἠνέῳξέν τις ὀφθαλμοὺς τυφλοῦ γεγεννημένου·
33 If this man were not from God, he could do nothing."	33 εἰ μὴ ἦν οὗτος παρὰ θεοῦ, οὐκ ἠδύνατο ποιεῖν οὐδέν.

Pharisees Revile the Man vv. 28–29

28 Then they reviled him and said,	
"You are a disciple	A
of that one (Jesus),	B
but we of Moses	B'
are disciples.	A'
29 We know that	A
God has spoken by Moses,	B
but this One,	X
we do not know	A
where he is from."	B

The above pattern defines the Pharisees as those who do not know Jesus. Knowing and not knowing becomes the issue in what has evolved into a heated synagogue debate between a former blind beggar (who increasingly appears to be a disciple of Jesus) and the Pharisees (disciples of Moses). The contrast between disciples of Moses and Jesus is chiastically expressed in v. 28 with a simple ABBA pattern. Verse 29 delineates what disciples of Moses know and do not know. They *know* that God has spoken through Moses. They do *not know* the origin of Jesus. More irony appears as the Pharisees claim they "do not know" Jesus's origin (v. 29) and yet claim they do "know" that he is a "sinner" (v. 24). In John, not knowing Jesus is also not knowing the Father who sent him. Jesus makes this claim in 8:19. Not knowing Jesus is also sin in John. Immediately after Jesus statement in 8:19, he goes on to say that unbelief will result in death in sin (8:21, 24).

The Man Outwits the Pharisees vv. 30–33

30 The man answered and said to them,	
For in this there is a marvel,	A: marvel
that you do not know from where he is,	B: from where
and he opened my eyes.	C: opened eyes
31 But we know that sinful ones	X
God does not hear,	Y
but if anyone is God fearing, and does His will,	X'
He hears that one.	Y'
32 From [the beginning of] the age it was never heard	A': never heard [marvelous thing]
that anyone opened the eyes	C': opened eyes
of one having been born blind.	
33 If this one was not from God, he could do nothing.	B': from God

The man states that it is a "marvel" or an "amazing thing" that the Pharisees "do not know" Jesus's origin, despite the fact that Jesus opened his eyes. In A and A', this marvel (v. 30) contrasts the marvelous act of opening the eyes of a man born blind (v. 32). The marvelous act demonstrates Jesus's origin. The height of sarcasm and irony is reached here in that, in the face of such an amazing miracle (ἐκ τοῦ αἰῶνος οὐκ ἠκούσθη, from the age unheard), religious leaders and disciples of Moses "do not know."

The word ἀκούω (hear/listen) continues to play an important role. As in v. 27, the Pharisees do not "listen" (ἀκούω, with the idea of responsiveness), so also in v. 31 the man describes how God will not "listen" (ἀκούω, with the idea of responsiveness) to sinners but does "listen" to the one who is "devout" (θεοσεβής) and does his "will" (θέλημα). Finally, to bring all this word play back to the foreground, the man says, "it has never been reported/heard (ἀκούω) that anyone opened the eyes of a person born blind."

The man's argument in vv. 31–33 progresses logically:

- Premise: God does not listen to sinners (31a)
- Premise: God listens to the pious and those who do God's will (31b)
- Premise: Jesus opened the eyes of one born blind (by implication 32)
- Conclusion: God listens to Jesus (33)
- Conclusion: Jesus is "from God" (33 stated negatively)

In terms of prominence, vv. 30–31 stand out since they contain the largest amount of spoken dialogue in the episode.[20] (In Greek this is 57 words of continuous dialogue. Jesus's speech in vv. 3–5 is second containing 42 words). The man's argument accomplishes two things: 1) through logical argumentation it establishes Jesus as one who is "from God" and therefore not a sinner; 2) through sarcasm it establishes the Pharisees as ignorant, those who "do not know." As far as rhetorical effect is concerned, sarcasm and humor are delightful to audiences. The listener will want to side with the man born blind. Middle ground is eliminated. One must either side with the disciples of Jesus or the disciples of Moses. The disciples of Moses are those who "do not know." The listener will want to avoid siding with the Pharisees. This will be explored further in the Irony, Wit, Humor, and Sarcasm chapter, but briefly stated, the knowledge that Jesus is from God is shared by the healed man, the narrator, and the audience. This shared knowledge creates an in-group bond.

Verse 34: Pharisees Expel the Man

34 They answered and said to him, You were born completely in sins, and you teach us? And they threw him out.	34 ἀπεκρίθησαν καὶ εἶπαν αὐτῷ· ἐν ἁμαρτίαις σὺ ἐγεννήθης ὅλος καὶ σὺ διδάσκεις ἡμᾶς; καὶ ἐξέβαλον αὐτὸν ἔξω.

The Pharisees highlight the fact of the man's blindness from birth and assume this is an indication of sin, "ἁμαρτίαις σὺ ἐγεννήθης" (born completely in sins). This assumption has been rejected by Jesus in v. 3. Instead, the result of the man's blindness will be to "make manifest God's works"

---

20. Westfall, "Prominence," 88. Under the heading *Prominent Material Supported by Elaboration/comment*, she discusses how the presence of expanded sentences increase prominence and draw audience attention.

(ἵνα φανερωθῇ τὰ ἔργα τοῦ θεοῦ, v. 3). The Pharisees reject the teaching of the one in whom God's works are made manifest.

Scene 7: Jesus Receives the Man, 35–38

35 Jesus heard that they had thrown him out, and finding him, he said, "Do you trust into the son of man?	35 Ἤκουσεν Ἰησοῦς ὅτι ἐξέβαλον αὐτὸν ἔξω καὶ εὑρὼν αὐτὸν εἶπεν· σὺ πιστεύεις εἰς τὸν υἱὸν τοῦ ἀνθρώπου;
36 That one answered and said, "And who is he, Lord, so that I might trust in him?	36 ἀπεκρίθη ἐκεῖνος καὶ εἶπεν· καὶ τίς ἐστιν, κύριε, ἵνα πιστεύσω εἰς αὐτόν;
37 And Jesus said to him, "You *have* seen him, and he is the one talking to you."	37 εἶπεν αὐτῷ ὁ Ἰησοῦς· καὶ ἑώρακας αὐτὸν καὶ ὁ λαλῶν μετὰ σοῦ ἐκεῖνός ἐστιν.
38 And he said, "I trust, Lord!" And he bowed before him.	38 ὁ δὲ ἔφη· πιστεύω, κύριε· καὶ προσεκύνησεν αὐτῷ.

An immediate contrast is developed between the Pharisees and Jesus in vv. 34 and 35. The Pharisees "throw out" (ἐκβάλλω), whereas Jesus "finds" (εὑρίσκω). The prominence of this scene is heightened with the presence of a subjunctive[21] and a perfect[22] verb in vv. 36 and 37 respectively. In v. 36, "that I may trust" (πιστεύσω subjunctive of πιστεύω), we have the subjunctive. In v. 37, "you have seen him" (ἑώρακας perfect of ὁράω), there is the perfect. Verse 38 closes the scene with two short two word cola: πιστεύω, κύριε (Lord, I trust) and προσεκύνησεν αὐτῷ (he worshipped him).

---

21. Westfall, "Prominence," pp. 80. Westfall argues that mood is an indicator of prominence.

indicative	unmarked	default
imperative	↓	3rd, 2nd person pl.
subjunctive	↓	1st person pl. command
optative	marked	rare, emphatic

22. Westfall, "Prominence," 79. Again, aspect/tense (n16) is an indicator of prominence.

This is the climactic scene. The healed man has yet to actually see Jesus physically, even though he has demonstrated great insight into who Jesus is and where he is from (from God, v. 32). Jesus, heard of the man's abolishment and then seeking and finding him (εὑρίσκω), solicits trust (v.35). While "εὑρίσκω" can mean find by chance,[23] it can also mean to find after searching.[24] The mention of Jesus hearing that he had been thrown out seems to indicate that this is an intentional seeking out. This is supported by 10:3–4 where the good shepherd "calls," "leads out," and "brings out" the sheep. Tension as to the fate of the healed man after being "thrown out" is resolved. This tension has been building since it was foreshadowed in vv. 22–23. He is now part of Jesus's community. Interestingly, the very next instance of ἐκβάλλω in the narrative is in 10:4 where Jesus the good shepherd has "brought out"[25] all of "his own." This ironically frames the actions of the Pharisees as part of the plans of the good shepherd!

If the rhetorical goal of both the narrative as a whole (by this I mean all of the Gospel of John) and of this episode is to elicit trust in Jesus and bring life,[26] then this scene serves that purpose in two ways. First, the cultural fear which comes from being removed from community and made an outcast (vv. 22–23, 34) is relieved by acceptance of the man into Jesus's community. Second, this acceptance happens specifically through trust in Jesus (v. 38).

---

23. εὑρίσκω, BDAG s.v. 1.b.

24. Ibid., s.v. 1.a.

25. The NRSV, because of context, renders ἐκβάλλω in 10:4 as "leads out" and in 9:34 and 35 renders it "cast out." This is a verbal thread that is missed in translation.

26. Cf. John 20:31, "but these have been written in order that (ἵνα) you might trust (πιστεύσητε) that Jesus is the Christ (cf. 9:22) the son of God and that by trusting (πιστεύοντες) you might have life in his name."

Scene 8: Jesus passes judgment upon the Pharisees, 39–41

39 And Jesus said, "I came into this world for judgment, so that those who don't see might see, and those who see might become blind." 40 And some of the Pharisees who were with him heard these things, and they said to him, "Surely *we* are not blind?" 41 Jesus said to them, "If you were blind, you would have no sin. But now that you say, 'We see,' your sin remains."	39 Καὶ εἶπεν ὁ Ἰησοῦς· εἰς κρίμα ἐγὼ εἰς τὸν κόσμον τοῦτον ἦλθον, ἵνα οἱ μὴ βλέποντες βλέπωσιν καὶ οἱ βλέποντες τυφλοὶ γένωνται. 40 ἤκουσαν ἐκ τῶν Φαρισαίων ταῦτα οἱ μετ' αὐτοῦ ὄντες καὶ εἶπον αὐτῷ· μὴ καὶ ἡμεῖς τυφλοί ἐσμεν; 41 εἶπεν αὐτοῖς ὁ Ἰησοῦς· εἰ τυφλοὶ ἦτε, οὐκ ἂν εἴχετε ἁμαρτίαν· νῦν δὲ λέγετε ὅτι βλέπομεν, ἡ ἁμαρτία ὑμῶν μένει.

39 And Jesus said,
    for judgment I into this world came,
    in order that the *ones* not seeing   A   ἵνα οἱ μὴ μὴ βλέποντες
    may see,   B   βλέπωσιν
    and the ones seeing   A'   καὶ οἱ βλέποντες
    may become blind.   B'   τυφλοὶ γένωνται.

There is a simple ABAB pattern in v. 39 which describes the effect that Jesus has upon the "world:" Not seeing → may see ↔ seeing → may become blind. Jesus reverses the fortunes of the seeing and the blind. The ἵνα + subjunctive expresses purpose here. Jesus's purpose in coming includes the reversal just described. The ἵνα . . . βλέπωσιν ("in order that they might see") matches the similar result construction in v. 3 ἵνα φανερωθῇ τὰ ἔργα τοῦ θεοῦ ("in order that the works of God might be revealed"). The man was born blind "so that" God's works might be seen, while Jesus has come "so that" the blind might see. These phrases complement one another in that the works of God, sight to a man born blind, are performed by Jesus, who comes in order that the blind might see. Taken together they help to define Jesus as the one sent to "work/accomplish" God's "works."

This "judgment" (κρίμα, v. 39) also has another side to it. The presence of Jesus in the world forces a judgment. One cannot remain neutral. In this case, the Pharisees, who claim to have sight, knowledge, and insight, are made blind. This is also the purpose (ἵνα ... τυφλοὶ γένωνται) of Jesus presence in the world.

40 And those of the Pharisees who were with him heard these things, and said to him,
    surely we are not blind?

---

41 Jesus said to them,
    If you were blind,   A
    you would have no sin.   B
    But now you say, We see;   A'
    therefore, your sin remains.   B'

In v. 41 there is an ABAB pattern: blind = no sin; claim to sight = sin remains. Verse 39 matches the ABAB pattern in 41 and the two verses together move from the general (39) to the specific (41).

---

	39 And Jesus said, for judgment I into this world came,	41 Jesus said to them,
A	in order that the *ones not seeing*	If you were *blind*,
B	*may see*,	you would have *no sin*.
A'	and the ones *seeing*	But now you say, We *see*;
B'	may *become blind*.	your *sin remains*.

The expressed purpose of Jesus's presence in the world (v. 39), to make the blind see and the seeing blind, is expressed more specifically in v. 41. Jesus's purpose is to make those who have a claim to understanding ("we see") become blind ("sin remains") and those who have no claim to understanding ("blind") able to understand and thus "have no sin."

The entire episode redefines sin. Sin is failure in recognizing/seeing/knowing Jesus as light of the world. At the end, the episode comes full circle. The man born blind in the beginning of the episode is assumed to be a product of sin. By the end of the episode he sees, is characterized as one who "knows," and is proven to be sin free. The Pharisees, generally assumed to be holy, by the end of the episode are declared to be blind and in sin and characterized as those who do not know.

Knowing and seeing are closely related in John (3:11). Twice the Pharisees *emphatically* claim "we know . . ." (ἡμεῖς οἴδαμεν[27], 9:24, 29). In 9:41, Jesus echoes back to them that they claim to see, νῦν δὲ λέγετε ὅτι βλέπομεν (but now you say, "we see"). Their claim to see or to know is the reason that their "sin remains" (9:41). The Pharisees are proven to be blind at the end of this episode, in as much as they cannot see Jesus for who he is, the one sent by God to do God's works. To follow the logic of John's narrative, any who see Jesus, also see God (12:45). By implication, those who cannot see Jesus do not see God.

This is a key point in relation to moving the audience toward a place of trust. The audience, like the man born blind, is transformed as they begin to see Jesus in the same way as the healed man sees him. As light (Jesus) now abides in the man born blind (whereby he has life), the same can happen for the audience as they begin to see Jesus (and therefore God) in te same way the healed man does.

Once again, the rhetorical impact is this: Do not be like the Pharisees who do not know, do not see, fail to recognize the "sign," and therefore "remain" in sin. Rather, be like the man born blind who sees, knows, is declared not a product of sin, and who in spite of facing terrible sanctions ("they threw him out," v. 27) trusts in Jesus. But more than simply "don't be like the Pharisees, be like the healed man," the story brings the audience to a point of decision and therefore a point of judgment (9:39). Now, like the characters in the narrative, the audience is also confronted with the reality of the light of the world, and must also decide. If the audience sees/knows Jesus for who he is, the one sent by God to do God's works, at that moment the audience also sees/knows God and receives life. In this respect, the passage leads the audience toward a place of courageous witness (like the healed man has demonstrated). The audience can also rest secure in the knowledge that, like the healed man, there is a community (the community of the good shepherd) who will receive them and that, also like the healed man, the good shepherd himself will care for them.

---

27. Again, the unnecessary use of ἡμεῖς (we) with a verb that already contains the "we" in the pronominal ending functions to add emphasis to the verb. See n16.

Special Johannine Terminology

The Gospel of John programmatically redefines a number of key terms. As the audience is carried along by the story, they learn the special language of the Gospel and the community of believers associated with it. This episode functions as a part of that program of redefinition. *Sin* is redefined in this episode as not trusting or accepting Jesus as the one sent by the Father. The conventional understanding of the day was that sickness is the result of sin. When the disciples apply this assumption to the man born blind, it is rejected by Jesus (scene 1). Likewise, the Pharisees (disciples of Moses) assume that Jesus must be a sinner since he has healed on the Sabbath. This assumption is refuted by the man born blind (scene 6).

Sight is also a special Johannine term which plays a role in this episode. The audience is initially invited to trust through the phrase "come and see" spoken by Jesus to the disciples (1:39), by Phillip to Nathaniel (1:46), and by the woman at the well to her villagers (4:29). In this episode, sight is redefined as the way in which one comes to know that Jesus is from God. In "seeing" Jesus, one sees God who sent him (12:45).

Judgment, another important Johannine term, comes as a result of the presence of the one sent (both ἀποστέλλω and πέμπω). As the one who is sent, Jesus acts as savior and as judge. His primary reason for being sent is to "save" (σώζω) the world 3:17. Those who trust in him are not judged/condemned (κρίνω), but those who do not trust are already (ἤδη) judged/condemned (κρίνω) (3:18). There are no judicial proceedings that need to occur. The judgment is "already" (ἤδη) pronounced according to one's response of trust in the one God has sent. In John 9:39, it is for the purpose of[28] "judgment" (κρίμα) Jesus claims to have come into the world. His presence and the "work" which he does in healing the blind man provide the occasion for judgment to be made. The healed man chooses to respond in trust (πιστεύω) where the Pharisees fail to see who Jesus is and fail to recognize the work done in healing the blind man as God's work. They are therefore judged as having sin which "abides/remains" (μένω, 9:41).

In fact, *remaining, abiding, dwelling*, all translate the Greek μένω. This Johannine term is used primarily to express the mutual indwelling

---

28. εἰς κρίμα ἐγὼ εἰς τὸν κόσμον τοῦτον ἦλθον ("for judgment I came into this world") where εἰς expresses reason or purpose BDAG, s.v. 4.f.

of the Father, the Son, the Holy Spirit, and the disciples.[29] All are said to "abide in" one another (1:32; 14:10, 15–17; 15:1–11). Additionally Jesus's purpose in coming "as a light to the world" is so that people would not "dwell" in darkness (12:46). This is precisely his effect on the man born blind. Jesus the light of the world frees the man from darkness. For those in the episode who do not trust, their sin "abides" or "remains."

Conclusion

One of the primary values of an analysis such as this is that the emphasis in the text is discovered. As one follows the patterns in the narrative one discovers where the narrator leads the attention of the audience. Another value is that the terms in the narrative will often define one another through the various patterns.

In the first scene, the man's blindness is characterized as an instrument for revealing God's works. This function becomes increasingly evident as the episode progresses. The common cultural assumption that his blindness was the result of sin is also denied. Jesus, as light of the world, performs God's works while it is day.

The second scene functions to further define Jesus as the sent one, expressed indirectly with wordplay on the pool of Siloam. The staccato phrases "he went, and washed, and came back seeing" increase the energy of the scene and move the episode to the next interaction.

In scene three the energy level remains high as "buzz" is generated about the healing. The neighbors are debating about whether the man they see now is actually the man born blind. The use of the imperfect (ἔλεγον) indicates an ongoing discussion. The man settles the discussion by saying "it is I." This culminates in the first questioning of the healed man in the next scene. Once Jesus is defined as light and the one sent by God, and the blind man is shown to be an instrument of revelation (Scene 1) the audience is swept along quickly (Scenes 2–3) from the healing to the first questioning (Scene 4).

The tension is heightened when the audience is told "it was" a Sabbath. The imperfect (ἦν) is a more proximate verb tense. Again "buzz" is generated as the Pharisees engaged in an ongoing discussion about whether or not Jesus is a sinner. The discussion is again settled by the

---

29. More on this see Brown, *John*, 1:510–12; Malatesta, *Interiority*; Neyrey, *Perspective*, 399.

healed man who answers, "He is a prophet." Twice now the man has settled an ongoing discussion. The Pharisees, however, do not accept his answer.

In scene 5, when the parents are questioned, they are asked "How does he now see?" The parents not only answer that they don't know "how" he sees but they go a step further and assert that they are ignorant of "who" opened his eyes, thus focusing the central issue on Jesus. The use of the pluperfect ("had already decided together" συνετέθειντο) in v. 22 draws dramatic attention to the decision that confessors of Jesus as Christ will be expelled. It is also ironic in light of the indecision about Jesus in the prior scene.

In scene 6, the man is questioned a second time and the Pharisees are characterized as those who do not "hear" and as those who do not "know." By contrast, the man born blind is shown to be one who does hear and does know. In the most prominent monologue of the chapter, the man argues that Jesus is "from God." The audience's attention, as well as the plot tension, is at its height as the man and Pharisees engage in heated and even volatile (v. 28, "they reviled him") debate. The man is expelled from synagogue life.

On the heels of this heated debate the climax of the episode unfolds. Jesus reappears in scene 7 and seeks out the man in contrast to the Pharisees who expel him. He elicits trust from the man who worships him as lord. A subjunctive and a perfect verb in vv. 36 and 37 respectively highlight the prominence of this scene which provides a welcome emotional relief from the tense scene preceding it.

In the final scene, Jesus, in the second most prominent speech of the episode, reverses the fortunes of the blind and the sighted. By means of metaphor and wordplay, those who are blind become those who see and recognize Jesus as light of the world. Those who claim the ability to see become blind, failing to recognize the light of the world. Those who recognize (man born blind/disciple of Jesus) have no sin, those who do not recognize (Pharisees/disciples of Moses) remain in sin.

As the episode progresses, one can see the development of the man born blind's character, in contrast to the Pharisees' characterization. As the man born blind gradually comes to a fuller understanding of Jesus and thus to true sight, the Pharisees become increasingly hostile and stubborn with respect to their understanding of Jesus. They are ultimately portrayed in the final scene as blind.

Rhetorically, the episode works to distance the audience from the "disciples of Moses" and to elicit sympathy for the man born blind. This is done by increasingly characterizing the Pharisees as ones who do not "know," do not "hear," and do not "see." The man born blind gains understanding, courage, and wit (both rhetorical skill and sarcasm) throughout the episode. After building sympathy for the healed man the author can then portray him as a positive example.

He is found by Jesus, trusts in Jesus, and finally worships Jesus. The courage and positive example of the healed man at this point is an attempt to convince the audience likewise to place faith in Jesus. Fear over loss of community is assuaged by the assurance that Jesus's community is waiting.

The episode forces a decision about Jesus. One must decide that Jesus is from God or not. The characters within the Gospel story, as within this episode, are forced progressively into two categories: those who *receive* Jesus (1:12) and are thus children of God (1:12–13), or those who *do not receive* him (1:11) and are children of the devil (8:44). Those who *receive* Jesus do so by trusting in Jesus (1:12;[30] 3:36; 20:31) *and* the one who sent him (5:24). Indeed trust in Jesus and trust in the one who sent him are one in the same (12:44). Those who have such trust also have life (1:4; 3:15–16), eternal (αἰώνιος,[31] 4:14, 36; 5:24; 10:28; 12:50; 17:2) and in abundance (περισσός, 10:10). Those who do *not receive* Jesus are those who do not trust (3:18) *or* trust but do not confess (ὁμολογέω,[32] 12:42; cf. 9:22). They die in their sins (8:21, 24), love darkness rather than light because their works are evil (3:19), and their sin remains (9:41). In fact, death (θάνατος) is the default state of humanity in John, since the one who trusts (πιστεύω) crosses (μεταβαίνω) from death to life (ζωή) (5:24 cf. 8:12). The "aha" moment in this passage is at 9:41 where those who claim to see have sin which remains. Will the audience remain in the

---

30. Here, τοῖς πιστεύουσιν εἰς τὸ ὄνομα αὐτοῦ, (those trusting in his name) is in apposition to "those" (αὐτοῖς) who have the authority to become children of God (ἔδωκεν αὐτοῖς ἐξουσίαν τέκνα θεοῦ γενέσθαι).

31. It indicates a divine quality of life in addition to simply everlasting life, cf. LXX Gen 21:33 where it is a quality of God.

32. The only other time ὁμολογέω is used is in 1:20 where John the Baptist confesses that he is not the Christ. The other two times it is used of those who "confess" that "Jesus is Christ" (9:22) and in the summary of the people's unbelief at 12:42. By implication one can assume that 12:42 is talking about a confession of Jesus as Christ since both 12:42 and 9:22 contain the same threat of ἀποσυνάγωγος (expulsion from synagogue community).

category of those who think "we see" and "we know" or will the audience accept the vision of Jesus that the author offers? As the audience "sees" Jesus as the healed man sees him, they too experience Jesus as light of the world—and the courage to testify to it.

This episode then serves the overall goal of the Gospel, trust in Jesus, by a combination of factors. First, Jesus is characterized in this episode as light of the world and one who is "from God" and "sent" to do God's "work." Second, Jesus finds the healed man who acts as a positive example and places his trust in him. Third, any fear of sanction from Jewish authorities is mitigated by acceptance into Jesus's community. Finally, sin is redefined. Instead of a traditional understanding of sin, sin is defined as failure to accept Jesus as the one sent from God to do God's work.

3

Narrative Analysis

IN THIS CHAPTER I will examine the passage according to the principles of narrative criticism.[1] This discipline analyses the passage according to the features present in a narrative: plot, character, setting, point of view, standards of judgment and rhetoric.[2] "Arguably, *everything* in the text contributes to its impact and our interpretation of it, and so everything has some rhetorical function."[3] While some narrative studies deal with a gospel as a whole,[4] or deal with particular aspects of narrative such as studying a particular character throughout a gospel,[5] it is also appropriate and useful to study a particular episode within a gospel.[6]

In a narrative, an episode can be a means through which one can understand more clearly the Gospel. In a narrative as tightly woven as the Gospel of John one sees ideas in a single episode that appear throughout

---

1. In general on this see: Beckson, *Literary Terms*; Boomershine, *Story Journey*; Marguerat, Bourquin, and Durrer, *Bible Stories*; Perkins, "Crisis"; Powell, *Narrative Criticism?*; Resseguie, *Narrative Criticism*; Rhoads and Syreeni, *Characterization*; Rhoads, Dewey, and Michie, *Mark as Story*.

Non-biblical Narratology: Abbott, *Introduction to Narrative*; Bal and Boheemen, *Narratology*; Fludernik, *Introduction to Narratology*.

For John specifically: Culpepper, *Anatomy*; Culpepper and Segovia, *Fourth Gospel*; Holleran, "Seeing the Light"; Moloney, *Belief in the Word*; Moloney, *Signs and Shadows*; Moloney, *Glory Not Dishonor*; Moloney, *Gospel of John*; Stibbe, *John as Storyteller*; Stibbe, *John as Literature*; Thatcher and Moore, *Anatomies of Narrative Criticism*.

2. Powell, *Narrative Criticism?*; Rhoads, Dewey, and Michie, *Mark as Story*; Boomershine, *Story Journey*. In relation to the power of a narrative to convince (rhetoric of a narrative) see also: Abbott, *Introduction to Narrative*, ch. 4.

3. Abbot, *Introduction to Narrative*, 40; emphasis is the author's.

4. Culpepper, *Anatomy*.

5. Thompson, "Voice, Form."

6. Rhoads, *Reading Mark*, 63.

the Gospel. Several of these appear in John 9. Jesus as light, where Jesus is from, sin, trust in Jesus as the one sent, judgment, expulsion from the synagogue community, and fear of "the Jews" all appear in this episode as well as in the rest of the Gospel. The overall narrative helps to inform these various concepts. The Gospel serves as a framework to understand the episode, while a given episode further shapes and nuances the various concepts, themes and values in the narrative.

All of these elements help to shape what is called the *story world*, a world with its own internal logic, values, structures and circumstances, all derived from the elements within the narrative itself. The author uses the narrative to weave a self contained "story world" that certainly has enough connection with the real world so the audience may follow, but also stands apart from the real world, so that the audience is drawn into it as the narrative unfolds.[7] Of this, Abbot writes, "scholars have sought to redirect the focus of narrative study from the story to the world that is generated in rendering the story. Narrative in this sense "is the art of making and understanding a world."[8] Obvious examples of this exist in the modern genres of fantasy and science fiction. In such stories the audience must follow the logic of a world "built" by the narrative where dragons and magic exist or where "the force" can "be with you." For the audience to follow the story at all they must engage and understand the elements of the story world. Powell also uses the example of a movie where:

> Once inside the theater, we may find ourselves involved with a view of reality distinct from that of the world in which we actually live. Nevertheless it is possible for our encounter with this simplified and perhaps outlandish view of reality to have an effect on us, an effect that may continue to make itself felt long after we leave the theater and return to the real world.[9]

Movies, particularly so called "cult classic" movies, may be a better modern analog to explain the impact of a story on an audience than the modern written story. Movies are experienced in a multisensory (sight and sound) way, in a group, literary stories are experienced silently and individually. A gospel most likely was experienced in a group and, since

---

7. Ibid., 4.
8. *Introduction to Narrative*, 164–65, Abbot quoting Doležel, *Heterocosmica*, 42.
9. Powell, *What is Narrative*, 90. An example of how a story has lasting effect on an audience in the real world might be the fact that after the popularity of the *Star Wars* trilogy many enthusiasts would express parting greetings with the phrase "may the force be with you."

most ancients could not read, performed by a storyteller who used gestures, body language, and voice inflection (thus an experience of sight and sound for the audience).[10] In all of these things, a performer seeks to draw the audience into the story world and create a rhetorical impact on the audience.

I will demonstrate through examination of the narrative components listed above that the implied audience[11] is asked by the implied author[12] to have courage and "trust in the Son of Man" despite potential negative consequences. The audience has already been told that Jesus is the life that is the light of all (1:4) and is the light of the world (1:9) which brings life (8:12). The episode of the man born blind serves within the whole narrative to show the audience how this narrative claim (cf. 9:4) is true.[13] In this episode, the man born blind receives a new life through the process of his encounter with and trust in the "light of the world." This process takes place concretely in the form of his restored sight (9:7, 39), his ability to witness (9:11-12, 13-17) courageously (9:24-34), and his expulsion from one community (9:34) and acceptance into a new community (9:35-38; cf. 10:4, 16).

Location in the narrative

In the narrated order of the Gospel, the episode appears in what Raymond Brown calls the "Book of Signs." The Gospel can be divided into two parts, the Book of Signs (chs. 1-12) and the Book of Glory (chs. 13-20 with 21 as an appendix or second ending).[14] The function of the Book of Signs is to demonstrate who Jesus is by presenting his works or signs as evidence of his identity. The works or signs of Jesus call people to have faith, to trust in him. (This will become more evident from a study of ἔργον and πιστεύω later in the chapter.) In the last half of the Gospel, the Book of Glory, the listeners are addressed as those who have trust;

---

10. Shiner, *Proclaiming*, 79ff. and 127ff.

11. The picture or profile of an audience that one can infer from the narrative. In narrative criticism this is usually called the implied reader, given the orality of antiquity I prefer the term implied audience. Powell, *What Is Narrative*, 15.

12. Powell, *What Is Narrative*, 5. The picture or profile of the author that one can infer from the narrative.

13. Also, Culpepper, *Gospel and Letters*, 174.

14. Brown, *John*, 1:cxxxviii.

trust is assumed rather than elicited. I would argue that in general this understanding holds true.

Thus, the episode of the man born blind is set in a section of the Gospel that deals with Jesus miracles as signs or works which testify to who Jesus is. This particular episode exemplifies true sight and true trust based on the evidence of Jesus works (9:32-33). In addition to calling listeners to trust and to have courage, this episode also functions in its larger narrative context to further sharpen the conflict between Jesus and the Pharisees (9:39-41; 10:1, 8), a conflict that reaches its climax in John 11:45-53 in the plot to kill Jesus (which was hinted at in 7:1). Finally, the passage serves to clarify the recurring theme about fear of the Jews (7:13; 9:22; 19:38; 20:19). The narrative comment in 9:22-23 explains the nature of this fear, namely, expulsion from the synagogue.

Setting

In this section, I will examine three elements related to setting. Every story has three basic parts: characters, events or plot, and setting.[15] All stories have *characters* or at least a character. The characters do something; this is the *plot*. The characters do not do their something in a vacuum. There is always setting. *Setting* is where and when the characters play out the plot.

Setting can be understood in three ways: location or place, time, and social context. *Location* refers to the place where events in the narrative happen. Is an event inside and private, outside and public, on holy ground, in Jewish or Gentile territory, and so on? Each of these options will likely affect how an event is to be understood.

Time can be expressed in a number of ways.[16] There is the time in the span of history or there is *locative* time when an event specifically takes place (Luke 1:5 or 2:2 for example). The kind or *type* of time when an event takes place, such as night (John 3:1), or on the "Sabbath" (holy time versus ordinary time as in John 5:9; 9:14) is also important. This kind of time also includes seasons such as Passover, for example. The *duration* of time that an event last is another factor to consider as well. These kinds of

---

15. Abbot, *Introduction to Narrative*; Bal and Boheemen, *Naratology,* 112ff, 201ff; 189ff; 133ff, 219ff.

16. Powell, *Narrative Criticism*, 72-73. Also, Bal and Boheemen, *Narratology*, 214-18; and 79-97.

settings in time just listed are the kinds of time the characters in a story experience. Another kind of setting in time has been called *monumental time*.[17] This kind of setting in time refers to the overarching span of all time, time that includes but also transcends history.

Social context encompasses many elements and is complex enough to deserve its own chapter in this work. Social context or social setting encompasses issues of social status, economics, political institutions, customs of the society, understanding of how the world works (cosmology), and class structures.[18] To be sure this list is not exhaustive. Essentially, these are all things that a first century Mediterranean audience and author would know and assume in common. These are the things that would be brought to the story telling table so to speak. Unfortunately these are also things that are often lost to a twenty-first century Western audience. To further complicate things, many of the assumptions of a twenty-first century Western audience are in conflict with the assumptions of a first century Mediterranean audience. For example, eyesight and how vision works is not understood by us in the same way as it was to John's audience. This is also true for sickness and disabilities.

Location

The apparent narrative setting for this episode is still Jerusalem. The temple is most likely nearby, for if the blind man, as the bystanders note, "sat and begged" (9:8) then it was likely near one of the gates. It is just under a half mile from the south gates to the Pool of Siloam. The significance of the Siloam Pool will be examined in the next section in relation to the Feast of Booths.

The setting in Jerusalem is for Jesus a place of danger. John's audience already knows that "the Jews" in Judea are looking for a way to kill him (7:1). The tension between Jesus and the Jewish authorities increases during Jesus's activity at the Feast of Booths (chs. 7–8). Jerusalem and the Temple are thought by the Pharisees and Chief Priests to be their domain of control or their "place" (τόπος, 11:49). Jesus is essentially in enemy territory, playing out the statement that his "own did not receive him" (1:11).

---

17. Powell, *Narrative Criticism*, 74, citing the work of Ricoeur, *Time and Narrative*.
18. Powell, *Narrative Criticism*, 74–75.

Time

The Gospel story as a whole encompasses the span of history from the creation of all that was made (1:3) up to the last judgment (12:48). More specifically, John's story narration begins at the time when "the true light ... was coming into the world" (1:9). The story as a whole, then, narrates that period of time in which the true light who "enlightens everyone" (1:9) and who "brings life" (1:4) was in the world. During this time the very world which that light created "did not know him" (1:10) and "did not receive him" (1:11). However, also during this time, some do receive him by trusting (πιστεύω) in his name (1:12). Those who do trust in his name subsequently become God's children born by God's will. In ordinary families, the male head of the household, the father (ἀνήρ), decides that children should be born. In the family created by trust in the name of Christ, God's will (θέλημα) is operative, making God the father of this new family (1:13). So then, John's Gospel narrates a time of pregnant opportunity when one can become a part of God's family through trust in the light of the world. Every episode in the Gospel story is therefore to be seen as presenting this choice in some degree or another. So also, the act itself of telling and hearing the story is a time of this same pregnant opportunity (20:31).[19]

The setting in time is somewhere between the Feast of Booths (7:2) and the Feast of Dedication (10:22).[20] It is unclear exactly when the episode takes place. In this respect, the episode has an ahistorical or perhaps, better stated, a "timeless" feel to it. Also of great significance is the fact that, in the story world, it is not an ordinary day; it is a Sabbath (9:14). We must keep in mind the narrative connection between the claim Jesus makes as light of the world in 8:12 and his claim in 9:5 that "As long as I am in the world, I am the light of the world." His first claim as light of the world takes place on "the last day, the great day" of the Feast of Booths.[21]

---

19. Of course the act of storytelling is beyond the scope of setting. Setting is an element of the story itself, something contained in the story. The telling of the story is an element outside of the story and deals with the effect on an audience. Even so, these two elements seem closely enough related to be mentioned together here.

20. Moloney, *Signs*, 120, and also n15 for a brief discussion on this.

21. If we assume that the section of 7:53—8:11, the woman caught in adultery, was a later insertion into the narrative, then the timeline is unbroken from 7:37. This places Jesus's statements about "living water" and "light of the world" on the same day.

The significance of the connection with the Feast of Booths is twofold. The first is in relation to the Pool of Siloam on the Sabbath.[22] In *m. Sukkah* 4:10b–c we read, "But on the eve of the Sabbath one would fill with water from Siloam a gold jug, which was not sanctified, and he would leave it in a chamber [in the Temple]."[23] An audience familiar with the customs of the feast would associate Siloam with the water libations performed on the last day of the festival (*m. Sukkah* 4:9–10). This would recall for an audience Jesus's recent statement about "rivers of living water" flowing from the believer's "belly" (κοιλία, 7:37–38).

The second connection of this episode with the festival is the statement "I am the light of the world" made in 8:12 and repeated in our episode in 9:4. On the evening of the last day of the feast, large lights using priestly garments for wicks and fueled with oil were lit.

> (5:2) At the end of the first festival day of the Festival [the priests and Levites] went down to the women's courtyard. And they made a major enactment [by putting men below and women above]. And there were golden candleholders there, with four gold bowls on their tops, and four ladders for each candlestick. And four young priests with jars of oil containing a hundred and twenty logs, [would climb up the ladders and] pour [the oil] into each bowl. (5:3) Out of the worn-out undergarments and girdles of the priests they made wicks, and with them they lit the candlesticks. And there was not a courtyard in Jerusalem which was not lit up from the light . . . (*m. Sukkah* 5:2–3)

Jesus's claim in 8:12 to be "the light of the world" surpasses the feast that lights up Jerusalem.[24] No doubt John's audience would remember this claim, and the aftermath of conflict with the Pharisees, upon hearing it again in 9:4.

The episode of the blind man's healing is an illustration of the effect the light of the world has on the world. Some trust (9:38), while others become more deeply entrenched in their rejection and ignorance (9:24, 29 cf. 3:19–21).

---

22. Also, Moloney, *Signs*, 122; Moloney, *John*, 194–98; Myers, *Characterizing Jesus*, 148.

23. My quotations from the Mishnah are from Neusner, *The Mishnah*, unless otherwise noted.

24. Moloney, *John*, 266, notes the connection to the lighting ceremony at the end of the festival.

Another aspect of setting in time relates to the kind of life a believer receives from Jesus. The life that Jesus brings is primarily described as "eternal" (αἰώνιος). Indeed, every instance of αἰώνιος modifies ζωή (life). In all other instances except one ζωή stands alone. The one other time ζωή is modified, the modifier is "περισσός," (10:10) which can mean *abundantly, in extraordinary amount* or *extraordinary in nature or quality*.²⁵ It is followed by ζωή modified by αἰώνιος in 10:28.²⁶ It is probably safe to say that "αἰώνιος" and "περισσός" help to define one another here. In 10:10 the good shepherd gives "abundant life" and in 10:28 he gives "eternal life" to the sheep. This "eternal life" involves no one being able to "snatch" (ἁρπάζω) the sheep out of Jesus's hand or the Father's hand (10:28–29 cf. 10:12). The word indicates stealing or taking away by attacking or seizing.²⁷ It describes what the wolf does to the sheep when the hired hand, who does not own or care for the sheep, runs away, failing to protect them. We can deduce that the idea of eternal life for John involves protection and safety, where one is cared for by both Jesus and God (10:28–29, cf. 17:12, 15). It also involves a deep or intimate knowledge of both Jesus and God (10:4–5, 14–15 cf. 17:2–3). According to John, those who receive life are ushered into a new "age" (αἰών, 10:28 cf. 6:51, 58; 8:51; 14:16) where they are cared for, protected, and never experience death. In as much as life is a new age in John, the gospel is set in this new age.

Social Setting

As was mentioned above, this aspect of setting receives its own chapter later in this work in which these ideas will be further developed. Nevertheless, I will outline the issues here. The *understanding of vision* in Jesus's (and John's) time was very different from our contemporary view of vision today. As we shall see in the chapter on social science, the primary difference is that vision is understood to be a light that shines forth from one's heart and out one's eyes touching the object beheld. It is more like the sense of touch in this respect than a matter of our being receptive of light (light entering our eyes), as we understand it today.

---

25. περισσός, BDAG, s.v. 2 and 1.

26. Although a new setting in time is announced in 10:22, the Feast of Dedication, the subject matter of Jesus's speech is still the sheep and the good shepherd.

27. ἁρπάζω, BDAG, s.v. 1.

Although often treated with compassion, the *sick and disabled* were considered to be less than whole. Often, illness was understood to be punishment for past sins. This is particularly true of those who are blind. Thus the man born blind, as I will argue in the social-science chapter, would be thought of by John's audience as pitiable, shameful, associated with sin, and ignorant. Therefore, after being healed by the light of the world, his progressive insight and courage in witnessing before the Jewish authorities is significant.

Additionally, there are issues of *Honor and Shame*, particularly in relation to debating with the Jewish authorities. Honor is a core value in Jesus's (and John's) culture. It is a publically recognized claim to worth and something sought by all people and groups of that culture.[28] The importance of Honor cannot be underestimated for the First Century Mediterranean personality.

Finally, there is the issue of the *dyadic personality* and the need to be embedded in a kinship or fictive, kinship group in relation to the man being thrown out of the synagogue community and then sought out by Jesus.

Characterization

Characterization is what the author gives the audience in order for them to be able to construct a character from the narrative.[29] Quite simply, a character is an actor in a narrative.[30] Characters are those who carry out the action of the story, even if that is something very simple like standing by and watching. We usually think of a character as a person but a character can be a group of people. Also, a character can be other personalities such as demons, angels, or depending on the kind of story, animals or natural phenomenon.

There are various ways by which an author can accomplish the task of characterization. In other words, an author has different means to help an audience build an image of what a particular character is like. This is done by either telling or showing.[31] Telling is when a reliable narrator tells the audience outright what a character is like ("Noah was a righteous

---

28. Pilch and Malina, eds., *Biblical Social Values*, 95–96.
29. Powell, *Narrative Criticism*, 52; Abbot, *Introduction to Narrative*, 130ff.
30. Powell, *Narrative Criticism*, 51.
31. Booth, *Fiction*, 3–22.

man . . ." Gen 6:9). The technique of showing is much more nuanced and invites deeper interaction of the audience with the narrative. In showing, the author invites the audience to compare and contrast various pieces of evidence based on what a character does or says and based on what other characters do or say about that character. As I have mentioned above, John 9 functions to show the audience that Jesus is the light of the world after having been told that by the author (1:4, 9).

The characters (or character groups) in this episode include: Jesus, the disciples, the man born blind, the people and onlookers,[32] the Jewish authorities and/or Pharisees, and the parents of the man born blind.

Characters who serve simple functions

The disciples serve to raise the question about sin and to address Jesus as "Rabbi." Both of these functions help to set up the episode to follow. After these functions are complete, they recede into the background no longer to appear in this episode.

The people who question the blind man after his healing serve the function of bringing the healed man to the Jewish authorities. They are characterized as curious and amazed at the healing, and also skeptical about the reality of the miracle. They also provide a platform for the healed man's first act of witnessing about "the man called Jesus" (9:11). It is important to note that the presence of bystanders provides a context for the other characters to interact with one another publicly. Interactions in the public arena involve challenges of honor and shame. A representative of a group wins honor or is shamed during interactions in the public arena.

The Parents

The Healed Man's Parents are quite simply "afraid of the Jews." Their fear stems from the decision to expel those who confess Jesus as Messiah. They provide contrast both with the Pharisees, on the one hand, and with the man born blind, on the other. They are not like the Pharisees who,

---

32. As a point of clarification I will refer throughout to this group as "onlookers" or "bystanders." Thus these characters (inside the Gospel narrative) should not be confused with those who are hearing the Gospel of John told or read to them (outside the gospel narrative), who I will simply call "the audience."

even though they initially show some openness to Jesus, remain blind to who Jesus is. Nor are they like the man born blind, who demonstrates progressive understanding and ultimate trust in Jesus. Due to their fear they take evasive actions. That is to say, they simply say what is needed in order not to anger "the Jews" and in order to avoid the risk of being thrown out of the synagogue (9:22). Even so, according to the values of the narrative, they are assessed negatively. Ultimately they do not demonstrate courage by supporting their own son. Speaking about all in the Gospel who remain silent because of "fear of the Jews" (12:42), the omniscient narrator puts them in the category of those who loved human glory more than glory from God (12:43).

The Pharisees

The Pharisees develop in character as the episode progresses. They are at first simply the Jewish religious authorities and experts. This is seen when the people who witness the miracle bring the healed man to them. This would have been a logical thing to do in the event of a miraculous healing. The Pharisees are divided in their opinion about Jesus when initially questioning the blind man (9:16), but then their opinion is solidified against Jesus (9:24).[33] In their second interrogation, they are portrayed as ones who are hostile to Jesus and who are dangerous enemies of those who might trust in Jesus. This is conveyed by the narrative comment about those who confess Jesus as messiah being put out of the synagogue. By the end of the episode, they are portrayed as ones who do not trust and, as sinners, are metaphorically blind.

The Pharisees are portrayed as those who think they "know" (9:24, 29) but are actually ignorant and blind (9:41). The Pharisees believe that they know the status of Jesus and have determined that he is sinful (9:24). When confronted with the reality of the blind man's healing they become hostile and entrenched in their position. They refuse to see the logical implications of the man's testimony (9:33): "If this man [Jesus] were not

---

33. It is important to note here that in 9:13–17 those who are questioning the man are identified as "the Pharisees" but in 9:18–23 the inquisitors are designated as "the Jews." When the man is questioned a second time (ἐκ δευτέρου) in 9:24–34 the inquisitors are not identified but we can surmise that they are still "the Jews" given the narrative connection between 9:23 "ask him," and 24 "so for a second time they called him." Since, in v. 27, the man answers their questions with, "I told you already" (ἤδη) we can understand, at least for chapter 9, the Jews and the Pharisees to be the same group.

from God, he could do nothing." Rather, they maintain their position that they "know"[34] more than what has been "revealed" (9:3) in the healing. They claim discipleship to Moses to whom "God spoke" (9:29). This may be a reference to Exod 33:11 where "the Lord spoke to Moses face to face (ἐλάλησεν κύριος πρὸς μωυσῆν ἐνώπιος ἐνωπίῳ) as one might speak to his own friend (φίλον)." While this is certainly an impressive pedigree for the "disciples of Moses," what they do not know, ironically, is that Jesus was "with God" (πρὸς τὸν θεόν) from the beginning (ἀρχή) (John1:1.2) before Moses existed (cf. 8:58). So then the disciples of Moses, the Pharisees, are characterized as entrenched in a position of not knowing where Jesus is "from" (πόθεν, 9:29).

John 9 fits into a progressively hostile characterization of the Pharisees throughout the Gospel. Initially the Pharisees are characterized as simply inquisitive. They send "priests and Levites" to investigate John the Baptist (1:24). Nicodemus, a "man from the Pharisees" (3:1) is also characterized as curious, but still does not seem to understand even after his conversation with Jesus (3:9–12). Even so, the Pharisees are not characterized as hostile but rather inquisitively guarded. After a Sabbath day healing in chapter 5, "the Jews," conceivably including many Pharisees, begin to persecute him (5:16). By 7:32ff. the Pharisees, along with the Chief Priests, send temple guards to arrest Jesus. Here they are characterized as both hostile and without belief (7:45ff.). Only Nicodemus provides a moderating voice here (7:50–51) but he is ridiculed (7:52). If "the Jews who trusted in him" (8:32) include some Pharisees, chapter 8 also fits into this picture of a progressively hostile characterization. By the end of Chapter 8, "the Jews" "picked up stones to throw at him," quite possibly in an effort to kill him.

As was mentioned above, in chapter 9 the Pharisees progress from those who are not sure whether Jesus is a sinner (9:16) to those who are fully convinced that he is (9:24). After the raising of Lazarus (11:38–34), the Pharisees are thoroughly entrenched in their opposition, planning with the Chief Priests to kill Jesus (11:53). Even when "many of the authorities trusted in him" they could not confess openly because they feared being cast out of the synagogue (12:42).[35] Finally it is the Pharisees

---

34. O'Brien, "Written," 293.

35. The language used to describe the authorities is emphatic, ὅμως μέντοι καὶ ἐκ τῶν ἀρχόντων πολλοὶ ἐπίστευσαν εἰς αὐτόν, literally, "*nevertheless indeed even* from the authorities many trusted in him" (italics mine). This emphatic language serves to convey just how much control the Pharisees had by using the threat of synagogue

along with the Chief Priests who arrest Jesus in league with Judas, a man described as one whom Satan has "entered" (13:27). Essentially then, the final mention of the Pharisees is that they are in league with Satan.

The Man Born Blind

The blind man's character develops as a contrast to the Pharisees. In the beginning of the episode, he is either a sinner or the son of sinners, because he was born blind. Blindness and sin are the two major hurdles an ancient audience would have to overcome if a sympathetic characterization of the blind man would be attained. In the social-science chapter, I will describe in more detail the kinds of attitudes, feelings, and assumptions that were associated with blind people in Jesus's culture. Here suffice it to say that based on just the cultural assumptions, the blind man would have been a character from which the audience would have withdrawn. He would have been perceived as pitiful, shameful, associated in some way with sin (cf. 9:2), ignorant, and dangerous.[36] These assumptions would have produced a deeply negative initial assessment by John's audience (at least for those hearing the story for the first time). This is a characterization that Jesus's words promptly dispel (9:2).

Even so, as the episode progresses the blind man becomes truly one in whom God's works are made manifest (cf. 9:3). In John 6:29, the work of God is defined as trust in the one whom God has sent. The healed man progresses in his understanding of Jesus,[37] as will be mentioned below in the section on Jesus's characterization. The final development in the healed man's character is narrated in 9:35–38. In these verses he responds to Jesus invitation to trust (9:35). He then vocalizes or confesses his trust (9:37a), and expresses that trust through worship (9:37b). Since God's work is described by Jesus (6:29) as trust in the one whom God has sent, when the healed man responds in trust, that work is accomplished. By coming to trust, the healed man becomes someone in whom "God's works" are "revealed" (φανερόω, 9:3).

---

expulsion. It is control exercised through fear. This same fear operates in 9:22.

36. As I will describe in the social-science chapter, the blind were thought to possess the very real (to that culture) and dangerous evil eye.

37. Keener, *John*, 1:775.

The contrast of the healed man with the Pharisees[38] can be illustrated as follows:

Table 3.1: Contrast of the Healed Man with the Pharisees

MAN	Sight	Witness	Trust
PHARISEES	Blindness	Denial/Rejection	Sin

The man born blind moves from one who is blind to one who truly sees and thus trust. He is also taken from a rather flat character to one who is witty and real. In the initial interaction between the blind man and Jesus, the blind man is a passive character who does not even solicit the healing from Jesus. It is of course possible that the man did not wish to solicit a healing on the Sabbath. It is also possible that he, being blind, did not know that Jesus, a healer, was nearby. For whatever reason, initially he is simply an object of discussion between Jesus and the disciples. In the final interrogation between the man and the Pharisees, he is witty (teasing the Pharisees by suggesting their discipleship to Jesus), and he is wise (logically demonstrating how Jesus is "from God"). As a result of his experience with Jesus, the healed man goes beyond being a literary stereotype, to a more complex, hence more real character. Because of his contact with the *light* of the world (9:5), he finds his own *life* (cf. John 1:4).

The man is portrayed as one who is not "afraid of the Jews" (7:13; 9:22; 19:38; 20:19). On the contrary, he responds to the Pharisees with increasing courage and boldness,[39] then engaging in a pressing theological argument that Jesus is "from God" (9:33). This courage results in the expulsion (9:34) which his parents so feared (9:22).

Finally, the healed man is portrayed as an excellent witness to Jesus.[40] Instead of shrinking in the face of opposition, he flourishes. Although the Greek words μαρτυρέω, μαρτυρία, or μάρτυς do not appear in this passage, "witness" is an important concept in the Gospel, appearing 39 times in 31 of the 879 verses in John. John the Baptist is characterized as the quintessential witness to Jesus. He testifies that Jesus is the one sent

---

38. Also, Brown, *John*, 1:377.

39. Neyrey, *Perspective*, 35, notes that the Gospel positively portrays those who demonstrate the virtue of courage.

40. Ibid., 45–46 also.

from God to the people (1:7, 8, 15), to the Pharisees (1:19, 32, 34), and to his own disciples (3:26–36) even accepting the idea that his own followers should leave him to follow Jesus (3:30). Next, the Samaritan woman is responsible for leading a whole town to trust in him (4:39). The works that Jesus does, as well as the scripture, are witness that he is from God (5:36) and brings life (5:39). The crowd present at the raising of Lazarus continued to bear witness to what had happened (12:17). Although the word is not used of Moses, he serves as a witness having written (1:45) about Jesus. Ironically, the man is more like Moses than the "disciples of Moses" (9:28), the Pharisees. The Holy Spirit will bear witness to Jesus (15:26), along with his disciples (15:27). And finally the "author" of the Gospel bears witness (19:35; 21:24). It is possible that 15:27, "And you also will bear witness, because you have been with me from the beginning" may not only be addressed narratively to the disciples within the episode but through the art of storytelling may be addressed to believers who are in the audience as well. The audience has also "been with" Jesus from the "beginning" of the narrative.

Jesus

Jesus as Light

The narrative presents Jesus as light. As was mentioned earlier, the narrator tells the audience in the prologue that Jesus is both life and light (1:4). This is done by an omniscient narrator[41] and the information would be seen as reliable to an audience. Even so, an audience will want a demonstration of such a grand claim. Jesus refers to himself as light which brings life (8:12), but still the audience awaits a valid demonstration of that claim. Such a demonstration finally comes in this episode.[42] There are three major aspects of light to be explored: light in relation to *life*; light in relation to *insight, wisdom, and/or knowledge*; and light in relation to the *presence of God* or the divine. In asserting that Jesus is light, the Gospel asserts that Jesus is the one who brings life, who brings insight,

---

41. Culpepper, *Anatomy*, 16, 19, defines the Narrator as the literary device who is "the voice that tells the story and speaks to the reader." An omniscient narrator, is able to supply " privileged information into the story which no ordinary observer of the action would have."

42. Moloney, *Signs*, 121.

wisdom, and knowledge, and who is the presence of the divine among people.

The concepts of *light and life* are linked in the Fourth Gospel. Not only is light connected with life in John (1:4; 8:12) but this is also the thought in general in Greco-Roman culture. The words φῶς and ζωή are often paired poetically[43] as in Aeschylus, *Persians* 299 where a messenger tells Atossa: Ξέρξης μὲν αὐτὸς ζῇ τε καὶ βλέπει φάος (Xerxes himself lives and beholds the light). Also, when informed of the death of his wife and two children who no longer "see light" (λεύσσει φάος, Euripides, *Phoenissae* 1547) Oedipus replies: ποίᾳ μοίρᾳ πῶς ἔλιπον φάος; ὦ τέκνον, αὔδα, ("by what portion did they leave the light; child speak?" Euripides, *Phoenissae* 1554). Another such example is in Sophocles where Clytemnestra has a dream about Agamemnon coming back to life, and she uses the description "returning to the light" (Sophocles, *Electra* 417–19).[44]

In addition to Hellenistic culture, the concept of light is linked to life in the Hebrew scripture as well. The beginning of John mirrors the beginning of the Hebrew Bible with the Greek phrase Ἐν ἀρχῇ ("In the beginning"). In Gen 1:3 light (LXX φῶς; Heb. אור) is the first act of creation, after which all the rest of creation and life follows. Light's relationship to life (LXX ζωή or ζάω; Heb. חי) is seen in passages such as Job 3:20, 33:28–30; Ps 27:1; 56:13 where they appear in poetic parallelism, and in Ps 13:3 where it is in antithetical parallelism with "death" (LXX θάνατος; Heb. מות).

Light in both the Hebrew scripture and the Hellenistic culture is also related to *insight and wisdom*. Light (אור) is clearly connected to both God's commands and to the possession of wisdom in Ps 19:8; 119:30; Eccl 2:13; 8:1; Isa 51:4, as well as truth (LXX ἀλήθεια; Heb. אמת) in Ps 43:3. Truth and light are also connected by Euripides (κλεπτῶν γὰρ ἡ νύξ, τῆς δ' ἀληθείας τὸ φῶς, "for the night belongs to thieves, the light to truth,"[45] *Iphigenia in Tauris* 1026), while several authors connect Light

---

43. ζωή, LSJ s.v. b. The entire subheading is dedicated to this meaning.

44. For fuller discussion of the connection between light and life, see Bernidaki-Aldous, *Blindness*, 11–18; Hartsock, *Sight and Blindness*, 61–63. Also, Myers, *Characterizing Jesus*, 148 n41 cites: Eur., *Pheon.* 1541–48; *ALC* 122–29; 268–69, 385; *Hec.* 376; Soph. *Aj.* 854–59; Hom. *Od.* 4.450; *Il.* 18.61; some of which I have already included in the body of my text.

45. From *Iphigenia in Tauris*, trans. Potter.

with knowledge and insight (Plato, *Phdr.* 261e; Sophocles, *Phil.* 581; Plut., *De recta ratione audiendi* 17).[46]

Finally the *presence of God* or the divine is symbolized and portrayed by light in both the Hebrew scriptures and Hellenistic culture. In the Hebrew bible light is related specifically to God's "face" or "presence" (LXX πρόσωπον; Heb. פנה) as in Ps 4:6; 44:3 56:13. The Aronic blessing (Num 6:25) is evidence of how God's face or presence (פנה) which shines (אור) upon the people brings well being (שלום) as well as grace and mercy (חנן). In the wilderness wanderings God is present with the Israelites as light. God's presence in the pillar of fire gave the Israelite host light at night (Exod 13:21; Ps 78:14) and the presence of God in the cloud also "lit up the night" as it interposed itself between the Egyptian army and the Israelites (Exod 14:20).

As early as Homer, light characterizes the divine and the realm of the divine. Olympus is described as "radiant" (αἴγλη)[47] and full of light (φῶς).[48] This is of course true in New Testament literature as well (Acts 9:3; 26:18; 2 Cor 4:6; 1 Tim 6:16; Jas 1:17; 1 John 1:5).

I will offer a more complete explanation of the concepts of how light and darkness are related to sight and blindness in the chapter on social-science issues. For now suffice it to say that in characterizing Jesus as light, the author also characterizes Jesus as one who brings life; who brings wisdom, knowledge, and insight; and as the presence of the divine.

Sent

John's Jesus is the one sent by God. He refers to himself as sent (9:4) and also the narrative comment about the translation of the pool as "sent" (9:7) reminds the listener that Jesus is also the one "sent" as I will explore further in the chapter. Jesus "works" prove that he has been sent (5:36) as this episode illustrates. Some forty times we are told by the author of John that Jesus is sent by the Father. While πέμπω is used to describe Jesus in this episode (9:4), ἀποστέλλω is also used here in 9:7 and throughout John. Indeed, the two seem to be used interchangeably (5:23 π., 24 π., 30 π., 36 α., 37 π., 38 α.; 6:29 α., 38 π., 39 π., 44 π., 57 α.; 7:16 π., 18 π.,

---

46. Ceslas Spicq and James D. Ernest, "φῶς, φωστήρ, φωσφόρος, φωτεινός, φωτίζω, φωτισμός," in *Theological Lexicon of the New Testament*, 3:473.

47. Homer, *Odyssey* 6.45

48. Plutarch, *Pericles* 39.3

28 π., 29 α.). Each word can be used of one who is sent with a charge or purpose.

As one "sent" by God, and as one who is "from" (πόθεν, 9:29, 30; παρά, 9:33) God, John's Jesus is intimately familiar with God to the point that he can make such claims as, "the father and I are one" (10:30; cf. 1:14, 18; 6:46). The idea here is that Jesus is acting as a commissioned agent of God. The way the world, Pharisees, etc., treat Jesus is how they treat God (rejection). So also, those who receive Jesus (those who come to trust in Jesus cf. 1:12), receive God and what God offers through Jesus his agent, namely life (1:4; especially 5:24–26, cf. 3:15–16, 36; 5:24–26).

Son of Man

The Son of Man is an apocalyptic end time judge according to Daniel 7:13 and Enoch 49:4; 61:9; 69:27; 2 Esdras 13.2ff. In the Gospel of John the phrase ὁ υἱὸς τοῦ ἀνθρώπου[49] occurs 13 times in 12 verses. Each time it is a self designation on the lips of Jesus, except in 12:34 where the crowd is speaking to Jesus after he uses it of himself in 12:23. Scholars have essentially three[50] understandings of the use of "Son of Man." In the first understanding, "Son of Man" refers to the humanity of Jesus.[51] In the second, it designates Jesus as a divine figure or person.[52] In the third, it is another way of saying "Son of God."[53]

The first appearance in John is at 1:51, where the Son of Man is likened to the ladder in Jacob's vision (Gen 28:12). The phrase "upon the Son of Man" in John 1:51 falls exactly where "upon it" (referring to the ladder[54]) falls in Gen 28:12. This effectively makes the Son of Man equiv-

49. In John 5:27 the phrase appears without the articles, υἱὸς ἀνθρώπου. It is unlikely, however, that this is not a Johannine Son of Man saying as Burkett argues. Burkett, *Son of the Man*, 41–45. The context of the verse is judgment, which fits with other Son of Man sayings in John (8:28; 9:35–41; 12:30–36) and Dan 7:13 uses the anarthrous phrase, as Reynolds ("Son of Man Idiom," 116) notes.

50. Reynolds, "Son of Man Idiom," 104. Depending on how nuanced one wishes to be, this list of categories could certainly be expanded.

51. Moloney, *Johannine Son of Man*.

52. Harris, *Prologue and Gospel*, 107; Reynolds, *Apocalyptic Son of Man*.

53. Burkett, *Son of the Man*; Brown, *Introduction to John*.

54. Compare John 1:51b, καὶ τοὺς ἀγγέλους τοῦ θεοῦ ἀναβαίνοντας καὶ καταβαίνοντας ἐπὶ τὸν υἱὸν τοῦ ἀνθρώπου (*son of man*) with LXX of Gen. 28:12b, "καὶ οἱ ἄγγελοι τοῦ θεοῦ ἀνέβαινον καὶ κατέβαινον ἐπ' αὐτῆς (*it*)" where αὐτῆς (it) has κλίμαξ (ladder) as its antecedent (italics mine).

alent to the conduit between heaven and earth, or "the gate of Heaven" (ἡ πύλη τοῦ οὐρανοῦ) as Jacob states it (LXX Gen 28:17).[55]

The idea is continued[56] in the next use of the term. In 3:13ff. Jesus will cast himself as the exclusive (v. 13, οὐδεὶς "no one") revealer of "heavenly things" (τὰ ἐπουράνια, v. 12). A corollary function of being the gate of heaven.[57] So we now have both *gateway to and revealer of heaven/heavenly things*.

But added to the mix in this passage is that of divine judgment, trust and life. The Son of Man "must" (δεῖ) be lifted up and this will result in either trust or unbelief. Trusting in the Son of Man (cf. 9:38) results in life (3:15) and not being judged/condemned (κρίνω). Not trusting results in perishing (ἀπόλλυμαι, v. 16) and judgment/condemnation (κρίνω, vv. 17–18). So now we have Son of Man as the *gateway to heaven, interpreter of heavenly things*, and *bringer of life and judgment*. One may also add 5:26–29 in support of the theme *bringer of life and judgment*.[58]

The theme of Son of Man as *bringer of life* is present in the next appearance of the phrase in 6:27, 53, 62.[59] Here, life is the result of the food that the Son of Man gives. This food is the Son of Man himself, in that "eating" and "drinking" the Son of Man is a metaphor for trust.[60] I would cite the similarity of 6:40 with 6:54 as evidence for this conclusion.[61] In 6:40 looking and trusting in the Son results in eternal life and resurrection. In 6:54 eating the flesh and drinking the blood of the Son of Man results in the same: eternal life and resurrection. John 6:40 frames the eating and drinking of 6:54 in terms of trust, much like if x=z and y=z then x=y. Trust equals eating and drinking. The eating of the Son of Man results in the mutual abiding (μένω) that is characteristic of the Johannine believer (15:4–7, 9–10, 16).[62]

---

55. Also, Reynolds, "Son of Man Idiom," 114; Harris, *Prologue*, 116–29; Ham, "The Title 'Son of Man.'" This function is central to Walker's understanding; Walker, "John 1:43–51 and 'The Son of Man.'"

56. The theme of ascent and descent (ἀναβαίνω and καταβαίνω) is also continued.

57. Also Harris, *Prologue*, 120; Ham, "Title 'Son of Man,'" 79.

58. Also, Reynolds, "Son of Man Idiom," 117; Martyn, *History and Theology*, 132–33. Martyn compares Dan 7:13–14 with 5:27 and the "authority" (ἐξουσία in both LXX Dan 7:13 and John 5:27) to execute judgment.

59. Also, Ham, "Title 'Son of Man,'" 81.

60. Dunn, "John 6."

61. Although Voelz sees a contrast between the passages. Voelz, "Discourse," 31.

62. Reynolds, "Son of Man Idiom," 117.

In 8:28 the idea of the "lifting up" of the Son of Man is re-visited. Just as in 3:14ff the Son of Man "must" be lifted up in order to bring both life and judgment, in 8:24 Jesus tells the crowds (apparently the Pharisees, cf. 7:24 but also the Jewish crowds in general) that they will die in their sins if they do not trust. The lifting up of the Son of Man is the instance that will cause the crowds to realize that the Son of Man does nothing on his own but is in perfect harmony with the Father's instructions or teaching (διδάσκω, 8:28). Again, this fits with the concept of Son of Man as revealer of heavenly things. This lifting up further reveals the Son of Man as the light (12:34-35, cf. 12:24). Lifting up (ὑψόω) and glorify (δοξάζω) are both Johannine euphemisms for the death[63], resurrection, and ascension (cf. 6:62; 17:5; 3:13) of Jesus.

Given the specific accumulation of functions of the Son of Man, it seems unlikely to me that the title is simply synonymous with "a person" or "this person" (as in me or I). It is possible that the title may be synonymous with the Son of God, but then why not simply use Son of God throughout?[64] So, to summarize Jesus, as the Johannine Son of Man, functions as 1) *gateway to and revealer of heaven/heavenly things* (1:51; 3:13ff.), 2) *bringer of life and judgment* (3:13ff.; 5:26-29; 6:27, 53, 62), and 3) *one in perfect harmony with the Father's instructions* (8:28).

Prophet

The healed man specifically identifies Jesus as "a prophet" (εἶπεν ὅτι προφήτης ἐστίν, 9:17, without the definite article, cf. 4:19 and implied in 4:44). This is a significant characterization of Jesus in the Fourth Gospel. In 6:14 and 7:40 Jesus is specifically recognized as "the prophet" (ὁ προφήτης, with the definite article, cf. 1:21, 25). Cho[65] identifies the prophetic aspects of Jesus's ministry in John. He defines four aspects of an Old Testament prophet and describes how each relate to Jesus activity in John: 1) acting as a spokesperson for God while in an intimate relationship with God (being sent by, and being in and abiding in the Father), 2) symbolic actions[66] (2:13-25), 3) using miraculous signs to legitimate the

---

63. As Judas leaves to betray Jesus unto death, Jesus's reply is, "now the Son of Man is glorified..." (13:31).

64. Also Harris, *Prologue*.

65. Cho, *Prophet*.

66. Also, Brown, *John*, 1:379.

prophetic message (the various signs), and 4) acting as mediator between God and the people (John 17). The Samaritan woman initially recognizes Jesus as prophet based on his supernatural knowledge of her marital situation (4:16–19, cf. 2:24). The man born blind recognizes him as a prophet based on his ability to heal blindness (from birth no less!).

Jesus as the expected prophet (*the* prophet with the definite article) is the fulfillment of Deut 18:15–22 (perhaps John 5:46 alludes to this.) This prophet will speak all things as God commands (Deut 18:18, cf. John 8:28; 12:49, 50). In 6:14 Jesus as "the prophet who is coming into the world" envisions Jesus as the prophet like Moses (Deut 18:15). The presence of Jesus on the mountain (6:3, 14, the synoptics do not contain the detail about the mountain) may allude to Moses on Mount Sinai.[67] Further the reference to Passover (6:4) provides for another Mosaic connection.[68] Of course the comparison to the feeding Miracle of Moses and that of Jesus in the aftermath of the miracle as well as the grumbling (γογγύζω, John 6:41, 43, 61 cf. Exod 17:3; Num 11:1; 14:27, 29; 17:6, 20) the crowd engages in, all point to Jesus as the prophet like Moses of Deut. 18:15. But of course the "bread" that Jesus provides will bring eternal life (John 6:58).

Other characterizations of Jesus

The disciples address Jesus as "rabbi," a title of respect and authority, by his disciples. The address of Jesus as "rabbi" (ῥαββί) by his disciples, coupled with the question of "who sinned . . ." helps to characterize Jesus as one having the authority to act as judge[69] in religious matters.

In this episode, Jesus re-frames what might be understood as common ways of thinking. He re-frames the disciples' question about sin and changes the topic to that of God's "work" (9:4–5). When the Pharisees confront him on the topic of blindness, he reframes the topic in relation to sin (9:40–41). In this way, Jesus responds to people continually on his own terms and by doing so brings to the audience alternative ways of thinking. These alternative ways of thinking must then be accepted

---

67. Cho, *Prophet*, 216.

68. Ibid., 217.

69. Verlyn D. Verbrugge, "ῥαββί," in *New International Dictionary of New Testament Theology: Abridged Edition* 508–9.

or rejected, much like John's Jesus, who must ultimately be accepted or rejected as light and life.

Jesus causes division and controversy. Not only are the Pharisees divided on the topic of whether Jesus is "from God" or a "sinner" (9:16). Jesus's very presence as light of the world forces a decision to be made. Thus another character trait of Jesus is that he is the occasion for judgment. Jesus was not "sent" into the world to act as judge but rather to save the world (3:17; 12:47). Even so, the act of judgment happens by his very presence in the world—when "people loved darkness rather than light" (3:19) and when one "rejects" Jesus "and does not receive" his "word" (12:48). Jesus's presence in the world is a paradox. On the one hand, he can speak of his authority in the world as judge: "for judgment (κρίμα) I have come . . ." (9:39); "The Father judges no one but has given all judgment (κρίσις) to the Son" (5:22). On the other hand, he can affirm that his presence in the world is not for the purpose of judgment/condemnation (κρίνω, 3:17, 12:47).

The characterization of Jesus as judge fits with the Son of Man title in 9:35. This Son of Man characterization of Jesus is continued in Jesus's interaction with the Pharisees in 9:38ff. Jesus pronounces, "now that you say, 'We see,' your sin remains." Jesus acts as judge upon the (narrative) representatives of "the Jews."

Conversely, Jesus is presented as one who elicits trust.

Figure 3.1: Widening of the Healed Man's Understanding of Jesus.

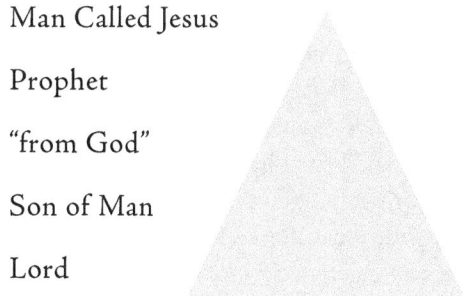

Man Called Jesus

Prophet

"from God"

Son of Man

Lord

The characterization of Jesus, within just this episode, develops as the healed man's understanding of Jesus widens and deepens.[70] Even though Jesus is absent in the narrative from v. 8 through v. 35, he is the topic of

---

70. Also, Brown, *John*, 1:377; Culpepper, *Gospel and Letters*, 178.

investigation in both of the scenes where the man born blind is questioned. As Jesus's character is progressively described by the man born blind, the audience is offered an increasingly broader characterization of Jesus. They will finally have to decide whether to accept or reject this characterization. Jesus is described progressively as: "the man called Jesus" (v. 11), "a prophet" (v. 17), and person who is "from God" (v. 33). When he finally reappears in v. 35 he seeks out the healed man and elicits trust ("Do you trust in the son of man?"). He is finally worshiped as "son of man" (v. 35) and as "lord" (v. 38) (see Figure 1).

Jesus is characterized not only as one who heals but also as one who brings insight. As proof that Jesus is "from God" the healed man offers his own experience of healing, "ἐκ τοῦ αἰῶνος οὐκ ἠκούσθη . . . (never since the beginning of time was it heard . . .)" (v. 32). He concludes that if Jesus were not "from God (παρὰ θεοῦ)" he could not have done this. Not only does Jesus heal the man's physical sight but brings the man spiritual insight—insight that ironically surpasses that of the Pharisees.

Transforming

Finally, and perhaps most important, John's Jesus transforms a person's life. The man born blind goes from a sightless beggar to an insightful witness. Not only does he gain insight along with his physical sight, he gains courage and trust as well. He is not only changed personally but his social group changes as well. He moves from being a member of his Jewish social network, to being ostracized by the leaders of that network. Then he is sought out by Jesus who invites trust. In trusting the man becomes part of the social network of those who trust in Jesus. In his encounter with Jesus, the man is transformed physically, inwardly, and socially.

John's Jesus constrains change in all who encounter him. On the one hand, he heals, transforms, and brings light; while on the other hand, this is matched by one who brings judgment. As if a bolder has rolled into the middle of a highway, one must choose whether to go to the right or left but continuing on is no longer an option. While the blind man is transformed into one who has the "light of life" (8:12 c.f. 1:4), the Pharisees become more deeply entrenched in their rejection of Jesus and are transformed into those who "die in their sin" (8:21, 24). As the character of Jesus develops, the pressure on the audience to choose between trust or rejection/sin increases.

Character Point of View

In addition to having character traits, characters have different points of view or ways of understanding the world and the events around them. For example, the man born blind and the Pharisees have a different opinion or *point of view* as to where Jesus is from (contrast 9:24 with 9:31–33). Each of the characters can be understood according to how they view and understand the various events of the episode.

The *disciples* regard Jesus with authority and consider him "rabbi" therefore knowledgeable in theological affairs. They have placed their trust in Jesus and have committed to follow him (6:67–69). Their initial impression of the man born blind is that he is associated in some way with sin. They must view healing on the Sabbath as permissible since they continue to follow Jesus after the previous Sabbath healing in chapter five.

The *bystanders* are skeptical of the healing. They trust the Pharisees as authorities in the law and consider them knowledgeable in synagogue affairs, demonstrated by bringing to them the healed man. We are given no suggestions about their point of view regarding Jesus.[71]

The *parents* would been relieved to have a pronouncement from a miracle worker that freed them of the shame of sin, since many in that society would assume their sinfulness to be the reason for their son's blindness. At the same time, they are fearful of what might happen to them when questioned by the Pharisees. It does not seem that they regard the Pharisees with respect only with fear since their answers are evasive, "ask him he is of age" (9:21). We do not know their view point on Jesus, although they may be one of the "many" who "trusted in him. But because of the Pharisees they did not confess it, for fear that they would be put out of the synagogue" (9:42).

The *Pharisees* seem to begin the investigation of the miracle with an open mind. They have conflicting points of view about the legitimacy of the Sabbath day healing. They are open to the opinion of the healed man as to whether Jesus is "from God" or a "sinner." Both of these things change, for they end the episode with the viewpoint that Jesus is a sinner who is not from God (9:24, 29). They do not respect the opinion of the healed man and take the viewpoint that the man was born "entirely in sin" (9:34). They are assured of their own authority and their knowledge of religio-political affairs, twice asserting, "we know" (9:24, 29).

---

71. Unless one considers ἐκεῖνος (that one) in v. 12 to be disparaging.

The *man born blind* has a developing view of Jesus, as was discussed above, but that point of view is always positive, ending in the same viewpoint of Jesus and the disciples. He places his trust in Jesus and worships him. His final argument (9:30–34) with the Pharisees indicates the following in relation to his point of view: First, Jesus is "from God" and *not* a sinner, because God obviously listened to Jesus in effecting the healing. Second, he does not regard the Pharisees with authority. Third, he does not consider them knowledgeable in religious affairs.

Jesus as one who is sent by the Father obviously understands himself to be "from God" and therefore not a sinner. He considers himself to be authoritative, but only in as much as he says (8:28) and does (8:29) what the Father wants. As the only one who has come down from heaven (3:13), he considers himself to have firsthand knowledge in theological affairs (3:11), firsthand knowledge of God (7:29), and believes his teaching is directly from God who sent him (7:16). He considers neither the parents or the man born blind to have sinned in a way that resulted in the man's blindness. However he believes any who do not trust in him will die in their sins (8:24). This may include the parents, but certainly includes the Pharisees (9:41).

From this analysis we can see that the characters who are closest in point of view are Jesus, the disciples, and the man born blind. Directly opposed to their point of view are the Pharisees. The point of contention centers around whether or not Jesus is "from God" or a sinner. Somewhere in the middle are the parents and the bystanders.

Internal Structure and Plot

Turning attention to the internal structure of the passage one actually finds that the passage may stand as a literary unit which runs from 9:1–10:21. There is no break at all between 9:41 and 10:1. The same situation is assumed for 10:1–21 as for 9:39–41.[72] The only change is in content, but in terms of the structure of the narrative itself, 9:41–10.18 are part of Jesus's response to the Pharisees' question about their own blindness. Chapter nine can be divided logically by content: miracle and dialogues; but also by the dramatic rule of twos where only two characters or

---

72. Also, Maloney, *John*, 291, 296, additionally see my n74.

character sets interact at a time.[73] Such a division produces eight scenes. I have outlined the passage as follows:

I. Miracle of Healing (9:1–12)

    A. Need presented (1–5) [Scene 1, Jesus and the disciples]

    B. Miracle (6–7) [Scene 2, Jesus and the man]

    C. Aftermath of the miracle (8–12)
    [Scene 3, The man and the neighbors]

II. Dialogues (9:13–41)

    A. Healed man and the Pharisees: interview 1 (13–17) [Scene 4, Pharisees and the man]

    B. "The Jews" and the healed man's parents (18–23) [Scene 5, The Jews/Pharisees and the man's parents]

    C. The healed man and the Pharisees: interview 2 (24–34) [Scene 6, The Pharisees and the man]

    D. Jesus and the healed man (35–38) [Scene 7, Jesus and the man]

    E. Jesus and the Pharisees (39–41) [Scene 8, Jesus and the Pharisees]

III. Discourse (monologue) and result (10:1–21) [Scene 8, Jesus and the Pharisees, seems to continue]

    A. Jesus is the gate for the sheep (1–10)

        1. Jesus the gate (1–6)

        2. Jesus the gate restated (7–10)

    B. Jesus is the good shepherd (11–18)

    C. The Jews divided by Jesus words and actions (19–21)

While I am focusing on John chapter 9, it is important here to note some points of connection and continuity[74] with 10:1–21. In v. 3, the "shepherd" calls out his sheep who hear his voice. In v. 4, the sheep follow the shepherd after being "brought out." The phrase translates the Greek ἐκβάλλω, which is used in 9:34–35 to describe the casting out of the man

---

73. Martyn, *History and Theology*, 37.

74. In her recent dissertation Lewis, *Shepherd Discourse,* also argues that based on numerous thematic links, Jesus's final speech to the Pharisees spans 9:39—10:21. Her dissertation advisor, Gail O'Day, also notes the same. O'Day, "John," 651.

born blind from the synagogue. This verbal thread could actually serve to frame the expulsion of the man as part of the activity or work of Jesus.

Also, throughout John 9 and 10:1–21 the activity of knowing (both οἶδα and γινώσκω)[75] is important. The parents, "know" (οἶδα) that the healed man is their son and was born blind, but do not "know" how he was healed nor who healed him (9:20–21). The Healed man claims to not "know" whether Jesus is a sinner but does "know" that he was blind and now sees (9:25). The Pharisees claim to "know" that Jesus is a sinner; they "know" that God spoke to Moses, but they do not "know" where Jesus is from (9:29). The man born blind points out the irony of their ignorance claiming that if Jesus were not from God, he could do nothing (9:30). It is this argument that results in his being "cast out" (ἐκβάλλω) (9:34). The sheep who are "brought out" (ἐκβάλλω) "know" the shepherd's voice (10:4) but will not follow a stranger's voice that they do not "know" (10:5). The Pharisees do not "understand" (γινώσκω) the figure of speech Jesus is using (10:7). Jesus as the "good shepherd" "knows" (γινώσκω) his own, and his own "know" him (10:14). So also, Jesus and the Father "know" one another (10:15). One comes to trust through the ability to "know" by both the activity of sight, seeing Jesus and his works (John 9), and sound, hearing his voice and following (10:1–21).

I will proceed to examine the development of the episode by scenes of interaction. The episode follows the rule of twos, from classical Greek drama, where no more than two characters or character groups interact at one time.[76]

Miracle of Healing (1–12)

Scene 1: Jesus and disciples (1–5)

A plot can be examined in (at least) two ways, plot tension and resolution, and conflict analysis. Plot tensions are questions, problems, issues, and the like which develop over the course of a narrative and must be answered, solved, or resolved in some way. (Table 3.2, p. 110) Conflict analysis is the analysis of how the viewpoints, wants, desires, needs and/ or goals of different characters come into conflict.[77] In relation to conflict

---

75. The two terms are more or less synonymous (Seesemann, "οἶδα," in *TDNT* 5:116), and particularly seem interchangeable in John (cf. 8:55).

76. Holleran, "Seeing the Light," 14; Martyn, *History and Theology*, 37.

77. Powell, *Narrative Criticism*, 42.

analysis two important concepts are introduced: *sin* and *works*. The first is the question of sin, first introduced by the disciples at the beginning of the episode. The conflict between the man born blind and the Pharisees about whether or not Jesus is a "sinner" (9:24) and by extension "not from God" (9:16) develops later in the episode. The assumption that the man born blind was born "entirely (ὅλος) in sin" will be used as the final words of the Pharisees in their conflict with the man before he is expelled from the synagogue. Sin, in addition to being an item of conflict between characters, is also the first plot tension in this episode to develop.

The episode begins as Jesus and his disciples are "walking along" (παράγων) and encounter a man born blind. Here *plot tension one, sin*, is introduced. The question, "who is a sinner," must be answered. The disciples establish Jesus's expertise on the matter of sin by addressing him as "Rabbi." The question that they ask assumes that the man is blind as a result of sin, more specifically, either his own sin[78] or his parents.' The idea that children are punished for their parents' sin comes from Exodus 34:7 and the book of Job is an indication that sickness was often seen as a punishment for sin. This understanding was present in Jesus's day as well. In terms of distance,[79] the blind man, as a sinner or the child of sinners, would be removed from the audience. Jesus's subsequent reframing of his blindness will bring the audience into a more sympathetic relationship with him. The question of "who sinned" is a mystery to be solved much later in the episode, but with a twist. For now, Jesus simply says that *neither* the blind man *nor* his parents sinned. The blindness of the man is not explained hamartalogically but apocalyptically, "so that God's works might be *revealed* in him" (ἵνα φανερωθῇ τὰ ἔργα τοῦ θεοῦ ἐν αὐτῷ) (italics mine). Correcting narrative misunderstanding is one rhetorical device in which an author convinces an audience of the "correct" viewpoint to

---

78. It was assumed that an infant could incur guilt from sin in the womb for a number of reasons. Punching and kicking beyond the normal rate of an infant is one example. The mother worshiping in a pagan temple causes the unborn infant also to commit idolatry. Beasley-Murray, *John*, 155; Brown, *John*, 1:371.

79. Distance has to do with how close (sympathetic) or far away (antipathetic) the audience should feel toward a character. The more a character agrees with or exemplifies the values that the narrative expresses, the closer (or more sympathetic) the audience should feel toward the character. The more a character conflicts with those values the farther away (more antipathy) the audience should feel. Cf. Powell, *Narrative Criticism*, 25, 56–57; Booth, *Fiction*, 125–33. Sympathizing with characters that portray the values of the narrative is one way in which an author goes about convincing an audience.

have. Audience members "learn to see things in new categories; they move beyond the earthly realm they know and begin to see the heavenly realm. Misunderstandings are a strategy to reorient the reader."[80] Here the audience is reoriented to a different way of thinking about sin. By the end of the story expectations will be reversed[81] and sin will be redefined as failure to trust in and hear/listen to Jesus.

It is quite ironic that the blind man is to be an instrument of revelation (φανερόω). Although one usually thinks of ἀποκαλύπτω with respect to revelation, it can be synonymous with φανερόω, which in addition to "reveal" carries the sense of "cause to be seen."[82] The word itself is a favorite of John's to indicate some truth revealed or reality made manifest. A sort of word play is involved here in that the man is *blind* so that God's works may be *seen*, made evident, demonstrated or manifested. This is an important concept in the gospel. John the baptist first uses it when he indicates that Jesus would be "revealed" or "made known" to Israel (1:31). It is next used to summarize the miracle of the water changed to wine at the wedding at Cana where Jesus's "glory" is "revealed" and as a result his disciples "trust" (πιστεύω) in him. Trust is also the result for the man born blind (9:38). During his prayer in 17:6–8, Jesus has "revealed" the father to his disciples and they have "trusted" as a result. Thus one can see how φανερόω is used in the gospel as a phenomenon that leads to trust (πιστεύω).

The second important concept in the Gospel that is introduced in this scene is the idea of *work* expressed both the verb and noun: "(to) work" (ἐργάζομαι) and "works" (ἔργον). Jesus's works *reveal* who Jesus is and *testify* to who Jesus is (John 5:36; 10:25; 10:37). It is Jesus's work which proves that he and the Father are mutually "in" one another (John 10:38; 14:10–11). Jesus's works are parallel with the works of the Father in such a way that the Father is actually showing Jesus the works (John 5:20).

I believe that an audience familiar with Old Testament scripture might understand the "works of God" in much the same way as Ps 45 (46, English) particularly v. 8, "Come and see the Lord's works (LXX ἔργον) which he placed as wonders upon the earth." The psalm is speaking of

---

80. O'Brien, "Writen," 287–88.

81. Working from Booth, *Fiction*, Boomershine notes the reversal of expectation is another rhetorical tool an author uses to convince an audience. Boomershine, "The Structure of Narrative Rhetoric in Genesis 2–3," 115.

82. "φανερόω," in L&N 2:255.

God's mighty deeds of salvation expressed concretely in history. Brown also notes that the LXX uses this to describe God's works of salvation on behalf of God's people, citing among others, Exod 34:10; Ps 66:5 [Eng.]; 77:11–12 [Eng.]. I would also add Ps 78:7 [Eng.] and 66:5 [Eng.], especially with the connection to "come and see" δεῦτε καὶ ἴδετε cf. John 4:29 δεῦτε ἴδετε). [83] These deeds reveal who God is, just as in this passage they reveal who Jesus is (John 9:31–33). And, in some sense, they reveal the *reality* of God. The expression in 9:4, "work the works" (ἐργάζεσθαι τὰ ἔργα) can be seen as giving rise to these deeds of salvation. Just as God gave rise to God's deeds of salvation "in the days of old" (ἔργον, ὃ εἰργάσω ἐν ταῖς ἡμέραις αὐτῶν, ἐν ἡμέραις ἀρχαίαις) (Ps 44:1 [Eng.]; 44:2 LXX) so now Jesus "works a work" of salvation in a man born blind! The work of God is defined as: trusting in him whom he (God) has sent. In other words, to trust in Jesus *is* to do the work of God (6:27–30). This is made possible by God's self-revelation in Jesus's works (5:36; 9:3; 10:32; 15:24 and particularly 10:38; 14:10–11). In some sense, the miraculous sign and the response of trust together form the whole work. Brown states, "the concept of 'work' in John is wider than that of miracles; in [17:4] Jesus can sum up his whole ministry as a work. Not only are Jesus's miracles works; his words are works too . . . [14:10]."[84] We will see the fulfillment of this work in the climactic episode in 9:38. In the final statement in this scene, Jesus declares, "I am the light of the world." The very next scene gives a demonstration of this.

Scene 2: Jesus and the man (6–7)

After reminding the disciples that he is the "light of the world," Jesus makes mud from spittle and spreads or smears (ἐπιχρίω) it on the blind man's eyes. Jesus commands the blind man to wash in the pool of Siloam. The narrator tells us that the word means "the one having been sent" (9:7). This verbal thread reminds the hearer that Jesus is indeed the one "sent" (ἀποστέλλω) by the Father (3:17, 34; 5:36, 38; 6:29; 57; 7:29; 8:42) and that contact with the "sent one" is what heals.[85] It also serves to connect the episode to what is yet to come (10:36; 11:42; 17:3, 8, 18–25).

---

83. Brown, *John*, 1:526–27.

84. Ibid., 527.

85. Culpepper, *Gospel and Letters*, 175; Moloney, *Signs*, 122. Contra Neyrey, *Perspective*, 266–67, who sees this as insider language. I would argue that this serves to

The episode of the healing and its aftermath incorporate elements of the healing miracle genre. Healings of the blind are found in all of the gospels (Matt 9:27–31; 20:9–34; Mark 8:22–26; 10:46–52; Luke 18:35–42), but strangely the formal element of the miracle story which is left out of John 9 is the *request* for healing! As was pondered above, there are some possibilities for this. It is possible that, because it was a Sabbath the blind Man did not wish to request the "work" of healing. Or perhaps, the man, being blind, may not have been aware of the presence of a healer nearby. It is further possible that Jesus wanted to take full responsibility for the healing so as to protect the blind man from Pharisaic sanction. Whatever the reason, the blind man is not an active participant until Jesus tells him to wash. This omission has two effects. First, he is initially presented as a flat and passive character to heighten the contrast with his characterization near the end of chapter. Second, the blind man is not a petitioner, but rather a *means for revelation* of God's work. The whole episode of chapter 9 can be summed up as "God's work revealed in a blind man." This is not however to downplay the man's response to Jesus's command. The succinct description of the man's response, "he went, and then he washed and he came seeing,"[86] indicates the man's obedient responsiveness to the light of the world. This will be seen in contrast to the Pharisees' lack of obedient response (cf., 9:27, where they "do not hear/listen/understand" ἀκούω).

Scene 3: *The neighbors and the man (8–12)*

Upon returning from the pool of Siloam, the man is met by astonished neighbors and onlookers. After a somewhat comical discussion amongst the neighbors as to whether this is really the man formerly blind, he keeps insisting that it is indeed him.

Through the course of this episode the blind man progressively becomes a more lively and vital character. This finally culminates in his trust in, and adoration of, Jesus as "lord" (κύριος, 9:38). This trust is, for John, life (20:31). The man, once healed, goes on to be a witness to Jesus and a faithful disciple. The healed man's function as a witness begins as soon as he returns from the pool "seeing." Some of the onlookers did not

---

draw the hearer into the world of the story by connecting with parts of the story already disclosed. It thus *creates* insiders by deepening engagement.

86. Moloney, *John*, 292. Moloney, *Signs*, 122.

think it was actually the same person who was born blind, but the healed man "kept saying" (ἔλεγεν) that it was him, and the bystanders "kept saying (ἔλεγον) to him how were your eyes opened?" Here we have the imperfect active indicatives[87] of λέγω. The impression is an *ongoing* process of questions and answers between the healed man and the people. At this point in the episode the healed man knows Jesus only as "the man called Jesus" (see Figure 1) but continues to witness according to his own experience with Jesus.

Dialogues (13–41)

Scene 4: Healed man and the Pharisees: interrogation 1 (13–17)

When Jesus was nowhere to be found, the onlookers deliver the healed man to the Pharisees. Although conflict with the Pharisees has been brewing since 7:32, a Pharisee was still a respected religious figure. In terms of distance, at the beginning of this narrative the Pharisees would have the respect of the listener.

More tension is introduced to the plot by the narrative comment about the healing taking place on the Sabbath (John 14). This comment reminds the hearer of the controversy in chapter 5 (cf. 9) which also took place by a pool. A second plot tension is introduced here: *plot tension two, Sabbath healing*. The issue of the Sabbath healing recedes into the background as the episode progresses, while the real issue, Jesus's identity and origin, becomes evident. Culpepper notes that narratively "the interest is not in how the cure happened but in the issue of sin and trust as it relates to each character in the story. Is the blind man a sinner? Are the Pharisees righteous? Is Jesus an imposter or one sent from God?"[88] This is true also for the second round of questioning by the Pharisees of the healed man. Thus, there is the third plot tension, *plot tension three, identity and origin of Jesus*.

After the healed man recounts his healing to the Pharisees, they are divided. Some judged Jesus as a sinner; others were not sure because of the "signs." "Sign" (σημεῖον) is used throughout the Gospel to point to the identity of Jesus (3:2) and to elicit trust (2:11, 23; 4:48; 7:31). The proper understanding of this "sign" now becomes a point of conflict.

---

87. I am interpreting these indicatives as imperfects of continuance expressing ongoing action, Smyth, *Greek Grammar*, §§1889–1890.

88. Culpepper, *Gospel and Letters*, 176.

The division leads the Pharisees to ask the healed man to comment on Jesus. This is the second opportunity the healed man has to comment on Jesus's identity, and shows the beginning of increased understanding[89] by the healed man. This time he calls Jesus "a prophet."[90]

This label is significant in relation to the issue of "signs." In the LXX simply performing a sign did not guarantee the legitimacy of the "prophet" (προφήτης). The Israelites are warned in Deut 13:1–4 that despite signs (σημεῖον) a prophet may still be false (cf. Deut 18:15–22) and that they should not be "deceived" (πλανάω). The remedy for a false prophet in the midst of Israel is death (Deut 13:5; cf. 18:15–22). This sheds light on the apparently unprovoked statement of Jesus in 7:19 that the Pharisees are trying to kill him (cf. 7:1, 5:18). If he is indeed "deceiving" (7:12, 47) the people and working signs then the death penalty may very well apply. The accusation that he is deceiving carries with it the implication that the Pharisees are "trying to kill" him.

In terms of conflict analysis, the question of whether or not Jesus is a "sinner" spurs internal conflict among the Pharisees (9:16). They attempt to resolve this conflict first by asking the man, "what do you say about him" (9:17) but his answer is apparently not satisfactory. In an attempt to resolve the conflict and answer the question of whether or not Jesus is a "sinner" (9:16), the episode moves to the next level—an interrogation of the man's parents.

Scene 5: "Jews" and Healed Man's Parents (18–23)

At this point the investigation changes from how the man was healed to whether he was healed at all. From the viewpoint of the Jewish authorities it may be possible that the apparent sign is not a sign at all. As the parents of the man are questioned by the Jewish authorities, it is obvious that they are reserved and careful in their answer. They point the investigation back toward their son. The reason for this caution is fear (9:22). The phrase "fear of the Jews," introduced in 7:13, is finally explained in 9:22–23. These two verses of narrative comment introduce a fourth plot tension: *plot tension four, fate of the confessor*. What will happen to those who "confess" Jesus as Messiah, in light of the decision to expel those who so confess?

---

89. Also, Culpepper, *Gospel and Letters*, 176.

90. See discussion of this in the earlier section about Jesus's characterization.

Confess (ὁμολογέω) may mean to *promise, assure,* to *agree, admit* or to *confess*. It can be used in a judicial sense as to *make a confession,* or in a religious sense, *to confess sins*. But it may also mean to acknowledge something, ordinarily in public, *acknowledge, claim, profess,* and even *praise*.[91] This is related to the important Johannine concept of *witness* discussed above. Those who make this kind of confession, "the Jews" will expel from synagogue life. This social isolation would be devastating since in first century Jewish life people must depend on relationships and alliances formed with others in their social group in order to get the goods needed for daily life and even survival.

In this scene there is definitely stress if not conflict between the parents and the Pharisees. Two issues may be operating here. First, the common assumption that the blindness of the man may have been the fault of the parents (cf. 9:2) may lead the parents to believe that they are being accused of sin by the Jewish authorities. Second, there is the threat of being expelled from the synagogue (ἀποσυνάγωγος, 9:22). Their fearful response leads them to refer the authorities back to their son. This conflict moves the episode to yet another level, a heated conflict between the man and the Pharisees.

Scene 6: *The healed man and the Pharisees: interview 2 (24–34)*

"A second time" the Jewish authorities call the healed man for questioning. This begins at 9:24 with the Jewish authorities commanding the man to "give glory to God." This is a masterfully ironic statement which the author places on the lips of the authorities, for the healed man gives them exactly what they ask for, but *not* what they want. The statement "give glory to God" is a traditional oath formula in which a person is charged to tell the truth[92] (Jos 7:19), much like our contemporary "so help me God" at the end of the courtroom oath. In addition to this, it may be used to charge a person to confess one's own sin (1 Sam 6:5; Jer 13:6).[93] The Jewish authorities most likely meant "agree with us against Jesus and confess your own sin and Jesus's sin." Instead, what they received was a powerful testimony to the truth of Jesus's identity.

---

91. ὁμολογέω, BDAG 708.

92. δόξα, BDAG, s.v. 3, p. 258, also Keener, *John*, 1:790; Culpepper, *Gospel and Letters*, 177.

93. O'Day, "John," 658.

The word δόξα means *brightness, splendor, or radiance*, and is used to denote the *glory, majesty,* and *sublimity* of God in general.[94] The word is associated with the Hebrew כבוד in the LXX, and picks up its meaning almost exclusively. It refers to people in relation to their respective honor and esteem (1 Kgs 3:13; Ps 8:6), but more importantly it also refers to God and God's glory expressed through historical acts of salvation.[95] With this Old Testament view in mind, Brown defines "glory" as having two elements: 1) visibility and 2) power—thus a *visible* demonstration of the *power* of God.[96] "Glory" is revealed in the signs (2:11) and work (17:4) that Jesus does. It is of this "glory" the healed man testifies in his second questioning.

Plot tension one, sin, introduced in the beginning of the episode, reemerges again near the climax. The tension of expulsion from the synagogue (*plot tension four, fate of the confessor*) is also heightened in this scene, as the conflict between the man and the authorities heats up. The man witnesses to his own experience by not addressing the issue of sin, but rather summarizing his own history: "I was blind, but now I see."

When the authorities continue to press the issue by asking, "what did he do to you," the man points out that he has responded already to their question but they did not "hear/listen" (ἀκούω). This word may mean simply to exercise the faculty of hearing sound, but also carries with it connotations of hearing and understanding and even hearing and responding.[97] The Pharisees are those who do not "hear" and respond or understand in contrast to the man who hears Jesus's commands (v. 7a, "go," "wash"), obeys, and receives sight (v. 7b). This is further verification of Jesus's indictment of them in 8:47. They do not (ἀκούω) hear the words of God because they are not "from God" (ἐκ τοῦ θεοῦ). Ironically, they have already determined that Jesus is not "from God" (παρὰ θεοῦ, v. 16; cf. 33) and "do not know where he is from" (οὐκ οἴδαμεν πόθεν ἐστίν, v. 29). Unlike the Pharisees the healed man is like the sheep who "hear" (ἀκούω) the good shepherd's voice and follow (10:3, 16).

The man then sarcastically asks if they wish to become disciples of Jesus! This is quite a change from his initial passive characterization. The conflict at this point is boiling, "they reviled (λοιδορέω) him." In response,

---

94. δόξα, BDAG 256.
95. Hegermann, "δόξα," in *EDNT* 1:344–48.
96. Brown, *John*, 1:503–4.
97. ἀκούω, BDAG, s.v. 1. To exercise the faculty of hearing, s.v. 7 to understand and s.v. 5 to pay attention. Also, it is a technical term for "hearing" a legal case, s.v. 2.

the authorities claim discipleship (μαθητής) to Moses (9:28), and state that they "do not know from where" (9:29) Jesus comes.

The last mention of Moses[98] was in 7:19–24. In that scene, Jesus is responding to the "amazement" (θαυμάζω, cf. θαυμαστός in 9:30) of "the Jews" that he was able to teach without formal training (μανθάνω, 7:15). Jesus then claims to understand the Law of Moses better than "the Jews" he is addressing. "The Jews" are astonished (again, θαυμάζω) at the work (ἔργον, see the discussion of ἔργον starting at p. 96) Jesus did in chapter 5 when he healed a lame man on the Sabbath (5:1–18). Jesus argues that if circumcision is lawful on the Sabbath then so is healing (7:23). He charges "the Jews" with judging superficially rather than righteously (δίκαιος). Ironically, Moses is actually a witness to Jesus (5:45–47) but the "disciples of Moses" (9:28) "do not know where he [Jesus] is from" (9:29).[99]

The metaphorical blindness of the authorities grows more evident now, for the "works" and "glory" that point to who Jesus is and to where he is from, are evident. The healed man points this out as he responds by saying, "here is an astonishing thing . . ." The Greek "θαυμαστός" (*amazing* or *astonishing*) is from θαυμάζω which means "*to look on with wonder and amazement, to wonder at, marvel at.*[100]" A translation that captures the irony and visually-themed humor for this may be, "now here is a sight to see . . ."

In v. 31 he begins to talk in the first person plural, but he is only one person! The "we know" (οἴδαμεν) of the healed man answers and perhaps even mocks the emphatic[101] "we know" (ἡμεῖς οἴδαμεν) of the Pharisees in 9:24, and 29. Its effect is rhetorical *within* the narrative, but it also draws in and includes the believing listeners. A person hearing the Gospel in its entirety, and understanding the signs and works of Jesus, can say along with the healed man, "we know" that Jesus is from God and not a sinner. In addition to including the already believing hearers, it rhetorically draws in those who do not yet trust, including those who say "we know" along with the healed man.

---

98. Not including 7:53—8:11, the woman caught in adultery, which is probably not original to the Gospel.

99. Culpepper, *Gospel and Letters*, 177.

100. Liddell and Scott, θαυμάζω and θαυμαστός, 359; Annen, "θαυμαστός," in *EDNT*, 2:135–36.

101. The pronominal subject (we) and the verb (know) is contained in οἴδαμεν. This makes the first person plural pronoun ἡμεῖς grammatically unnecessary. It can be translated emphatically (we ourselves know . . .).

In 9:33, the tension of Jesus's origin (*plot tension three, identity and origin of Jesus*) is resolved, at least from the viewpoint of the healed man and the implied audience. Indeed Jesus could do nothing if he were not παρὰ θεοῦ (from God). This argument is based on the contemporary belief that God does not answer the petitions of sinful people. We see this understanding in Old Testament passages such as Job 35:13; Ps 66:18; Prov 15:29; and Isa 1:15. This also partially answers *plot tension one, sin*, in relation to who is a sinner (cf. 16, 24–25)? Jesus is not a sinner since God does not "hear sinners" (v. 30).

Although sarcastic in v. 30, the man's four verse argument is logical and cogent:

- Premise:
  - Jesus opened my eyes
  - God does *not* hear sinners
  - God does hear one who is devout (θεοσεβής) and who does God's will (θέλημα)
- Therefore Jesus is:
  - Not a sinner
  - Devout and does God's will

As additional fuel for his argument he adds that such a sign has not been heard of since the beginning of time (ἐκ τοῦ αἰῶνος).

In the next verse (9:34), the authorities cite the man's sin as the reason to dismiss his testimony. Here *plot tension four, fate of the confessor* is partially resolved, but at the same time heightened. The tension is resolved, but in a disturbing way. The audience learns what happens to one who confesses Jesus as Christ. That person is expelled or thrown out (ἐκβάλλω). The man is punished for speaking about what should have been plain from Jesus's works. Tension is heightened in that the audience must now ask, "What happens to the one who is thrown out?" The next scene (9:35–38) answers this question.

Conflict analysis can be seen not only in terms of the, disagreement, or opposing ideas or goals among characters or character groups, but also it can be understood in terms of the *threat* one group poses to the other.[102] In terms of conflict analysis, no scene in this episode is clearer

---

102. Powell, *Narrative Criticism*, 43.

that this one. There is conflict between the Jewish Authorities/Pharisees and those who trust in *and* confess Jesus. There is also conflict between the Pharisees and those who believe but do not confess openly (cf. 12:42). In this episode it is unclear whether the parents fall into the latter group but it is quite clear that the healed man falls into the former. The threat that the Pharisees pose to the believing confessors and non-confessors alike is expulsion (ἀποσυνάγωγος) from the synagogue (9:22; 12:42). In both 9:22 and 12:42, "confession" (ὁμολογέω) is the key term in relation to ἀποσυνάγωγος. The threat related to expulsion becomes even more ominous in 16:2 where killing (ἀποκτείνω) a believer as a service to God is added as a step beyond expulsion.

The threat that those who are in authority pose to those who are not seems clear but what threat could those who are not in power, believers in Jesus, pose? Though it is not quite as obvious, there are a number of clues throughout the episode that indicate the way in which "the Jews" and the Pharisees are threatened by Jesus and those who trust in Jesus.

First, healing which takes place on the Sabbath was a violation of sacred time. I will talk more about the nature of such a purity violation in the next chapter but for now suffice it to say that purity violations jeopardize the continued presence of God with the nation and in the temple.

Second, Jesus was claiming status as an agent or proxy for God, hence the accusations that he is "making himself equal to God" (5:18; 10:33 cf. 10:30; 19:7). Popular belief that Jesus is sent by the father would directly threaten the established authoritative interpretation of the Torah and the will of God, which was the domain of the Pharisees and the Jewish authorities. This is evident when "the Jews" are "amazed" that Jesus is teaching without formal training (7:14–15). Jesus appeals to an authority that comes from being "sent" (πέμπω) from God rather than an authority which comes from training (7:16). It is this authority that allows Jesus to be the interpreter of God's "will" (θέλημα) (7:17). Thus, from the perspective of the Pharisees, Jesus is deceiving (πλανάω) people (7:11, 47) and leading them away, to the point that "the whole world has gone after (ἀπέρχομαι) him" (12:19).

Third, the Pharisees are threatened by the potential to lose both their "place" (τόπος) and "nation" (ἔθνος) at the hands of Rome (11:47–50). Place (τόπος) can refer to a geographical location such as an area of land or a building such as the temple,[103] or it can refer to one's station or office

---

103. τόπος, BDAG, s.v. 1a and 1b.

such as a position of authority.[104] It is more likely that τόπος means the temple in this instance. Nowhere else in John does it refer to a person's station or position. Nation (ἔθνος) refers not to a geographical region but a body of people "united by kinship, culture, and common traditions."[105] Therefore the chief priests and Pharisees see popular belief in Jesus as a direct threat to the security of the temple and the nation itself. By extension however they would also see it as a threat to their own authority over the temple and the people.

These threats to the secure "place" (in both senses of the word) of the Pharisees prompt their action in this scene. They immediately make good on their threat of expulsion from synagogue life. After the healed man produces a cogent logical argument that Jesus is "from God," v. 34 describes emphatically[106] the response to the threat that such an argument poses to their security and, from their viewpoint, the nation's security.

The result of their action, the expulsion of the man, prompts the action in the next scene and motivates Jesus to "find" or "seek" (εὑρίσκω) the man.

Scene 7: Jesus and the healed man (35–38)

What happens to those who are thrown out? Jesus "finds" them. Jesus finding (εὑρίσκω) the healed man after his expulsion reminds the hearer of Jesus "finding" Philip (1:43) and calling him to "follow," as well as Jesus "finding" the healed paralytic after his encounter with the Pharisees (5:14). After finding the man born blind, Jesus elicits a confession of trust. This scene (9:35–38) is climactic in the episode, because not only is Jesus's identity revealed (Son of Man), and the fate of those who confess Jesus as Christ revealed (rejected by "the Jews" but accepted by Jesus), but it also provides the occasion for the fate of the Pharisees to be revealed in the next scene (9:39ff).

Jesus asks, "do you trust in the Son of Man?" The healed man asks who the Son of Man is, and Jesus identifies himself as the Son of Man. The episode reaches its climax as the man says, "Lord, I trust" and then

---

104. Ibid., s.v. 3.

105. ἔθνος, BDAG, s.v. 1.

106. καὶ ἐξέβαλον αὐτὸν ἔξω, literally "and they threw him out out." The adverb ἔξω is redundant and adds emphasis.

worships him. The plot tension regarding the fate of those who are "expelled" (*plot tension four, fate of the confessor*) is resolved here.

The threat of expulsion from synagogue life and the community would ordinarily be quite devastating. Instead, those who are "cast out" (ἐξέβαλον αὐτὸν ἔξω) are "found" by Jesus who does "not cast out" (μὴ ἐκβάλω ἔξω) anyone (6:37). Further, they will never be "snatched" (ἁρπάζω)[107] from Jesus's hand (10:28b cf. 10:12; 17:12, 15). This security is possible because it is the Father who gives them to Jesus (10:29). Finally, to those who are protected Jesus gives eternal life ("κἀγὼ δίδωμι αὐτοῖς ζωὴν αἰώνιον," 10: 28a cf. 10:10). This is essentially a new family of those who are born by the will of the Father (1:12–13) and who "love one another."

Jesus effectively defeats the threat of expulsion for confessing believers and "ups the ante" by promising eternal life, absolute security, and (unlike the Pharisees) to never cast out his people.

The redundant emphatic phrase "ἐκβάλλω" plus "ἔξω" occurs four times in the Gospel. It occurs twice in this episode, in vv. 34–35, when he is cast out and when Jesus hears that he was cast out. Prior to that it occurs after the miracle of the loaves. As Jesus addresses the crowd he states that whoever the Father gives him will come to him and the one who comes he will "never cast out" (μὴ ἐκβάλω ἔξω) (6:37). Finally, near the end of his public ministry Jesus declares that the "judgment" has come to the "world" and that "the ruler of this world will be cast out" (ὁ ἄρχων τοῦ κόσμου τούτου ἐκβληθήσεται ἔξω) (12:31). These phrases work to place what happens to the blind man in the larger framework of the Gospel. He is an example of the one who trusts, witnesses and is cast out, yet Jesus comes to him and receives him into a new community and family where he will be a child of God (cf. 1:12–13 and 12:36). Even though believers are "cast out" of synagogue life, the ruler of this world will ultimately be the one "cast out" (12:31). This clears the way for Jesus to be "lifted up" and to draw all people to himself, drawing them into this new family of eternal life and security discussed above (12:32).

The idea of faith or trust in the Gospel of John is always expressed as a verb (πιστεύω). The fact that the noun (πίστις) is never used indicates that, for John, being a believer and being a disciple are almost synonymous. That John prefers the verb to the noun shows the author is not thinking

---

107. The idea here is that of a forceful or violent seizure. ἁρπάζω, BDAG, s.v. 2.a, 134.

of faith as an internal disposition, but as an active commitment.¹⁰⁸ Trust (πιστεύω) is bound to Jesus's miracles. The purpose of Jesus's "signs" is to lead people to trust (2:11, 23; 4:53; 7:31; 11:15, 42, 45; 12:37; 20:31). Jesus's works also should lead to trust (10:25, 37ff; 14:11). On the one hand, there is a demand for miracles to prove Jesus's identity. This demand is the result of an unbelieving world (2:18; 4:48; 6:26ff). On the other hand, there is a kind of seeing and trusting whereby the signs of Jesus testify to who Jesus is.¹⁰⁹ The (formerly) blind man could see the sign or work of the healing as evidence that Jesus is "from God." The Pharisees could not see this. In John 6:40 seeing (θεωρέω) and trusting (πιστεύω) are brought together,¹¹⁰ along with eternal life and resurrection. Also, 12:44–45 uses seeing and trust as parallels. Thus, trust and recognition are related. So the signs and works of Jesus help one to trust, *but also* the one who trusts is able to comprehend or "see" the signs and works.

In this episode, the "works of him who sent" Jesus are fulfilled. The man trusts in the "sent one" (cf. 6:29). Jesus's odd answer to the question of "who sinned" is explained by the climax of the episode. The works of God are truly worked (6:28—τί ποιῶμεν ἵνα ἐργαζώμεθα τὰ ἔργα τοῦ θεοῦ; 9:4—ἡμᾶς δεῖ ἐργάζεσθαι τὰ ἔργα τοῦ πέμψαντός με) in the healed man as he comes to trust.

The Son of Man is an apocalyptic end-time judgment figure according to Dan 7:13 and *1 Enoch* 49:4; 61:9; 69:27. His coming will mark the beginning of God's judgment; and in 2 Esdras 13.2ff. the Son of Man is portrayed as functioning for both judgment and salvation (cf. 5:27).¹¹¹ Bultmann observed that the healed man is not referring to a future figure, but a present one, as evidenced by his asking, "Who is (ἐστιν, present tense) he sir?"¹¹² It is "into" this Son of Man that the healed man trusts. In John, the Son of Man is presented as having the words of life (6:60ff). As I have mentioned before, we see from the developing character of the man born blind that he finds life. Jesus acts as the Son of Man bringing

---

108. Brown, *John*, 512–13. This is why I tend to use "trust" throughout, rather than "believe" or "faith."

109. Barth, "πιστεύω," in *EDNT*, 3:91–97.

110. Ibid. πᾶς ὁ θεωρῶν τὸν υἱὸν καὶ πιστεύων εἰς αὐτὸν ἔχῃ ζωὴν αἰώνιον, καὶ ἀναστήσω αὐτὸν ἐγὼ [ἐν] τῇ ἐσχάτῃ ἡμέρᾳ (all who *see* the Son and *trust* in him may have eternal life, and I will raise him up on the last day.) italics mine.

111. Hahn, "υἱός," in *EDNT*, 3:388

112. Bultmann, *John*, 338.

salvation to the man born blind. In the next episode, Jesus will act as the Son of Man bringing judgment to those who claim to see.

From the perspective of conflict analysis there is no real conflict between Jesus and the healed man, however it is the man's trust (πιστεύω) in Jesus coupled with his confession or witness that Jesus is a "prophet" and "from God" which produces the conflict in his life that results in his being thrown out (ἐκβάλλω) (vs. 34–35). This adds an additional meaning to Jesus's statement in 10:4 that when the good shepherd has "brought out" (ἐκβάλλω) all his own he goes ahead of them and they follow him. The Pharisees are acting to limit and control Jesus's popularity by threatening expulsion from the synagogue. However, ironically, it is the very act of expulsion that brings people into Jesus's "sheep fold" (cf. 10:4). Once in that fold, they will have "eternal life" (10:28a) never be "cast out" (6:37) nor will anyone "snatch" or "seize" them from Jesus's hand (10:28b).

Scene 8: Jesus and the Pharisees (39–41)

The Pharisees overhear Jesus's conversation about judgment, blindness, and sight. They ask a question (9:40) using μή, which expects a negative answer.[113] "We are not blind are we?" In v. 39 and 41 their failure to see (βλέπω) is contrasted with the healed man who sees (βλέπω). In secular Greek, like English, the verb may mean to see optically or to see insightfully,[114] and in reference to the healed man it means both.

The question of sin (*plot tension one, sin*) is finally answered. "Who sinned?"—the Pharisees who claim to "see." The understanding of sin is reversed in this narrative. The assumptions made about blindness being a sign that someone has sinned are negated by Jesus statement to the Pharisees in 9:41. If they were blind they would *not* have sin. Sin in John is essentially *not trusting* in the one whom the Father has sent. The audience will be told that the Paraclete convicts the world of the sin of unbelief (John 16:9). Two things produce death in ones sins (John 8:24): Failure to trust in Jesus the divine revealer, and failure to trust that his works testify that he is from God (10:25, 37, 38).

---

113. Newman, *Concise Greek-English Dictionary*, 116.
114. Müller, "βλέπω," in *EDNT*, 1:221–22.

Table 3.2: Plot Tensions and Resolution in John 9

Plot Tension Developing:	Resolution:
plot tension one, sin (2, 16, 19?, 24–25, 30–33)	(41)
plot tension two, sabbath healing (16)	(33)
plot tension three, identity and origin of Jesus (16, 24–25)	(33)
plot tension four, fate of the confessor (22, 34)	(34 partial, 35–38 full)

General Observations Relating to Trials and Witnessing

The bulk of John 9 can be framed in terms of a forensic investigation or a trial scene. After the blind man returns from washing he is questioned by neighbors who take him to Pharisees who also question him and then question his parents to verify that he indeed was born blind. Once again he is questioned, essentially under oath, "give glory to God." The ideas of confessing (ὁμολογέω)[115] and witnessing (μάρτυς, μαρτυρέω, μαρτυρία, μαρτύριον)[116] both carry forensic or judiciary weight in their range of meanings. Additionally, in v. 39 Jesus states that he "came" (ἔρχομαι) into the world for the purpose of "judgment" (κρίμα), clearly a forensic term.

In fact, Lincoln sees the trial motif as a major and "integral"[117] way to understand the plot of the Fourth Gospel. He notes the judiciary themes throughout the first part of the gospel (chapters 1–12). He cites 2:25; 3:11, 17–19, 26–28, 32, 33; 4:39, 45; 5: 22, 24, 27, 29–39, 45; 7:14–52; 8:13–18, 26, 50 and John 9 all as part of an ongoing trial motif which is dominant enough to color the way in which the audience would interpret these conflicts.[118]

John 9 can be seen as part of an overall plot where "judgment" has come into the world (9:39 cf. 18:37) through Jesus. Lincoln sees Jesus's statement in the climactic trial scene before Pilate as the major revelation of Jesus's purpose: "For this I was born, and for this I came into the world, to testify to the truth (18.37)."[119] Jesus, throughout the gospel performs

---

115. ὁμολογέω, BDAG, s.v. 3.b.

116. Strathmann, "μάρτυς, κτλ.," in *TDNT*, 4:476.

117. Lincoln, *Truth on Trial*, 21; Lincoln, "Trials, Plots." Also Neyrey, *Perspective*, 265.

118. Lincoln, "Trials, Plots," 5.

119. Ibid., 8; Lincoln, *Truth on Trial*, 25–26.

"signs" (6:14; 7:31; 9:16) or "works" (5:36; 10:25)[120] which testify that he is sent from God and that he has a function of judge with respect to the world. Lincoln notes that Jesus functions in John as both a witness to the truth and as judge of the world.[121]

I will now trace the plot thread of judgment through Jesus's public ministry (John chs. 1–12) and take note of how John 9 fits into the schema. The first mention of Jesus's role as judge in the world is actually a denial of his role as judge. As an act of love, God has given God's only son that the world might be saved (3:16) and not "ἵνα κρίνῃ (from κρίνω)" (in order to judge/condemn) it (3:17). In the next verse the tone with respect to judgment is set for the rest of the gospel. The one who trusts (πιστεύω) in the Son is not judged/condemned and the one who does not trust is judged/condemned (v. 18). Judgment in John then becomes self adjusting according to the response of any given character or group to the Son. In v. 19 the verdict or judgment (κρίσις) is that the world has chosen darkness rather than the light (of the world). Having set trust versus not trusting as the tone with respect to judgment, the idea plays out in the rest of the Gospel.

The next scene having to do with judgment is in the aftermath of the Sabbath day healing of the debilitated man (5:19–30). In 3:19, judgment and light as well as life (3:16) were connected. Here the concept of judgment is connected with the act of giving life (5:21). As was discussed above, light and life are interrelated concepts in antiquity and explicitly connected in John's prologue (1:4). In what appears to be a one-hundred and eighty degree reversal of 3:17, we are told that the Father does not judge but rather all judgment (κρίσις) is given to the Son. The criteria for life or a favorable judgment is to hear Jesus's words and trust God (5:24). In 5:26 and 27, life and judgment are again connected. The father has "granted"[122] (δίδωμι in both 26 and 27) the Son both to "have life" and to "pass judgment." It is the fact that Jesus obeys the "will" (θέλημα) of God (cf. 9:31), which makes his judgments "righteous" or "fair" (δίκαιος) unlike the Pharisee's judgments (cf. 7:24), which are according to outward appearance and by implication not "righteous" judgments.

The apparently opposing statements about Jesus not judging (3:17) and then being given authority to judge (5:27) are brought together in

---

120. Lincoln, "Trials, Plots," 6.
121. Ibid., 7
122. δίδωμι, BDAG, s.v. 13, "to grant by formal action, *grant, allow,*" 243.

8:15–16. In contrast to the activity of the Pharisees who "judge by human standards" Jesus "judges no one." However, when the conditions arise[123] that Jesus does judge, he judges along with the Father. Jesus's intimate connection with the Father make him both Judge *and* one who does not judge in that he does not act *on his own* as Judge.

When we finally arrive at the episode of the man born blind, as mentioned above, it is filled with judicial themes of witnesses and interrogation. Both the man and the parents witness to what they know and have experienced. The parents know "this is our son, and that he was born blind." The healed man knows "he made mud, put in on my eyes, I washed, and now I see." He also knows that if "this man were not from God he could do nothing!" Once the parents testify, and twice the man testifies before the Pharisees who are presented in the role of judges who "judge by outward appearances" (7:23–24) but fail to see the meaning of the sign which Jesus has accomplished. It is this failure to see, and therefore failure to trust, that is their judgment (cf. 3:18–19). Because they claim to see and yet do not trust, they remain in sin (9:41). Even though the Pharisees have been cast throughout the episode as judges, Jesus is the one who appears at the end to act as judge. He pronounces a verdict (cf. 9:39) that has been developing since 9:16. Jesus acts as judge in that he announces what has already taken place. The Pharisees do not trust and therefore their sin remains (9:41).

Finally in the last few verses of the first half of the gospel (12:44–50), at the end of Jesus's public ministry, Jesus sums up his activity as judge. When one sees and trusts in Jesus, that person actually sees and trusts in God who sent him (12:44–45). But there are those who hear Jesus's sayings and reject Jesus and his sayings (12:46). Jesus does not directly judge such a person because Jesus did not come to judge but to save the world (12:47 cf. 3:17). Instead, the "word" that Jesus has spoken acts as judge (12:48). Jesus has not spoken on his own but rather has spoken in cooperation with God who sent him (12:49; cf. 8:16 where Jesus and the Father judge together).

---

123. ἐάν, BDAG, s.v. 1.a, "used w. subjunctive to denote what is expected to occur, under certain circumstances," 268. Here there is ἐάν plus the subjunctive κρίνω.

Conclusions

As the episode progresses one can see the development of the man born blind's character, in contrast to the Pharisees' characterization. As the man born blind gradually comes to a fuller understanding of Jesus, and thus true sight, the Pharisees become increasingly hostile and stubborn with respect to their understanding of Jesus, and thus move toward blindness. This blindness, which equals failure to trust in Jesus and therefore in God who sent him, results in the pronouncement of a judgment or verdict of sin.

The man born blind receives a whole new world and a whole new life from Jesus. The reception of new life is also evident in his character development. He moves from a flat passive character to a wise, witty, and faithful disciple. This new life puts him in a difficult, if not dangerous position with the Jewish authorities. Even so, the man exhibits courage in witnessing to what he knows to be the truth: "I was blind, but now I see." As was mentioned earlier, even though μαρτυρια or μαρτυρεω do not appear in John 9, the concept is here and is considerably important in the Gospel. This portrait of courage is painted against a backdrop of his parents "fear" of "the Jews." Thus courage and the ability to witness is highlighted as a narrative value.

Although he is cast out of the synagogue community, Jesus "finds" him, reveals himself to the man, and elicits trust. Jesus then pronounces judgment on the Pharisees, naming them as sinners, because of their claim to see, when indeed they have remained blind to the sign and work of God in their midst: "Never since the world began has it been heard that anyone opened the eyes of a person born blind. If this man were not from God, he could do nothing."

Message and Rhetorical Impact

The episode demonstrates that Jesus is *from* God. Jesus is the one who can heal and give life to one who previously had none. This is part of Jesus's function as one who, "works the works of God." Jesus is also judge. He pronounces judgment on the Pharisees who refuse to see and thus trust.

The episode illustrates that Jesus's action on the Sabbath trumps the law. While the law came through Moses (and the Pharisees are disciples of Moses), grace and truth came through Jesus Christ (1:17). This means that Jesus actions to do the works of God transcend the law. Jesus is in the unique position to do this since he is the only one who has ever seen God (1:18 cf.) and since he is the one who "makes God known" (1:18c).

In addition to what the text says about Jesus, the episode speaks to the audience promising that courageous trust will be rewarded by acceptance into Jesus's "fold" (10:16). Jesus is the good shepherd who "goes ahead" (10:4) of the sheep and who "finds" (9:35) those who have been thrown out. He does not abandon them, but he lays down his life for them (10:15, 17, 18).

Function

The episode would function in the life of the audience in a number of ways. It functions to encourage and exhort. The historical context of hostility and expulsion of those confessing Jesus as Christ was no doubt unpleasant for those who trusted. It was at least uninviting for those who might have trusted or were considering trust. The text encourages a person in such a situation to "trust in the Son of Man" (9:35).

The text promises that the one who trusts will not be abandoned. The believer, or potential believer, is exhorted to be courageous and to witness to the self evident truth contained in the signs and works of Christ. It is these signs that witness to who Christ is and to where Christ is from and also to where he is going (8:14). The healed man is lifted up as an example of a courageous witness in the face of adversity and serious consequences.

Here the listener is given a choice. Just like in other parts of chapters 1–12, the hearer is presented with the *choice* to trust. Trust or do not trust. Trust the signs and works, or choose to remain blind and receive judgment. To the one who chooses to remain blind, assuming to know the truth already, that person's sin remains, because sin is unbelief. But to the one who becomes like the man born blind, sight is given—sight brings trust and trust brings life. The episode urges the audience to trust in Jesus. In as much as it triggers that trust in the audience, the audience, at that moment begins to experience life.

For John, life (ζωή) is given by both God and the one whom God has sent (3:15–16, 36; 4:14; 5:24–26, 40; 10:10, 28; 17:2–3; 20:31). Just as God has "life in himself," so also the sent one has "life in himself" (5:26). Having "life in oneself" means being a source of life. So Jesus can speak of himself as being the source of life (17:3) or the source of the water of "eternal life (4:14)."[124]

This eternal life (ζωή modified with αἰώνιος) is the typical way John speaks of life. This is a quality of life, not just an everlasting life. It is characterized by the mutual indwelling of God, the Son, and the disciples (14:20). In John, God/the Father and Jesus/the Son are described as *abiding in* or *being in* one another (10:38; 14:10-11, 20). The Son/Jesus and the disciples also are *in* one another or *abide in* one another (14:17, 20; 15:4). This is further expressed as abiding in love. God/the Father, Jesus/the Son, and the disciples are all said to abide in one another's love (15:9-10; particularly 17:26).

This Johannine mutual indwelling is key to understanding the quality of life expressed by αἰώνιος (eternal). Eternal life is knowing God *and* knowing God comes from knowing the one God sent (17:3). It is precisely life in the community of believers, namely the sheepfold (10:1-18), where eternal life, namely knowledge of God and the Son (10:13-14, cf. 10:4-5), is experienced. As the man is expelled from the synagogue community, he is ushered into a new community of believers in Jesus. This is a community that knows and is known by Jesus (10:14). Knowing Jesus is knowing God (14:7, 9; 17:3). Knowing God and Jesus is eternal life (17:3). As an audience is led to trust, they become part of the community of believers where they may experience life and the love of God and the good shepherd (13:1, 34-35).

---

124. Note Jer 2:13, where God's people forsake "the spring of the water of life" and dig cisterns for themselves that are broken and unable to hold water—forsaking the source for their own devices.

4

Social-Science Analysis

I WILL PROCEED IN this chapter to investigate the major themes in the passage from a social-science point of view. I will use models from cultural anthropology that help to illuminate the social and cultural dynamics of the ancient world as they are relevant to the Gospel of John and to this episode in particular. The models are not templates to be imposed as absolutes onto the text. Nor are the templates references to actual things. Rather, the templates are pliable, heuristic abstractions designed to enable us to see more clearly the dynamics of the narrative world of John's Gospel. The models enable us to see connections and meanings of people, actions, and events that might otherwise escape our attention, because they are dissimilar to the dynamics of our own modern Western culture. The text itself is the final arbiter of meaning.

    I will apply these models in the following order. First, I will look at the understanding of sight in the time of Jesus, as well as the ancient understanding of blindness and ancient attitudes toward the blind. Then, I will also investigate models relevant to the ancient understanding of the human make-up, sickness and healing, sin, purity and holiness, honor and shame. In addition, I will examine the system of patronage and brokerage in Jesus's time. And I will look at the man born blind's behavior in relation to speech and dissimulation in cultures of oppression. Finally, I will examine the language of the episode through the lens of "anti-language." Such analyses are useful in order to understand the story better and to grasp the potential responses of an audience hearing the Gospel.

Core Values of Honor and Holiness

Honor

Anthropologists and historians tend to agree that the core value of the first century Mediterranean culture was honor.[1] A core value is that which all human beings in a particular time and culture seek. Honor is a claim to worth that is socially recognized.[2] One's initial "cache" of honor comes from one' birth, one's father and one's social strata. Ben Sira writes, "The glory of one's father is one's own glory" (NRSV).[3] Adoption into an honorable household, such as Octavian into Julius Caesar's house, gives one an increased level of honor or socially recognized worth.[4] This is significant for those in John who through trust become "children of God" (1:12–13).

As a core value in ancient Mediterranean society honor is an end in and of itself. David deSilva writes,

> Seneca, a first-century Roman statesman and philosopher, wrote: "The one firm conviction from which we move to the proof of other points is this: that which is honorable is held dear for no other reason than because it is honorable" (*Ben.* 4.16.2). Seneca claims that his peers regard honor as desirable in and of itself, and dishonor as undesirable in and of itself. Moreover, he understands that the concept of "honor" is fundamental and foundational to his contemporaries' thinking. That is, he expects them to choose one course of action over another, or to approve one kind of person over another, and, in short, to organize their system of values, all on the basis of what is "honorable."[5]

So it is a value in and of itself and an ancient Mediterranean personality views other things, actions, speech, goods, wealth, all as means to the end of honor. In other words, one gives away goods to acquire and maintain honor. Money, for example, is valuable not for the things which one can gain from it (as in dominate American culture); rather, in ancient society the proper use of money will gain/maintain one's honor. Acting as benefactors, wealthy citizens in ancient cities would donate large sums of

---

1. DeSilva, *Honor*, 22.
2. Malina, *New Testament World*, 31.
3. DeSilva, *Honor*, 28.
4. Ibid.
5. Ibid., 22.

money in order to effect improvements and ultimately gain honor in the eyes of the citizens.[6] In Ps 21:21 "Honor" (כבוד), along with "life" (חי), is the motivating factor for "righteousness" (צדקה) and "loyal love" (חסד).

Honor is continually lost and gained in a dynamic social "game" of give and take. This is called *challenge and response*. The challenge and response interaction is always public since honor is a socially recognized claim to worth.[7] Finally, honor is collectively held. Honor is won or lost by and for the social group (family, village, guild, and so on). For the purpose of this work I will not launch into a complete discussion of honor and the challenge/response interaction. The reader is referred to Bruce Malina's discussion and explanation.[8] One final note relevant to John 9: resorting to violence and insults (9:28, 34) is an indication that the challenge has been lost.[9]

Holiness

A second pivotal or core value for the biblical stories of the New Testament is *holiness*. While this is not a core value for all of the ancient Mediterranean peoples, for the ancient Israelite it is central. It hearkens back to the command to "be holy for I am Holy" (Lev 11:44–45; cf. Lev 19:2; 20:7, 26; 1 Pet 1:15). This core value of holiness is intricately related to the concepts of purity and defilement.[10] The entirety of the law of Israel might be understood as laws that maintain holiness.[11] This concept revolved around keeping the people, and by extension the temple and land of Israel, pure.[12] The danger of defilement lay in the fear that if the land or temple were too badly defiled, then God would withdraw God's protection and presence from the sanctuary and from the land! Purity was therefore the concern of every Israelite; and every Israelite was concerned to see that other Israelites maintained purity (cf. Matt 15:2 par. Mark 7:2–3).

6. Ibid., 35.
7. Ibid., 29.
8. Malina, *New Testament World*, 27–57, especially the chart on 34.
9. Malina and Rohrbaugh, *Social-Science Commentary on John*, 173.
10. For an overall understanding of purity see: Nelson, *Faithful Priest*; deSilva, *Honor*; Douglas, *Purity and Danger*.
11. Rhoads, *Reading Mark*, 154.
12. This was already a near impossibility in Jesus's time because of Roman (gentile = unclean) occupation.

Holiness and purity were organized according to time, space, and people. For example Sabbath days (time) were more holy than other days, the inner sanctuary of the temple was more holy than the outlying area (space), and the high priest was more holy than another Israelite male. A correlation of these three dimensions (time, space, people/things) can be seen when one notes that only once a year on the Day of Atonement (time) could the high priest (person) wearing the priestly garb (things) enter the innermost sanctuary of the temple, the holy of holies (space).

To better understand the concept of purity one can look to the seminal definition of the anthropologist Mary Douglas who essentially understands purity as things that are in their proper place, and defilement as things that are out of place. Therefore a person who bleeds or has an open sore produces matter (blood or pus) which is out of place and thus defiles. Seminal discharge (a life producing fluid), which is good and valuable since it is used in fulfilling the divine command to multiply, is still matter out of place and defiles (Lev 15:16–18, 32; cf. 22:4). Menstrual blood is especially dangerous in its ability to defile, since it is both blood (life containing/giving fluid cf. Gen 9:4; Lev 17:11, 14; Deut 12:23) and symbolic of reproductive power. Even something as seemingly harmless as spittle can defile if the source is from one who already has a defiling discharge (Lev 15:8; cf. Num 12:14). Also, that which is not complete or whole, such as a physical deformity, is out of place and defiles (Lev 21:18). Therefore the episode of the woman with a flow of blood (matter out of place) has purity/defilement issues at its core (Mark 5:25–34). So also, the healing of a man born blind (incomplete/not whole) on the Sabbath (more holy time) was an issue of purity and defilement.[13] A word of caution is necessary here, I am not suggesting that anyone in the list of Lev 21:18 is in a perpetual state of impurity. The list was meant for priests in particular sacrificial service. However one can glean a general sense of greater versus lesser suitability to approach the divine related to physical appearance and the presence of physical disabilities.

Although it is not expressed, one can extrapolate that those who are not whole (blind, lame, deformed, deaf, mute, blemished, breaks in skin integrity, etc.) are also seen with less honor.

---

13. Above from Neyrey, "Purity in Mark's Gospel"; Malina, *New Testament World*, 161–73.

Sight in Jesus's Time

In antiquity, the act of seeing was not conceived of in the same way as in modernity. Both Hans Dieter Betz and Dale Allison following Betz's earlier work have noted that there were three ancient theories of how vision worked.[14]

- **Intromission:** "Effluences," or material continually streaming from things that are seen, enter the eye. This is a minority theory held mostly by atomist thinkers such as Leucippus (5th cent. BCE, of Miletus?), Democritus (born ca. 460 BCE, of Abdera), and Epicurus (341–270 BCE, of Samos).[15] This is the view closest to our modern theory of how vision works, in which light enters the eye from objects reflecting a light source. Aristotle understood sight in this way.

- **Extramission:** light exits the eye from the lamp or light or fire of the soul, falls upon an object; and sight is accomplished. This is the most widely held theory in antiquity.

- **Combination:** Plato, among other authors, proposed some combination of the intromission and extramission theories. This is a less widely held theory.

Intromission

The minority opinion is held by Aristotle, who believed there is a transparent medium (such as air) which connects objects and observers. This medium is activated by color; and the eyes are acted upon by the medium for sight to occur. In this understanding, the eyes are passive receptors. Even so, in explaining his theory of vision (Arist. *de Sensu* 437a ff.), Aristotle states that most of the general population (not just philosophers) believe that the eye has in it a fire (πῦρ, 437a 26) or light (φωτός, 437b 26) that comes forth to enable sight.[16]

---

14. Betz, "Matthew 6:22f," 46ff.; Allison, "Eye Is a Lamp"; Moss and Stackert, "Blurred Vision," 757–76.

15. Allison, "Eye Is a Lamp," 62–63.

16. Ibid., 63.

Extramission

The majority of other ancient authors held a simple extramission theory of vision. Of these, Allison writes: "Alcmaeon (early 5th cent. B.C., Croton), Parmenides, the Pythagoreans, and the Stoics held to versions of the so-called extramission theory of vision, according to which the eye produces or is the channel for some sort of visual ray. This ray reaches out and comes into contact with objects in the world."[17] This is also the theory to which Philo of Alexandria holds. He states that the eyes go forward to meet objects of sight (Philo *de Abr.* 150). A good example of this is from Sophocles's *Ajax* where Athena has turned Ajax mad and vows to protect Odysseus by turning away the "beams" (αὐγάς)[18] of Ajax's eyes (Soph. *Aj.* 69–70)

Combination

Finally, Plato holds a combination theory of vision. He holds that vision takes place by a cooperation of external light and the light that flows out of the eye. The "light-bearing eyes" (φωσφόρα . . . ὄμματα, Plat. *Tim.* 45b) produce light (extramission), which flows out and intermingles with the light of day (45c) and carries (intromission) the objects "touched" (ἐφάπτω) to the soul (ψυχή). This produces the sensation of "seeing" (ὁράω) (45d). Plato's explanation is important, since the act of seeing is related to touching (ἐφάπτω) or, more accurately, "laying hold of" or "grasping."[19] Thus sight is not a passive but an active process that involves one's inner light (φαοσφόρος) exiting the eyes to "lay hold" (ἐφάπτω) of an object. Given that sight can refer both to understanding/insight as well as to physical sight, it is not surprising that ἐφάπτω can metaphorically mean to grasp with the mind as well as to grasp physically.

In the above discussion, two things are of note in relation to the man born blind. First, *inner light is required for sight*, whether one holds to a combination theory or extramission theory (as noted above, it is unlikely that an intromission theory would have been held by the average first century hearer of the Fourth Gospel). The fact that the man was blind meant that he was without inner light. Second, to the average first century

---

17. Ibid.
18. αὐγή, LSJ defines this as, "*light of the sun,* and in pl., *rays, beams.*"
19. ἐφάπτω," LSJ, 336.

person, the function of the eye is active not passive. Seeing is akin to touching. This phenomenon of touching something or someone with the eyes explains somewhat why the blind were regarded with such intense trepidation. This will be explored further in the following section on the characterization of the blind, particularly in relation to the evil eye.

Characterization of a blind person

Having examined how sight works and how it does not work in the case of a blind person, let us look at what an ancient audience might have thought and felt when confronted with a blind character.[20] As mentioned in the narrative analysis chapter, an ancient audience would have had a certain set of assumptions and preconceived notions about a blind person (whether that is a literary character or someone physically present). I stated that the man born blind would have been viewed by an ancient audience as "pitiful, shameful, associated in some way with sin (cf. 9:2), ignorant, unclean, and dangerous." I will unpack that statement in the paragraphs following.

The phenomenon of judging character based on physical characteristics is called physiognomy. While modern Western culture tends to dismiss such an endeavor as unscientific and even prejudicial, the practice was the norm in antiquity, to the point that there were even several handbooks and writings dedicated to the practice.[21] What this means is that an ancient audience would not dismiss or gloss over a physical description or trait as readily as a modern audience might. The assumption behind physiognomy is that physical characteristics and inner character are linked. They are linked so closely that when one changes the other changes![22] Such a change can be "seen" in the way the character of the man born blind develops once he is healed.

As discussed above, the eyes are (to an ancient mind) closely related to the soul or inner person. Because eyes provide a direct window to

---

20. On this section see: Allison, "Eye Is a Lamp"; Berger, "The Evil Eye"; Bernidaki-Aldous, *Blindness*; Bridges and Wheeler, "Evil Eye"; Eastman, "Evil Eye"; Elliott, "Paul"; Elliott, "Sermon"; Gilmore, "Anthropology"; Hartsock, *Sight and Blindness*; Kalmin, "Evil Eye"; Kern-Ulmer, "Evil Eye"; Lieu, "Blindness"; McAllister, "Theology of Blindness"; Moss, "Blurred Vision"; Nuño, "Pathologies"; Olyan, "Blind or Lame"; Opatrny, "Blind Man"; Thomsen, "Evil Eye"; Wazana, "Evil Eye."

21. Hartsock, *Sight and Blindness*, 1.

22. Ibid.

the soul they are the most important feature to be examined physiognomically.[23] So important that almost a third of Polemo's handbook on physiognomy is dedicated to understanding the eyes.[24]

Pitiable

From the point of view of physiognomy, perfection is ideal. Therefore, disabilities in general were viewed in a negative light.[25] The disabled, including the blind, were often the objects of mockery in antiquity.[26] Even the god Hephaestus is mocked by the other gods because of his lameness (*Il.* 1.597–600).[27] Specifically, blindness is almost always seen as a negative condition and often thought of as worse than death.[28] Hartsock notes that the Chorus counsels Oedipus that he would be better dead that to live blind (Soph. *OT* 1367)![29] Thus, the man born blind would have been seen as a pitiable character.

Shameful and Associated with Sin

As a pitiable and pathetic condition, blindness is often considered to have been inflicted upon persons as punishment for some sort of sin or transgression. Sometimes the transgression is intentional, and sometimes it is unintentional. The punishment is dealt sometimes by the gods and sometimes by other people. This happens so frequently that an audience would readily assume (like the disciples, John 9:2) that the blindness is related to some transgression or shortcoming.[30] There is the case of Lycurgus who

23. Ibid., 17.

24. Ibid., 17. Polemo of Laodicea, a highly influential rhetorician in the era of Hadrian, authored *de Physiognomonica*, one of the major works in this area. For a fuller discussion of Polemo see Hartsock, 15ff.

25. Ibid., 53.

26. Opatrny, "Blind Man," examines references to the blind in the papyri and notes the case of several letters written by a blind man to the authorities in protest of his ridicule and mistreatment including even the theft of his property and crops.

27. Hartsock, *Sight and Blindness*, 57.

28. Ibid., 66.

29. Ibid., 67.

30. Ibid., 68–69. Brant, *John*, 164, however, notes that not every instance of blindness was associated with sin. She points to Tobit who is blinded (Tob 2:7–10) while doing a good deed!

was blinded by Zeus for his treatment of Dionysus (Hom. *Il.* 6.130–140). Also, for entering into a contest with the muses, Thamyris was blinded (Apollod. *Bib.* 1.3.3).[31] After surveying blindness in ancient Egypt, Mesopotamia, Hittite Anatolia, McAllister concludes:

> Blindness also carried a number of meanings in the Ancient Near East. In all three cultures, blindness, viewed as caused by a curse or divine punishment, would carry the meaning of such ... The blind in such a culture would ever be denied opportunities and rejected because of the stigmas placed on them by such superstitions. The blind, then, could be understood as either cursed for things they had done and/or as omens concerning bad things that would come to pass. When used figuratively, blindness was a universal symbol of weakness or ignorance in all three cultures.[32]

He also notes that in certain "limited cases" God seeks the blinding of those who attack the vulnerable and set themselves up against God's people and purposes (Gen 19:11; 2 Kgs 6:17–20; Zech 11:17; 12:4; 14:12; Psalm 69).[33]

Ignorant

Physiognomists also ascribed to the physically blind the inward condition of "blindness" or ignorance.[34] An example of the relationship between functional eyes and lucid thought is found in *Ajax* when Athena "puts madness" on Ajax's eyes (Soph. *Ajax* 69ff.). The powerful Ajax is confused and, thinking that he is fighting valiantly in battle, is instead battling against farm animals that he takes prisoner, brings home and tortures![35] The rare exception to this view of blindness was that of an ironic depiction of a "blind seer." This is, however, not a frequent character in ancient literature.[36] In Hebrew literature we find a connection

---

31. Ibid., 70. These are only two examples of several Hartsock offers.
32. McAllister, "Theology of Blindness," 62.
33. Ibid., 353.
34. Hartsock, *Sight and Blindness*, 73.
35. Ibid., 73.
36. Ibid., 76–77. It may be of note here that Ophioneus is a seer who was blind at birth. He regained sight when taken by a sharp pain in the head but later lost his sight and became "as he was at first" (Paus., *Descr.* 4.10.6, 4.12.10, 4.13.3). Brant, *John*, 165, notes that this is present in Hebrew literature as well (1 Kgs 14:1–14). I would note

between "madness," "confusion of mind," and "blindness." In Deut 28:28, the three concepts are included in parallelism as part of the curses that accompany breaking the Sinai covenant.[37] We see blindness used to signify being oblivious to another's faults (Gen 27:1–4; 1 Sam 3:2), and also to signify the general unwillingness of the Israelite people to follow God (Isa 6:9; 42:18).[38]

The two other characteristic from my above description of how an ancient audience would have seen the man born blind are dangerous and unclean. These will be covered later in the section on the evil eye.

Darkness and the Evil Eye

Specifically with respect to the illness of blindness, one must note that light is matter or stuff in antiquity. Also, darkness is matter or "stuff," it is a presence and not simply the absence of light as we think of it today. As we noted in the section on theories of vision, the commonly held belief is that light emerges from ones heart and moves out through the eyes in the seeing process. One can reason, then, that blind people are those who have darkness (matter, not just the absence of light) in their heart. This understanding of the outflow of darkness from one's heart out through one's eyes is key to the pervasive ancient Mediterranean fear of the *evil eye*.[39] People who have the evil eye may be aware of it and may choose to use the ability to harm others, but are often totally unaware of their condition and quite unintentionally cause harm. Pilch writes, "In this scheme of things, darkness emanates from the eyes of sightless persons because their hearts are presumably full of darkness. Similarly, harm emanates from the 'evil eye' of the envious-hearted person" [40] (Mark 7:21–22; where in v. 22 the NRSV's "envy" is literally "evil eye").

There are several places in the Bible where "evil eye" appears; however, since it is not a familiar modern western concept, English translations usually translate the phrase with some sort of expression of envy, stinginess, or miserliness (Deut 15:7–11; 28:53–55; Prov 23:6–8; 28:22;

---

particularly that the prophet could not be fooled despite his dim eyesight.

37. Also McAllister, "Theology of Blindness," 362–63.

38. Brant, *John*, 164–65.

39. For the concept in general: Elliott, "Fear of the Leer"; Berger, "Evil Eye"; Maloney, ed., *The Evil Eye*; Thomsen, "Evil Eye."

40. Pilch, "Blindness," 480–81.

Sir 14:3, 5–7, 8, 9; 31:13; 37:11; Matt 6:22–23; Mark 7:22; Luke 11:33–34). This is inadequate, however, since the evil eye involves much more than feelings of envy and greedy behavior. The evil eye is a phenomenon whereby the evil (perhaps envy or perhaps other kinds of evil) within one's heart reaches out through one's eyes and touches another person or thing. The person or object beheld is subjected to real danger. From the first century Mediterranean cultural perspective, the evil eye is often thought to be responsible for the failure of crops, the death of children and livestock, and the sudden illness of a person or animal.

One can see the relationship between the heart and the evil eye in Mark 7:20–23 (NRSV)

> {20} And he said, "It is what comes out of a person that defiles. {21} For it is from within, *from the human heart*, that evil intentions come: fornication, theft, murder, {22} adultery, avarice, wickedness, deceit, licentiousness, *envy (lit. the evil eye)*, slander, pride, folly. {23} All these evil things come from within, and they defile a person." (Italics mine)

In Matthew 6:22–23 and the parallel in Luke 11:33–36 one sees the relationship between light, darkness, and the eye.

> {22} "The eye is the lamp of the body. So, if your eye is healthy (lit. eye is pure, ἁπλοῦς), your whole body will be full of light (φωτεινός); {23} but if your eye is unhealthy (lit. if your eye is evil, ὁ ὀφθαλμός σου πονηρός), your whole body will be full of darkness (σκοτεινός). If then the light (φῶς) in you is darkness (σκότος), how great is the darkness! (Matt 6:22–23, NRSV)

> {33} "No one after lighting a lamp puts it in a cellar, but on the lampstand so that those who enter may see the light. {34} Your eye is the lamp of your body. If your eye is healthy (lit. eye is pure, ἁπλοῦς), your whole body is full of light (φωτεινός); but if it is not healthy (lit. if it is evil, πονηρός), your body is full of darkness (σκοτεινός). {35} Therefore consider whether the light (φῶς) in you is not darkness (σκότος). {36} If then your whole body is full of light (φωτεινός), with no part of it in darkness (σκοτεινός), it will be as full of light (φωτεινός) as when a lamp gives you light (φωτίζω) with its rays." (Luke 11:33–36, NRSV)

It is important to note that the lamp representing the evil eye fills the body with darkness (σκότος). How can a lamp produce darkness? In these passages "light" (φῶς) is either "illumination" (φωτεινός) or "darkness" (σκοτεινός). The explanation is that "darkness" is a thing in and of itself, not simply the absence of light, as we think of it today. As a thing, it functions like light. It can fill a room like light can; and, indeed, in the passages above, it fills the body of the one who has the evil eye. In Isaiah 45:7 darkness is a creation of God just like light. This understanding of darkness seems to be present in Gen 1:1–5 where God separates light from darkness as two different things. Pilch also notes:

> In the beginning there was only darkness (Gen 1:2). Darkness was a positive entity existing in its own right, not the absence of light, since light was not yet created. Moreover, darkness had no dependent relationship upon any source. This concept so plainly set out in Genesis is fundamental to understanding human blindness and its significance in the ancient Israelite world. God created light (Gen 1:3), also a positive entity existing in its own right. Light was not dependent on any source such as the sun, moon, or stars, since these did not yet exist. God would create them on the fourth day (Gen 1:14–19).[41]

In addition to the envious-hearted, those who were thought to possess the evil eye are persons with unusual physical features such as those with joined eyebrows, those with physical problems with the eyes, and especially the blind.[42] One can understand then why the blind are often thought to possess the evil eye.[43] Keep in mind that the commonly held theory of vision in Jesus's and John's time was that of extramission, gazing upon someone or something is akin to touching or grasping.[44] Of this Gilmore writes, "Vision also expresses concepts of ego-boundary and fears about personal integrity and bodily intrusion. The "seer" visually incorporates the object, consumes it, dominates it: 'in these parts, to look is to steal.'"[45] In terms of the evil eye, the darkness or envy in one's heart moves out through the eyes and falls upon, touches, or grasps (ἐφάπτω)[46] that which is beheld. This can cause (from the point of view

---

41. Ibid.
42. Elliot, "Sermon," 56; Elliott, "Paul," 265.
43. Malina, *John*, 170. Elliot, "Sermon," 56. Also see the excellent discussion of blindness and the evil eye in Bernidaki-Aldous, *Blindness*, 99–100, as well as Berger, "Evil Eye"; Maloney, ed., *The Evil Eye*; Elliott, "First Testament."
44. Elliot, "Sermon," 54.
45. Gilmore, "Anthropology," 197–98.
46. Plat. *Tim.* 45d. See above discussion under "Site in Jesus's Time."

of that society) real harm, such as causing young children or animals to become sick or die or causing crops to fail. For example, Plutarch writes:

> ὅταν οὖν οὕτως ὑπὸ τοῦ φθονεῖν διατεθέντες ἀπερείδωσι τὰς ὄψεις, αἱ δ' ἔγγιστα τεταγμέναι τῆς ψυχῆς σπάσασαι τὴν κακίαν ὥσπερ πεφαρμαγμένα βέλη προσπίπτωσιν, οὐδὲν οἶμαι συμβαίνει παράλογον οὐδ' ἄπιστον, εἰ κινοῦσι τοὺς προσορωμένους

> Now, when men thus perverted by envy fix their eyes upon another, and these, being nearest to the soul, easily draw the venom from it, and send out as it were poisoned darts, it is no wonder, in my mind, if he that is looked upon is hurt. (Plut., Quaes. Conv. 5.7.3)[47]

It is clear here that Plutarch believes that something in the soul (ψυχή) which is harmful or literally "bad" (κακία) is actually "sent out" through the eyes, using the metaphor of being "attacked" or "fell upon" (προσπίτνω) by "poison arrows" (πεφαρμαγμένα βέλη).

Also, the chorus in *the Oedipus at Colonus of Sophocles* clearly depicts the blind Oedipus as able to cause them to be cursed because of his blindness (150–54).[48] Oedipus, guided by his daughter, wanders into a sacred grove at Colonus and sits upon a stone (19). He first encounters a stranger from the city who tells him he is on sacred ground. His next encounter is with a group of elders (the chorus). When the chorus of elders first encounter him, prior to knowing anything about his history, their initial reaction is shock and fear (140), ἰὼ ἰώ, δεινὸς μὲν ὁρᾶν, δεινὸς δὲ κλύειν ("Oh! Oh! How dreadful to see and dreadful to hear!"). They react not to the character's history, since they do not yet even know his name, but to the fact that a blind man is present in a holy place.

So to summarize, those who are envious, but also those who have compromised eyes, especially the blind, are thought to have an evil or darkness in their heart.[49] Just like the inner light of a sighted person moves out of the heart through the eyes and touches objects beheld, the inner darkness of an envious or blind person moves out of the heart, through the eyes and touches the things beheld. This inner darkness, when it touches vulnerable persons, can cause death, illness, or other harm such

---

47. Translation from Goodwin, *Plutarch's Morals*.
48. Bernidaki-Aldous, *Blindness*, 99–100.
49. Also, Bridges and Wheeler, "Evil Eye," 76–77. Further, Eastman notes that the *Testament of Solomon* (18:36; cf. 18:2) links the evil eye (βασκαίνω) with darkness. Eastman, "Evil Eye," 85.

as crop failure. So then the blind man in our episode constitutes a threat. He would be perceived as one associated with shame and sin (either his or his parents), and he is a potential source of danger to those around him who may be susceptible to the evil eye.

Summary of the Blind Man's Characterization

In this section I have tried to demonstrate from a social-science perspective how an ancient audience would have initially perceived the character of the man born blind, that is, someone pitiable, shameful and associated with sin, ignorant, dangerous and unclean. Admittedly, an undertaking that attempts to "know" what an audience is thinking based on cultural issues spanning language and history is precarious. Also, the various perceptions and attitudes about the blind discussed in this section were most likely believed, by the people of Jesus's and John's time and local, to varying degrees. (for example not everyone would have spit three times[50] while passing in front of the blind beggar but also not everyone would have felt entirely comfortable with his presence either. I believe that there is enough evidence to get a general impression of how the blind, and therefore our episode's man born blind, would have been perceived. In summary, he would have been at best, pitied and looked down upon, and at worst feared and despised. I will argue in the Analysis by Scene section of this chapter that the action of Jesus as light of the world reverses the presence of darkness within the man and transforms him into a witness that demonstrates insight. He will change from an unsympathetic to a sympathetic character, because of the effects of the light of the world on him.

Model of Human Being

Dyadic Personality

In the mind of an ancient Mediterranean person, the model of the human being was very different from our modern Western notions. Anthropologists refer to the first century Mediterranean personality as a *dyadic*[51]

---

50. Spitting three times is one of a number of things one can do to avoid the effects of the evil eye. Elliott, "Fear of the Leer"; Elliot, "Paul," 268–269.

51. Technically since dyadic refers to a relationship between two, I prefer something like "group-oriented personality" or "collectivist(ic) personality" as opposed to an individualistic personality.

personality.[52] As opposed to an individualistic personality type, a dyadic personality type considers people to be inextricably bound or embedded in a collective or a group. This group orientation is called collectivism. Psychologically, a group oriented personality derives his or her self-image and understanding from the group in which they are embedded. This group is usually the family; but by extension it can also be the tribe, village, nation, ethnic group. Fictive kinship occurs when a group that is bound together by a social commonality other than birth substitutes in some way for the family group.[53] The various communities of the early church were fictive kinship groups (Mark 3:32; Matt 12:50; John 1:12–13; 20:17).

The collectivist personality type will conceive of herself or himself as always being in inter-relationship with those who are on an equal social stratum as well as with those who are on higher and lower social strata. This horizontal and vertical interrelatedness is essential for being human.

Those who are of this communal orientation will understand other individuals not as individuals, but rather as part of the group in which they are embedded. Individuals are judged based on the family, tribe, village, or nation in which they are embedded. Likewise, a group is judged based on the actions of an individual member of that group.[54]

Because the individual exists for the purpose of being part of a group, honor (socially recognized claim to worth) is collectively held,

---

52. On this: Bowe, "Filipino Eyes"; Crook, *Reconceptualizing Conversion*; Crook, "Structure"; Esler, "Mediterranean Context"; Gowler, "Characterization"; Joubert, "No Culture Shock?"; Klingbeil, "Individualismo Y Colectivismo"; Lawrence, "Structure"; Malina and Neyrey, *Portraits of Paul*; Malina, "Individual and Community"; Malina and Neyrey, "First-Century Personality."

53. DeSilva, *Honor*, 194–97.

54. This should not be taken too extremely nor too lightly. Certainly individualistic personalities like Westerners can think of themselves as part of a group and feel great social (peer) pressure as a result. So also, collectivistic personalities can conceive of concepts like personal responsibility and individual desires or needs etc., as Crook, "Structure," 266 aptly notes. The idea is a *spectrum* of orientation. The characters in our Biblical stories, the audiences, and the authors, as well as the recipients of our Biblical letters and epistles etc. would all be on the collectivistic side of the scale. As such, issues of embeddedness would be of significantly more importance to them than to, for example, the typical North American. A simple example from my (admittedly) modern and personal experience may suffice. A female parishioner of mine was once engaged to be married to an American born Easterner of Islamic faith. His parents disapproved of the marriage and as a result he broke the engagement. Even though this caused him immense personal (individualistic personality) pain, he was unable to break away from the wishes of the kin group into which he was embedded (collectivistic personality).

not individually held. Any honor or dishonor that an individual incurs is reflected in the group in which that individual is embedded. Responsibility for honor, morality, holiness, and purity belongs to that of the group rather than that of the individual. Since honor and purity are the responsibility of the group, those who are not whole (a leper or the deformed for example) are removed from the group in order to protect the honor and purity of the group (not in order to punish the individual). This happens because the individual exists *for* the group or network, not the reverse.[55]

This is why the threat of expulsion from the synagogue *community* (ἀποσυνάγωγος)[56] is so powerful, for those who are collectivistic rather than individualistic. This would result in a shaming of the individual and the family in which he or she was embedded. Such an expulsion would result in a kind of "social death"[57] that would cut one and one's family off from the security and benefits, both physical and emotional, of belonging to a social structure.

---

55. Above from Malina, *New Testament World*, 62–67; Malina and Rohrbaugh, *Synoptic Gospels*, 343–45.

56. At this point let me discuss further the phenomenon of "ἀποσυνάγωγος" (expulsion from the synagogue community). The word only appears three times in our know ancient Greek texts—all in the Gospel of John (9:22; 12:42; 16:2). Early interpreters of John, such as J. L. Martyn and Raymond Brown believed that there was a widespread expulsion of believers in Christ from the Jewish Synagogues in the late first century because of the *Brikat ha-Minim* (benediction against the heritics) instituted after a Rabbinic council at Yavneh around 80 CE. This benediction called a curse upon the "Nazarenes" (cf. John 1:46), that is to say, followers of Jesus as the Christ. This would force those who believed in Jesus as the Christ to no longer be able to worship in the synagogues—a kind of expulsion. This theory has come under great criticism since the 1980s. Meeks declared the benediction a "red herring" (102–103). Scholars such as Kimelman, Cohen, McCready, Reinhartz, and Boyarin have all helped to paint a picture of the supposed events at Yavneh as suspect. It is unlikely that there was a widespread organized expulsion of the believers in Jesus from the synagogues post 80 CE. The organizational structure would have been too lose and informal for such an event. It is more likely the ἀποσυνάγωγος is a localized phenomenon, but one that impacts the life of John's audience perceiving themselves as being thrown out of the social structure of the synagogue community. This "throwing out" would carry with it a social stigma that would be devastating to a collectivistic personality living in a honor-shame culture. Some of the above is from Brant, *John*, 166–68.

On the issue of Yavneh and synagogue expulsion see Meeks, "Breaking Away"; Kimelman, "Birkat ha-Minim; McCready, "Johannine Self-Understanding; Cohen, *The Beginnings of Jewishness*; Reinhartz, "the Word Was Begotten; Boyarin, "Justin Martyr Invents Judaism."

57. Brant, *John*, 168.

The man born blind will end up embedded in a different social group than that in which he began (9:35–38). The story begins with him embedded in his family and synagogue (a social group not a building). He is thrown out of that social group as a result of his defense of Jesus as one who is "from God" (9:33–34). After he is "thrown out" (ἐκβάλλω, v. 34 and 35), Jesus "finds" (εὑρίσκω) him and elicits trust (πιστεύω, v. 35). Jesus, using the extended metaphor of himself as the good shepherd, speaks of himself as "bringing out" (ἐκβάλλω, 10:4) all of his own. This reframes the "throwing out" of the man from the synagogue by the Pharisees as the "bringing out" of the man into the sheep fold by Jesus. The story ends with the man embedded in his new fictive kinship group of believers in Jesus, i.e. those who have "the authority to become children of God" (1:12).

Three-Zone Person

Just as an individual is embedded in a group and interrelates both vertically and horizontally within the social order, so also an individual is conceived differently. One way to grasp the ancient concept of a person is too consider the model of three interrelated "zones of interaction," which seems to reflect faithfully the way some ancient people depicted themselves:

- Emotion Fused Thought
  (it is this zone which is of interest for John 9)
- Self Expressive Speech
- Purposeful Action

Each of these zones is symbolized by a related range of body parts. Each zone is responsible for a range of human activities which together make up a totality of human activities. It is difficult to say whether the ancient Mediterranean person was explicitly aware of the zones. It is more likely that the zones, as symbolized by their respective body parts, were simply their way of imagining and speaking about the human and about human activity.

The zone of *self expressive speech* is symbolized primarily by the *mouth and ears*. This zone is responsible for a range of human activities, which include speaking, listening, obeying, telling, praising, and so on. It is responsible for the activities of listening and responding, which are of great importance to the interrelationships in a collectivistic culture. It has to do with the ability to reveal oneself to others and to receive similar self-revelation from others. It is a means through which one can give honor or can shame another and through which one can be honored or shamed. (Job 13:17, "Listen carefully to my words, and let my declaration be in your ears.")[58]

The zone of *purposeful action* is symbolized primarily by the *hands and feet*. This zone is responsible for doing, acting, accomplishing, working, coming, going, touching, and so on. The activities of observable action are covered within this zone. This deals with the ability of a person to act upon their desire and will. (Mark 9:43, 45, "If your hand causes you to stumble . . . if your foot causes you to stumble.") The use of the hand/s often symbolize a transfer of past deeds or the transfer of power or ability. When Jesus heals, he often lays his hands upon the ill.[59]

Finally the zone of *emotion fused thought* is symbolized primarily by the *eyes and heart*. This zone is responsible for the human activities of seeing (perceiving), knowing, understanding, remembering, choosing, feeling, thinking, considering, contemplating, meditating and similar activities. It has to do with both cognition and emotion. (Ps 19:14, "meditation of my heart" and Mark 7:21, "from the human heart, that evil intentions come.")[60] So, from an ancient Mediterranean perspective the blind are affected not just in their ability to see objects but are affected in the zone of emotion fused thought.

For our understanding of the character of the man born blind we must note again that blindness indicates an inability to know and to understand. This fits with the earlier discussion of the blind as, physiognomically speaking, spiritually and morally ignorant.

This is pertinent to John 9 in that the man born blind becomes a "teacher" (9:34) and representative of the gospel's position about the person of Jesus. He does things a blind person in that society should not be able to do. He presents a logical argument about exactly why Jesus is from God (9:31–33). He is clever enough to answer an attempt to compel him

---

58. Above from Malina, *New Testament World*, 69; Malina and Rohrbaugh, *Synoptic Gospels*, 419; Pilch and Malina, eds., *Biblical Values*, 25–26.

59. See Matt 8:3, 15; 9:18, 25 for example. Above from Malina, *New Testament World*, 69; Malina and Rohrbaugh, *Synoptic Gospels*, 419; Pilch and Malina, eds., *Biblical Values*, 92–94.

60. Above from Malina, *New Testament World*, 69; Malina and Rohrbaugh, *Synoptic Gospels*, 419; Pilch and Malina, eds., *Biblical Values*, 63–64.

to condemn Jesus by indirectly disagreeing (9:25). He expresses wit and sarcasm during his debate (9:27). The audience can attribute all this to the man's healing and the influence of Jesus, the light of the world, on the man. Perhaps this dynamic also helps to explains why some people in the story were not sure he was the same man after he received his site.

Sickness and Healing

Ancient Understanding of Health

With respect to ancient understanding of sickness and healing,[61] it is necessary operationally to define some terms.[62] *Well-being* is defined as the normal state of human existence. Health is one aspect of well-being.[63] *Sickness* is defined as the loss of some aspect of health (and therefore the loss of some aspect of well-being). The terms *disease* and *illness* describe two different understandings of sickness.

Disease is the explanation of sickness in modern day biochemical, microbiological and physiological terms. This explanation focuses on signs and symptoms, the expected course of the sickness, and the expected outcome. It is individualistic and sickness can be described as disease irrespective of the social context or acknowledgment of it.[64] Disease is successfully resolved by a cure. A *cure* is the restoration of biochemical, microbiological and physiological processes to their normal function. It is done on an individual basis, and usually relates to the cause of the disease, such as infection with a microbe that needs to be eradicated.[65] According to this definition then, *disease* and *cure* are necessarily both modern constructs and *not* ancient ones. John's audience could not

---

61. Albl, "'Are Any Among You Sick?'"; Avalos, *Illness and Health Care*; Carroll, "Sickness and Healing"; Craffert, "Medical Anthropology"; Guijarro, "Healing Stories"; Hahn, *Sickness and Healing*; Hatfield, "Sin, Sickness, and Salvation"; Kleinman, *Patients and Healers*; Pilch, "Leprosy"; Pilch, "Healing in Mark"; Pilch, "Understanding Healing"; Pilch, *Healing in the New Testament*; Pilch, "Improving Bible Translations"; Seybold and Müller, *Sickness and Healing*; Simundson, "Health and Healing"; van Eck and van Aarde, "Sickness and Healing."

62. The following makes claims that are agreed on by social-science scholars but not necessarily all others about what constitutes health.

63. Pilch, "Improving," 130.

64. Ibid.; Pilch, "Healing in Mark," 143.

65. Pilch, "Improving," 132; Pilch, "Understanding Healing," 31.

understand disease and cure in the way it has been defined since present day scientific tools and worldview were not in place.

Illness is the explanation of sickness from the perspective of the human condition. It explains the human perception of the experience of the sickness. Of particular concern in this understanding is the effect the sickness has on the social interactions of the sick person, and the effect of the sickness on the social group.[66] The remedy for illness is healing. *Healing* is defined as providing social meaning for the problems created by illness. Healing is social and communal and the sick person gains a degree of satisfaction through the alleviation or elimination of the experience of the symptoms. This may or may not involve elimination of the sickness itself, however, in healing, meaningful interaction with the social group is restored.[67]

The value orientation of the New Testament world emphasizes *being* over doing, a *collectivist* (see "collectivist personality" section above) rather than individualistic personality, orientation toward the *past* with a sense of the importance of history, a tendency to *be subject to nature* rather than attempting to dominate it, and an assessment of human nature as a *mixture of good and evil*.[68] Overall, these values and cultural perceptions of reality make up the definition of health for the ancient Mediterranean person. Pilch notes that, "The 'sickness problems' presented to Jesus in the Second Testament are concerned with a state of being (blind; deaf; mute; leprosy; death; uncontrolled hemorrhaging; and so forth) rather than an inability to function. What a Western reader might interpret as a loss of function, namely lameness, is in actuality a disvalued state of being." [69] In other words, function is important *not as an end* but in as much as it allows one to continue in a *valued state of being* and in a state of proper social relationship. This is an issue for the sick or disabled—who see themselves as embedded in the family as part of the whole, not individually[70]—because they could not contribute in the most

---

66. Pilch, "Improving," 130; Pilch, "Healing in Mark," 143.

67. Pilch, "Improving," 132; Pilch, "Understanding Healing," 31; van Eck and van Aarde, "Sickness and Healing," 27–54; Albl, "'Are Any Among You Sick?'" 126; The contrast between these two concepts is also discussed in Hahn, *Sickness and Healing*.

68. Pilch, "Understanding Healing," 31.

69. Ibid., 22.

70. Albl, "'Are Any Among You Sick?'" 126, notes that both illness and healing are understood as a "socially organized response," citing Kleinman, *Patients and Healers*, 24; also Guijarro, "Healing Stories," argues that that healing is defined in social rather

meaningful way possible to the family/household work or business. The man born blind, as a beggar, was able to make some contribution, but not in the way a sighted person could. When Peter's mother-in-law is healed (Mark 1:31) she returns to an honorable social function of serving an honored guest, Jesus.

Health for the New Testament person includes an emphasis on a *valued state of being* (*honor*, a socially acknowledged claim to worth, as a *core value*), the ability to be *in relationship* with ones kin group (collectivist personality), the ability to maintain integrity with ones history, and the ability to remain *pure and undefiled* (*holiness* as a *core value*).

From this perspective we can understand the man's blindness as not simply loss of function but rather a *de-valued* state of existence.[71] As a beggar (9:8) and (assumed) sinner (9:2) and the general pitiable condition of a blind person (as discussed above) he would have *lacked honor*. The fact of his deformity may have attached *purity issues*.[72] Due to others wishing to avoid the evil eye (see below) and again the generally pitiable condition of a blind person, his blindness would have been to some degree isolating, a particular difficulty for people in a culture with a *collectivist personality*. It is important to note that the simple restoring of sight (function) did not necessarily constitute full healing. The reversal of his deformity (and perhaps washing in Siloam[73]) may have made it possible to maintain a state of purity. Restoring the man to a valued state of being (honor) is in process.

Also, restoring relationships with a social group (collectivist personality) is in process. He is brought by the bystanders (community of people) to the Pharisees, who are representatives and gatekeepers of the synagogue *community*. Neyrey writes about transformation in relation to the man's healing.[74] He identifies four stages of "rights of status transformation." They are: separation, a liminal stage, rite of passage,

---

than physical terms and that the healing of (blind) Bartimaeus integrates him socially.

71. Pilch, *Healing in the New Testament*, 13–15; van Eck and van Aarde, "Sickness and Healing," also describe the concept of sickness as being in a "disvalued" state of being.

72. One of the notions that Avalos, *Illness and Health Care,* argues is that the issue of purity was flexible and not consistently applied, but applied in ways to insulate society from populations such as the disabled.

73. Brown, *John*, 1:372; and Keener, *John*, 1:781, observe that Siloam is noted for its purification abilities.

74. Neyrey, *John*, 175.

acknowledgment of new status. He is separated from the world of beggars, the disabled, and the unclean by the healing and washing. The liminal stage is a time of training and enduring of hardship, represented by the two questionings (9:13–17; 24–33). During this liminal stage he proves himself able to reason like one who is part of Jesus's in-group or fictive kinship group. The rite of passage comes when he is excommunicated (9:34) by the gatekeepers of the synagogue community and welcomed (9:35–38) by the "gatekeeper" (θυρωρός, 10:3) of the community of believers.

The reactions of the various characters are interesting in relation to the man's healing and changing of social status. The bystanders recognize the change and begin a process of incorporating him into the synagogue community by bringing him to the community's gatekeepers, the Pharisees. The Pharisees begin a process of evaluation. To be sure, they are investigating the healing in relation to Jesus, but are also evaluating the man born blind as well, (9:17, "What do you say about him?"). It is conceivable that the healed man could have been incorporated into the synagogue community if he had acquiesced to the desires of the Pharisees in 9:24. The implication of their statement, "Give Glory to God. We know this one is a sinner," was to compel the man to swear by oath[75] that Jesus is a sinner, and therefore not from God. However, he does exactly the opposite, arguing that Jesus is from God (9:33). Therefore he is expelled by the synagogue gatekeepers.

Personal Causality

It is important to note at this point that from the ancient Mediterranean point of view sickness was understood by default to have a *personal cause* of some sort.[76] This may be the evil eye, mischievous or evil spirits that occupy the air and routinely interfere in human affairs, or personal or corporate sin. Having personal causes, sicknesses therefore also required a personal remedy of some sort, such as a healer with "power."[77]

For example, Deuteronomy 28: speaks of "blessing" and health for those who follow the covenant stipulations (28:1ff.) and curses for those who fail to "obey" (28:15ff.) Specifically, failure to keep the covenant

---

75. For "give glory to God" as an oath formula, see p. 113.
76. Neyrey, *John*, 47; Dawson, *Healing, Weakness and Power*, 25.
77. Malina, *NewTestament World*, 102.

results in illness of various kinds (Deut 28:22, 27–28, 35). The plot of Job suggests that other spiritual entities, Satan (1:6) in the case of Job, are able to afflict while still under the constraints of God (1:12; 2:6–7). The young man in Mark 9:14–39 (par. Matt 17:14–21; Luke 9:37–43a) from a modern perspective may be thought to have a neurological disorder (Mark 9:18, falling down, foaming at the mouth, grinding of teeth, full body rigidity are signs of a grand mal seizure); however, his plight is attributed to a demon (Mark 9:17). In the case of Deuteronomy 28, it is clear that the person afflicted is responsible, in part, for the affliction. In the case of Job, it is his own "blamelessness" (תם) and "uprightness" (ישר) that causes Satan to afflict him (Job 1:8, 2:3). The general assumption, however, is the perspective shared by the disciples, namely, that sin was a cause for illness.[78] Ben Sirach assumes this when he counsels the sick person to pray for healing *and* "cleanse your heart from all sin" (Sirach 38:9–10). As far as the man's condition of blindness at birth, given the dyadic personality and the tendency to consider people as part of a group (primarily a family group) rather than individuals on their own, punishment for sin stays in the family. This is seen in such passages as Exod 20:5–6 and its parallel Deut 5:9–10, where God punishes "children for the iniquity of parents, to the third and the fourth generation." Thus, the illness (2 Sam 12:15) and death of David's son is seen as having a familial personal cause, David's sin (2 Sam 12:14–19).

It is of note that Jesus uses spittle in the healing of the man born blind. While there is no hard evidence that spittle constitutes a purity threat[79] to Jews in the time of Jesus (or John), the use of a bodily fluid to perform an act of power, a healing, tells the audience something about the character of Jesus. Fluids that might otherwise contaminate can heal or remove impurity if drawn from a particularly pure or powerful specimen.[80] Examples of this are blood from a perfect animal sacrificed. Blood that would normally defile, when drawn from a perfect animal reverses defilement. An interesting similarity to John 9:6 (also Mark 7:33; 8:23)

---

78. Also, Simundson, "Health and Healing," 331; Carroll, "Sickness and Healing," 130 and 140 n2; Seybold and Ulrich, *Sickness and Healing*, 95.

79. Keener notes that spittle found in Jerusalem, except for the market place frequented by Gentiles, was ritually clean according to a 2nd century rabbi. Also, gentile spittle required immersion afterwards but not spittle from a Jew. *John*, 1:780.

80. Smith, "Jesus and the Pharisees," 153–54.

can be found in Tacitus, *the History* in which Vespasian uses his saliva to heal a blind man:[81]

> In the months during which Vespasian was waiting at Alexandria for the periodical return of the summer gales and settled weather at sea, many wonders occurred which seemed to point him out as the object of the favour of heaven and of the partiality of the Gods. One of the common people of Alexandria, well-known for his blindness, threw himself at the Emperor's knees, and implored him with groans to heal his infirmity. This he did by the advice of the God Serapis, whom this nation, devoted as it is to many superstitions, worships more than any other divinity. He begged Vespasian that he would deign to moisten his cheeks and eye-balls with his spittle. Another with a diseased hand, at the counsel of the same God, prayed that the limb might feel the print of a Cæsar's foot. At first Vespasian ridiculed and repulsed them. They persisted; and he, though on the one hand he feared the scandal of a fruitless attempt, yet, on the other, was induced by the entreaties of the men and by the language of his flatterers to hope for success. At last he ordered that the opinion of physicians should be taken, as to whether such blindness and infirmity were within the reach of human skill. They discussed the matter from different points of view. "In the one case," they said, "the faculty of sight was not wholly destroyed, and might return, if the obstacles were removed; in the other case, the limb, which had fallen into a diseased condition might be restored, if a healing influence were applied; such, perhaps, might be the pleasure of the Gods, and the Emperor might be chosen to be the minister of the divine will; at any rate, all the glory of a successful remedy would be Cæsar's, while the ridicule of failure would fall on the sufferers." And so Vespasian, supposing that all things were possible to his good fortune, and that nothing was any longer past belief, with a joyful countenance, amid the intense expectation of the multitude of bystanders, accomplished what was required. The hand was instantly restored to its use, and the light of day again shone upon the blind. Persons actually present attest both facts, even now when nothing is to be gained by falsehood. (Tac. *Hist.* 4.81).[82]

Of interest in this story is that healing (*remedium*) a blind man with his spittle is included as one of the "many wonders (*miracula*)" that occurred

---

81. Also, Keener, *John*, 1:780.
82. Church, Brodribb, Bryant, *Complete Works of Tacitus*.

"which seemed to point him [Vespasian] out as the object of the favor of heaven and of the partiality of the Gods." This is precisely the argument the man born blind uses to demonstrate that Jesus is "from God" (9:33).[83]

Patronage and Brokerage

Another sociological system that I shall explore pertains to the characterization of Jesus throughout the Gospel of John. The patronage system refers to a system of generalized reciprocity between social unequals. In this system, a lower status person in need (client) receives help in the form of favors from a higher status person (patron) who has access to needed resources for well-being and survival. The client is then indebted to the patron. Service through various, usually menial tasks was expected. The *primary duty* of a client was to honor the patron and to give the patron public praise.[84] A broker is one who mediates between the patron and the client. First order resources such as land, food, shelter, and jobs are controlled by patrons. Second order resources, contact with people (such as a patron), are controlled by brokers. Jesus is cast in the light of God's broker who is sent (πέμπω, ἀποστέλλω) by the Father (cf. 5:27; 17:2).

Forty times we are told by the author of John that Jesus is sent by the Father. "Sent" language is language which belongs to the semantic field of patronage.[85] As discussed in the narrative chapter's section on Jesus's characterization, πέμπω is used to describe Jesus in this episode (9:4), but ἀποστέλλω is also used throughout John in a seemingly interchangeable way. As such, Jesus is the one and only one (John 14:6b) who controls access to the Father who "sent" him. This access is to the resources which the Father has to offer, namely life (John 14:6a). In John 9, Jesus puts the man born blind in touch with the resources which God offers, life and light. Once this light is kindled within the man, he gains both sight, and insight. As a result of gaining insight into who Jesus is, one "from God" (9:33), he becomes part of the community of those who trust in Jesus. As a result of trust in Jesus, he gains life (John 20:31; cf. John 1:4; 3:15–16, 36; 5:24, 26, 29; 6:40; 11:25).

---

83. Carroll, "Sickness and Healing," 135–36, notes that the healings as well as other "works" and "signs" are used specifically to demonstrate that Jesus is the Son of God and source of both health and eternal life.

84. deSilva, *An Introduction to the New Testament*, 132–33.

85. Malina, *John*, 117–19; Pilch and Malina, eds., *Biblical Values*, 133–37.

Hidden and Public Transcripts

James Scott writes about the kind of interaction that takes place between a member of a dominated or subjugated class and the dominating class.[86] In New Testament studies Scott's work has often been used to describe the relationship of those subjugated under Roman authority.[87] I will however apply the work of Scott to the interaction between the man born blind and the Jewish authorities questioning him. I believe such an application is valid since this is an interaction between a beggar (9:8) born (according to common thought) in sin/shame and dishonor, on the one hand, and the honorable and respected (again, according to common thought) synagogue rulers, on the other hand. In these unequal interactions between subordinate and one who dominates there is a "public transcript."[88] This is the way a subordinate acts and speaks with those who dominate—because of "prudence, fear, and the desire to curry favor, shaped to appeal to the expectations of the powerful."[89] Essentially this is *saying* what those in power want to hear and *acting* amiably toward them—as a "survival skill"[90] to "produce a public transcript in close conformity with how the dominant group would wish to have things appear."[91]

Using the metaphors of "on stage" and "off stage," Scott describes two different ways of speaking and acting. While "on stage" the subordinate performs the act of the public transcript. But if this public transcript is an act performed "on stage" how can we truly know what the subordinate thinks?[92] This dilemma is answered by what Scott calls the "hidden transcript" which takes place "off stage" when those in power are neither present nor able to observe the actors. This does not mean that everything the subordinate says in the public transcript is always pretense nor can we say that all in the hidden transcript is reliable. What we can say is that the hidden transcript is produced for an audience who is considered trustworthy and safe by the speaker.[93]

---

86. Scott, *Domination*.
87. For example, Horsley, ed., *Hidden Transcripts*.
88. Scott, *Domination*, 2.
89. Ibid.
90. Ibid., 3.
91. Ibid., 4.
92. Ibid.
93. Ibid., 6.

The act of dissimulation mediates between the public and the hidden transcripts. This happens when it is too dangerous for the subordinate to speak the hidden transcript "on stage" in the presence of the dominate class, and yet must for some reason speak while under the observation of the dominate. When this happens, a "partly sanitized, ambiguous and coded version of the hidden transcript is always present in the public discourse of subordinate groups."[94] Such speech takes place in public view but is designed to have a "double meaning."[95] When the subordinate says what he or she really means, but in a way that sounds like what the dominate wants to hear, she or he is dissimulating.

If public transcripts, hidden transcripts, and dissimulation represent three different types of "political discourse"[96] then a fourth type happens when the pretense is broken in the public arena and a subordinate speaks plainly the hidden transcript for all, including the dominate, to hear. Scott refers to this as "the rupture of the political *cordon sanitaire*."[97] The man born blind moves from dissimulation (9:15, 25) to all out rupture (9:27) during the course of the episode.

Scott notes that such instances of open defiance usually provoke "a swift stroke of repression."[98] He claims that such ruptures constitute "a throwing down of the gauntlet."[99] When this happens the challenge poses a threat to the legitimacy of the dominate power structure that "offstage heresy" alone could never pose. In other words, dissimulation and keeping the hidden transcript hidden, even though they are forms of resistance, do not challenge the power structure like making the hidden transcript public. In addition to "a swift stroke of repression," Scott notes that those in power often define the challenger as "deranged, thus depriving his act of the significance it would otherwise have."[100] Of this practice he writes, "there is little doubt that it often serves elites to label revolutionaries as bandits, dissidents as mentally deranged, opponents as traitors, and so on."[101] In Scott's "so on" I would include labeling those

---

94. Ibid., 19.
95. Ibid.
96. Ibid., 18–19.
97. Ibid., 19.
98. Ibid.
99. Ibid., 203
100. Ibid., 205.
101. Ibid., 206.

who challenge a group's theological position and religious power as sinners, thus 9:34a.

What follows is an overall "social science" review of the episode scene by scene, at the same time detailing the nature of the various "transcripts" as they develop in the plot.

Anti-Language

Anti-language is a model used by some[102] to understand the highly specialized language present in the Fourth Gospel. Anti-language is used as a socialization tool of alternate societies or anti-societies. These are societies that exist outside the usual social constructs, either by choice (such as a cult) or by some sort of social expulsion, quarantine (such as prisoners within our penitentiary system), or socially necessary isolation (such as street gangs who have their own terminology and become like family to one another). Anti-language uses the language of the broader society, but gives specialized or redefined meanings to the words. The effect is that the members of the anti-society share a socially unifying linguistic symbology. The anti-language of an anti-society is used in two ways. It functions to increase cohesion and loyalty within the group, and it functions to socialize newcomers to the society, teaching them the values of the group and also bonding them psychologically and emotionally to the group. It expresses an understanding of reality that is peculiar to the anti-society. It also tends to be highly affective, so as to bond the group members to one another and to bond them to the central figure of the group. This serves to maintain group identity, cohesion, and loyalty in the midst of pressure or perceived pressure from the broader society.

While the specific historical situation of the Fourth Gospel (particularly in relation to issues such as expulsion, the so called benediction against the heretics, and the community's relation to Judaism in general) can be argued, it seems clear from the narrative that the implied audience (if not the real audience) sees themselves as having been rejected by the broader society (9:22; 12:42) and even under threat of real harm (16:2) from it. It is also clear that the central figure of the Johannine society is perceived to have been rejected as well (1:10–11).

As I have stated in the introduction, John 9 seems to almost provide a template for the socialization of a member of the Johannine community.

---

102. Malina and Rohrbaugh, *John*, 7–15; Petersen, *John and the Sociology of Light*.

It is the story of a person who receives his sight, both physical and spiritual, is then cast out from his own people for witnessing that his healer is from God. He is sought out by his healer, trusts and worships. The central figure of the Johannine community then pronounces that the representatives of the broader (expelling) community abide in sin.

To further cement the bond the man has with both the community and its central figure, a long and emotive dialogue (10:1–18) ensues about how the "good shepherd" leads his sheep who know his voice. These sheep do not follow strangers because they do not "know"[103] the voice of strangers (note the we versus them mentality). Jesus identifies himself as "the door" and promises pasture, i.e. safety. Jesus is the one and only one who lays down his life for his sheep (group members, 10:11, 15). The one who does not enter by the gate, (the gate is Jesus cf. 10:7), is a thief (10:1). The thief (anyone else that hasn't entered through Jesus the gate) comes to kill, steal and destroy (10:10). Jesus is therefore the only one who comes to bring abundant life to the sheep (10:10).

The use of anti-language reflects the anti-society's perception of reality. Jesus is light (9:4 cf. 1:4, 9; 8:12) and therefore life (1:4; 8:12). The world (the expelling community) does not receive this light (1:11) therefore does not have life. The world does not "know" the light (1:10) but his sheep "know him," and he "knows" his sheep. So also he "knows" the Father and the Father "knows" him.[104] The message is: there is no life, no knowledge of God, outside the sheepfold! The rhetorical effect is to urge the audience to get in the sheepfold and stay in the sheepfold, because only there will one be cared for and live "abundantly" (10:10).

Analysis by Scene

Scene 1: Jesus and disciples (1–5)

The episode begins with the disciples making the very natural assumptions that illness had some personal cause at its root and that in the case of a blind person, sin was that cause. This assumption is quickly challenged by Jesus. True to his character throughout the gospel, Jesus re-frames the issue not in terms of illness, sin, and personal cause, but rather in terms of God's work being revealed. This re-framing would have

---

103. The word is οἶδα both in 10:4 and 10:5, and can carry the connotation of intimate acquaintance or close relation, BDAG, s.v. 2. In 10:14–15 the verb is γινώσκω.

104. γινώσκω in each instance.

had a shocking effect on the ancient mind and would have peaked the interest of an ancient audience. At best, the re-framing would have been difficult to accept with all of the stigma attached to blindness: sin, shame, impurity, ignorance, being better off dead, the danger of the evil eye. How can one who is blind (who is all those things) possibly be an instrument of God's revelation (φανερόω, 9:3)? *How* remains to be seen in the rest of the episode.

After reframing the blind man's initial characterization, Jesus speaks of his own character. He is both "sent (πέμπω)" and the "light of the world" (9:4–5). As was discussed in the Patronage and Brokerage section above, the notion of Jesus as the "sent" (both πέμπω and ἀποστέλλω) one of God occurs throughout John, as one who is sent with a purpose, namely to bring life (cf. 10:10b). This purpose is related to Jesus's function as light of the world. As was discussed in the narrative chapter's section on Jesus's characterization, light and life are nearly synonymous in antiquity and are clearly related in John (1:4). It is important to note that from the point of view of patronage and brokerage, to receive the broker is to receive the patron and to reject the broker is to reject the patron (John 13:20 cf. Matt 10:40 // Mark 9:37 // Luke 9:48).[105] Jesus is then the only one who can offer the resources of life and healing that God possesses, and to reject the broker is to reject abundant life (10:10) and healing.

Scene 2: Jesus and the man (6–7)

The use of spittle in this scene to heal, as mentioned above, characterizes Jesus as one having great power and/or purity. The use of spittle may have suggested to the Pharisees a claim by Jesus to have religious authority. This would therefore constitute a threat to their religious authority. Also in this scene, Jesus acts as light of the world which cannot be overcome/overtaken/destroyed (καταλαμβάνω) by darkness (σκοτία, cf. John 1:5). In this case the darkness of blindness (and perhaps also the evil eye) is no match for the light of the world. In the final scene, we will see how the Pharisees fail to understand/comprehend (καταλαμβάνω) that same light thus are blind themselves (vv. 39–41).

---

105. deSilva, *Introduction*, 135.

Scene 3: The neighbors and the man (8–12)

In a collectivistic society comprised of dyadic personalities, very little introspection took place. People knew only what they observed in others; the human heart was hidden and known only to God (Ps 44:21; 139:23; Sirach 42:18). A public healing accomplished at least two things. First, the man is placed in a different social relation; he is no longer a blind beggar. He begins to interact with social groups in a different way. His interaction with the bystanders does not indicate that he is unclean or dangerous. Second, he is now associated with the "man named Jesus" who healed him. His behavior from this point forward will be scrutinized in relation to his healer. His healer's behavior will reflect on him and his behavior will reflect on his healer. This will be increasingly an issue as the story progresses (9:17, 28).

Scene 4: The man and the Pharisees (13–17)

The narrative comment in 9:14 locating the healing on a Sabbath brings more drama and tension to the episode. Sabbath day rules were not arbitrary or without purpose. The goal of these rules was to maintain purity within the nation so as to secure God's continued presence in the land and with the people. The participation of the healed man in a potential transgression of these rules, although passive, would have placed him in a precarious situation in relation to the authorities. Also, as an honorable recipient of a benefaction of healing at the hands of God's "sent" one, he would of course want to protect Jesus from suspicion. This can be seen in the dissimulating and careful language that the man uses when answering this first round of questioning.

Comparing his answer to the Pharisees in v. 15b with his answer to the neighbors in v. 11, we see a very important omission. The man does not choose to relate the fact that Jesus "made" (ποιέω) mud, since creation (ποιέω) was potentially a Sabbath violation.[106] The primary job of a client in relation to his patron is to speak his praise publicly and to remain loyal.[107] The man must cleverly walk a fine line between doing honor to his patron's broker and not offending the authorities. He

---

106. This may be an issue of kneading on the Sabbath as seen in *m. Shabb.* 22:6, which prohibits kneading in the case of medicine but allows anointing, and 24:3, also Brown, *John*, 1:373; Keener, *John*, 1:786.

107. DeSilva, *Introduction*, 140. Arist., *Nic. Eth.* 1163b 12–15.

does this in two ways. First, there is his omission of "making" mud. Second, when asked "what do you say about him," he paid Jesus honor by calling him "prophet."

Scene 5: The Pharisees and the parents (18–23)

The parents of the man make no attempt to walk such a fine line. When called and questioned they simply refer the Pharisees back to their son. Another piece of information is related in this scene which heightens the tension even more. The "Jews" had "agreed together" (συντίθεμαι, which was more than they could do in the prior scene when there was a σχίσμα among them!) to "expel from the synagogue" (ἀποσυνάγωγος) anyone confessing Jesus as the Messiah. Expulsion would have been particularly threatening in a society that was characterized by dyadic personality and that was concerned with gaining honor and avoiding shame. Expulsion would bring shame and cut the parents off from their social network. This would not only have been difficult emotionally and psychologically, but it would have made it very difficult to acquire the goods for daily survival since such goods were acquired through social networks.

Scene 6: The Pharisees and the man again (24–34)

The second questioning is the most emotionally charged of all the scenes. The Pharisees and the man born blind question and answer 3 times (24–25; 26–27; 28–33) before he is thrown out (34). Each question/answer cycle becomes increasingly charged.

First Q and A (24 and 25)—Dissimulation

The Pharisees begin by charging the man to "give glory to God"—an oath formula to tell the truth (cf. Joshua 7:19). The Pharisees are asking him to agree under oath that Jesus is a "sinner" (ἄνθρωπος ἁμαρτωλὸς) and therefore not "from God" (παρὰ θεοῦ) (cf. 9:16). As was discussed in scene 4, the man must walk a fine line between not offending the authorities and giving praise and loyalty to the one who restored his sight. The fine line has here become even thinner! Even so, the man once again finds a clever way to walk that line. He answers in a way that does not overtly disagree with his social superiors ("I don't know if he is a sinner") and yet maintains praise and loyalty ("I do know that being blind I now see") to the one who restored his sight (v. 25).

In terms of the work of Scott, discussed above, the man is speaking publicly in a way that does not directly challenge his superiors yet the hidden transcript is cleverly formulated. The man is in fact dissimulating. He *does* know if Jesus is a sinner or not. He will argue the point passionately and logically in just a few more verses. However, for now he maintains the social status quo. Still, the clever ear would hear the hidden transcript of protest in the last portion of his statement ("one thing I do know . . ."). As some of the Pharisees have already stated, a sinner could not perform such a sign (9:16b).

Second Q and A (26 and 27)—the beginning of a rupture

The Pharisees continue to push the issue and continue to push the man born blind to conform to their conclusions about Jesus. At this point, the man's response is insubordinate; nevertheless, he has yet to say what he really thinks. He is not directly challenging his social superiors but he is clearly moving in that direction with statements such as, "you did not listen" and the sarcastic question "you certainly[108] don't want to become his disciples [do you]?" The clever insubordination is met with slander and expulsion.

Third Q and A (28–29 and 30–33)—the hidden transcript becomes public

The response to insubordination is slander[109] (v. 28, λοιδορέω). The authorities reassert their power by appealing to Moses as their rabbi ("we are disciples of Moses" v. 28) and by casting doubt on Jesus's origins ("we don't know from where he comes" v. 29). The man's clear response has brought the hidden transcript fully to light. The quite logical argument is one that the Pharisees themselves pondered in v. 16b. The argument spans three verses (vv. 30–33) and culminates in the conclusion that Jesus could do nothing if he were not from God. The response of the man is

---

108. Intensifying use of καί. καί, BDAG, s.v. 2.b.

109. Scott, *Domination*, 205. As noted above, those in power often define the challenger as "deranged."

what Scott calls a rupture.[110] The man is speaking openly, passionately, and sarcastically[111] to authority in public! "Here is a sight to see! He opened my eyes but *you* don't know where he is from!"

Social control is swiftly exercised (34)

As one would expect, the authorities are swift to respond with an act of social control.[112] In order to diffuse the public challenge to their authority they do two things. First, they continue their program of slander by labeling the man "born completely in sin." They then quarantine him from the society over which they exercise authority by "casting him out." This casting out (ἐκβάλλω) is no doubt related to the earlier reference to being banned from the synagogue community (ἀποσυνάγωγος, v. 22, cf. 16:2). As it turns out, this was a very effective type of social control, as 12:42[113] indicates.

Two more things are left to discuss in relation to scene six as a whole. First, issues of honor and shame: Malina has asserted that the challenge and riposte interaction is reserved for social equals.[114] If this is true then it does not directly apply in the interactions between the man born blind and the Pharisees. Even so, it is still important to note that all public interactions dealt with the maintenance of honor. With this in mind, an ancient audience would note that the man born blind acted honorably toward his patron by remaining loyal and witnessing to what was done for him. He did not back down even in the face of intense interrogation. He also made every effort, until pushed to the limit, to walk the fine line between not disrespecting the Jewish authorities and yet still maintaining loyalty to his patron. This required both wit or cleverness, and a sense of shame.[115] The man's behavior throughout his interrogations demonstrates the opposite of what is assumed to be true of those who are blind.

---

110. Scott, *Domination*, 19.

111. As noted in the narrative chapter, Ἐν τούτῳ γὰρ τὸ θαυμαστόν ἐστιν can be read sarcastically as a play on the visual theme. The message being: my healed eyesight is not the spectacle but your refusal to see that Jesus is from God is a spectacle.

112. Scott, *Domination*, 19.

113. "Nevertheless many, even of the authorities, believed in him. But because of the Pharisees they did not confess it, for fear that they would be put out of the synagogue (ἀποσυνάγωγος)," John 12:42 NRSV.

114. Malina, *New Testament World*, 35.

115. A sense of shame can be defined as knowing when one is about to act

Crook has convincingly argued, however, that some honor challenges may take place across boundaries of unequal social status.[116] Crook cites the writings of Tacitus and particularly Aulus Gellius. Tacitus complains about the practice of those of lesser social status openly disrespecting their social superiors (*Ann.* 3:36) and praises Tiberius's practice of charging with treason those who produced writings challenging social elites (*Ann.* 1.72). Gellius describes a type of punishment (τιμωρία which he says is from τιμή, honor) designed to protect the honor (*conservatione honoris*) of social superiors that are dishonored (*Noc. Att.* 7.14.3). He argues that punishment seems unnecessary (*sane dignum*, not fitting) if, among other things, loss of status (*iacturam dignitatis*) were not possible (7.14.4). The idea here is that, from the viewpoint of the elites, it is possible to lose face in the public eye (honor: publicly acknowledged claim to worth) from not responding swiftly and decisively to challenges from social inferiors. Crook writes, "Dio (58.5.3–4) comments that to forgive an offense from someone of higher status is a virtue . . . but to forgive an offense from below is folly, a sign of weakness."[117] In addition to the "swift stroke of repression"[118] to preserve their authority, the Pharisees, having been bested by the wit of the healed man, must react forcefully to save face and preserve their honor in the court of public opinion.[119] This sheds more light on why the man was thrown out. In addition to the theological difference of opinion about the origins of Jesus, the Pharisees have been "one upped" by someone who, from their perspective, was born "entirely" in the dishonor of "sin" (v. 34).

Just as the bystanders (within the narrative) hearing the interaction must make a judgment about who won the honor challenge, so also, John's audience must make a judgment. It is becoming increasingly clear to an audience that the healed man's honor is on the rise, while the Pharisees are being characterized with progressively less honor.

---

shamefully and then not acting in that manner thus maintaining honor.

116. Crook, "Honor, Shame, Status," 599–600.

117. Ibid., 600.

118. Scott, *Domination*, 19.

119. The court of public opinion is those present to hear the interaction of challenge and riposte and judge a winner. In a narrative that is twofold. First, those characters *in* the narrative assumed to be standing by to hear the interaction. But second, and more importantly, the court of public opinion is the actual hearers of the story, John's audience. The audience makes a judgment as to who won the honor challenge between the healed man and the Pharisees.

Second, the issue of a collectivist personality: As a result of his honorable actions toward his patron, he is ironically removed from his social group (ἀποσυνάγωγος and ἐκβάλλω). As mentioned above, this would be a devastating thing for one with a dyadic personality.

Scene 7: Jesus and the man (35–38)

In v. 35 Jesus "finds" or "seeks" (εὑρίσκω) the man after he is thrown out of the synagogue. As discussed in the narrative chapter, Jesus's speech begun in 9:41 actually runs through to 10:18. In 10:1–18 Jesus describes a community of sheep cared for by the good shepherd. All in this community have been "brought out" (10:4 ἐκβάλλω cf. 9:34 and 35) by the shepherd who cares for them. When Jesus "finds" the man and elicits "trust" (πιστεύω), we can understand him to have been ushered into this new community of care. This community is in fact a new family that is defined by "trust" rather than blood kinship (John 1:12–13).

As discussed above under "dyadic personality," the community of care defined by trust is a fictive kinship group.[120] deSilva notes that the idea of fictive kinship was present in Philo. Philo writes,

> "For we should acknowledge only one relationship, and one bond of friendship, namely, a mutual zeal for the service of God, and a desire to say and do everything that is consistent with piety. And these bonds which are called relationships of blood, being derived from one's ancestors, and those connections which are derived from intermarriages and from other similar causes, must all be renounced, if they do not all hasten to the same end, namely, the honor of God which is the one indissoluble bond of all united good will. For such men will lay claim to a more venerable and sacred kind of relationship. (*Special Laws* I 317).[121]

Johannine fictive kinship is defined entirely by trust in Jesus (1:12) and *not* by blood relationships (1:13). In this new family, one is "born from/of God" (ἐκ θεοῦ ἐγεννήθησαν, 1:13). This is also stated as birth "from above" (3:3) or birth "from/of the Spirit" (ἐκ τοῦ πνεύματος, 3:6, 8). This fictive kinship is seen also in First John, where those who "love one another" are "born of God" (ὁ ἀγαπῶν ἐκ τοῦ θεοῦ γεγέννηται, 4:7) and those who "trust that Jesus is the Christ" are "born of God" (Πᾶς ὁ πιστεύων ὅτι

---

120. DeSilva, *Honor*, 194; Osiek and Balch, *Families*, 39, 54.
121. Yonge, trans., *The Works of Philo*, 564.

Ἰησοῦς ἐστιν ὁ χριστός, ἐκ τοῦ θεοῦ γεγέννηται, 5:1 cf. 5:4, 18). This new family of those who trust also considers itself to be protected by Jesus (1 John 5:18; cf. John 10:11–16, 17:12). From an honor/shame perspective, the man is an adopted child of God (1:12–13) and brother of Christ (20:17). Although the notion of sin is rejected by Jesus in v. 3, this is quite a step up from his dubious status at the beginning of the episode.

Conclusion

In looking at the episode of the man born blind through the lenses of a number of different social-science scenarios one gains a fuller understanding of how an ancient audience would have understood the events narrated. Particularly useful is the insight one gains into the development of the man born blind's character. Because of the assumptions about the blind in antiquity the man in our episode begins as a character who is pitiable, shameful and associated with sin, ignorant, "better off dead" and perhaps even dangerous to society because of the evil eye. He is transformed in the episode to one who honorably praises and is loyal to his benefactor. He proves himself to be clever enough to walk a fine line between loyalty to Jesus and not disrespecting the authorities, at least until pushed to the limit; and then he proves to be courageous in the face of imposed social isolation.

There are some very specific things that happen in the narrative to transform the man born blind from an initially undesirable and unsympathetic[122] character, into a desirable model[123] of trust and witness. In *scene one*, the notion that the man is a product of sin ("who sinned, this man or his parents . . .") is quickly dispatched and the potential shame of that reversed by Jesus. This is not a result of sin; on the contrary he will have the honorable task of God's works being revealed in him. In *scene two*, he demonstrates perfect obedience to Jesus and returns with his sight. The shame and stigma of blindness, along with the cultural assumptions, is removed. In *scene three* we see him begin to develop as a character who (although the very important Johannine term itself is not used) witnesses about "the man called Jesus." By this time in the narrative, the audience already knows that witnesses are cast in a positive

---

122. The audience would view him with antipathy. Cf. Powell, *Narrative Criticism*, 25, 56–57 and n79, chapter 3.

123. The audience would view him with sympathy; ibid.

way.[124] In *scene four* the man is continuing as a witness, but under more dangerous circumstances. He cleverly protects his patron, by omitting the detail of kneading on the Sabbath and demonstrates the dawning of understanding, Jesus is a prophet. In *scene 6* he becomes progressively bolder, first maintaining honor by finding a clever way to "give glory to God," circumventing the Pharisee's desired result. Then he presents a well formulated argument that Jesus is "from God" in a way that highlights the Pharisee's own ignorance. If seen as an inter-status[125] challenge riposte scene, he wins the honor challenge by his argument, which causes his social superiors to resort to expulsion. In *scene 7* the man is sought out and received into new community by the hero[126] of our narrative—an adoption into the honorable family of God (1:12–13; 20:17).

The total healing of the blind man from the beginning of the episode to the end reaches its completion. The darkness of blindness is reversed by the light of the world. He proved himself to be honorable, not shameful, and was restored to a social group, the new family of God (1:12–13).

---

124. See my discussion of "witness" and the characterization of the blind man in chapter 3.

125. As originally a blind beggar, he would have significantly lower status than the Pharisees.

126. Neyrey, *Perspective*, 275 also notes the progression and transformation of the healed man into a "hero" in the narrative.

5

Irony, Humor, Sarcasm, and Wit

JOHN 9 MAY ARGUABLY be one of the most ironic and witty stories in the Gospel.[1] Indeed, the entire episode is filled with humor, sarcasm, wit, and irony. This is true to such a degree that these phenomena play a significant rhetorical function in the episode. In this chapter, I will analyze the rhetorical effect of the presence of irony. I will also make note of humor, wit, and sarcasm, but the main interest here is irony and how it leads an audience to "stand" in the same place as the narrator of the story in determining that Jesus is the "Christ, the Son of God" and that "trusting" brings "life" (John 20:31).

Because of the highly subjective and cultural nature of irony, humor, sarcasm and wit, they tend to elude definition. Irony will be defined in the following section. Culpepper defines humor and wit as follows:

> Humor exploits the observation of the absurd, the incongruous, and the comical, often poking fun at the foibles of human life. Wit is the quick perception of cleverness and ingenuity. Both humor and wit delight in deviations from what is expected or what is required in various social situations.[2]

Humor and wit are expressed by subtleties of language and roundabout ways of speaking. Irony, humor, and wit are dependent on continuity of culture. In other words, they tend not to translate well into other cultures.[3] In the case of irony, Wayne Booth has noted that the further away from the original culture an audience is, the less likely they are to

---

1. Duke, *Irony*, 117; Moloney, *John*, 290. Schneiders, *Written That You May Believe*, 155.

2. Culpepper, "Humor and Wit" 3:333.

3. Ibid.

understand the irony and the longer it takes for them to comprehend it.[4] Therefore, in spite of the adage "if you have to explain it, it isn't really funny," I shall attempt to dismantle, explain, and, where necessary, fill in the cultural gaps of the irony, humor, and wit appearing in John 9.

Understanding of humor

In the *Linguistics of Laughter*, Partington studies instances of spontaneous laughter during briefings by the presidential press secretary from 2000–2006. One of the things he examines is "is the tactical use of laughter-talk to achieve specific rhetorical ends, for example, to construct an identity, to make an argumentative point, or to threaten someone else's face or boost one's own."[5] Each of the things listed is present in the episode of John 9. The man uses humor to argue his point and to increase his honor in the minds of the audience while diminishing his opponents' honor.

According to Parrington, when discourse[6] begins, the audience attempts to understand the discourse based on contextual clues both within and outside of the discourse. The audience adopts the most likely frame of reference for understanding the discourse. The anatomy of humor starts when a frame of reference (way of understanding a particular discourse) is met with an anomaly. An anomaly is an event or statement that cannot be understood according to the adopted frame of reference. Another frame of reference must be used to make sense of the anomaly. So a shift in the frame of reference takes place. The second frame of reference is inconsistent with the original frame of reference in a way that produces humor.[7] The point in the discourse (narrative, speech, or joke) where one realizes that a shift in frame of reference is needed, is called variously the *scriptswitch trigger*, the *disjunctor*, or as Partington calls it, the *backtrack trigger*.[8] He uses this term because when one reaches this point one must backtrack and reevaluate the narrative, speech, or joke according to a new frame of reference. This newly adopted frame of

---

4. Booth, *Irony*, 222–23.
5. Partington, *Laughter*, viii.
6. I am using the term "discourse" in order to summarize Parrington. By discourse I mean an act of communication such as a joke, narrative, conversation, speech, etc.
7. Partington, *Laughter*, 2.
8. Ibid., 4.

reference is incongruent with the first frame of reference in a way that is humorous. It can be diagramed as follows:

Table 5.1: How Humor Works

What is happening:	Why it is happening:
Frame of reference A is adopted as the humorous discourse begins.	The audience must make sense of the discourse and adopts a likely scenario to understand it, frame of reference A.
Something in the humorous discourse cannot be understood using frame of reference A	Backtrack Trigger: In order to continue making sense of the discourse, the audience backtracks and reevaluates the discourse according to a different frame of reference.
Frame of reference A is rejected as inadequate to explain the entire discourse and frame of reference B is adopted.	Frame of reference B makes better sense of the entire discourse including the backtrack trigger.
Laughter or comical realization occurs.	There is a humorous incongruity between A and B.

But just because two frames of reference are incongruent does not necessarily make for humor. There must be a sense of *oppositeness* involved.[9] Partington identifies three types of oppositeness that result in humor.

First is the *proper to improper shift*. This is a shift from what is proper behavior to what is improper real world and first-frame-of-reference world behavior. In other words it is improper from the viewpoint of the first frame of reference, prior to the backtrack trigger, *and* improper according the usual rules of real world behavior. This may be a contrast between the seemly and the unseemly, the noble and the ignoble, the lofty and the mundane, etc.

Second is the *reversal of evaluation*. In this scenario what is normally evaluated as good, useful, beautiful, worthy, or valuable is evaluated as bad, worthless, or ugly and vice versa. The reversal of evaluation, presenting something as desirable in the second frame of reference where it seemed undesirable in the first, produces a humorous effect.[10]

9. Ibid., 19–20.
10. Ibid, 23–24.

A third type of oppositeness that produces humor is *absurd, abnormal, and quirky logic*. Like the proper to improper shift, the logic of the first frame of reference must seem reasonable in the real world. The logic of the second frame of reference must be incongruent and opposite the first frame of reference but *also* incongruent with real world logic.[11]

Some examples using the above framework to understand humor:

Table 5.2: Shift from Proper to Improper

A priest, a rabbi, and a protestant minister are on a nature hike. They come to a stream.	Setting the scene.
The priest walks across the stream to the other side. The rabbi does the same. The minster, thinking his faith to be equal to theirs, also begins across but falls in.	Frame of reference established: miracle story.
The rabbi says to the priest, "We should have told him where those stones are."	*Backtrack trigger*: audience is forced to evaluate the scenario according to a non miraculous frame of reference: that of deception, practical joke, or at least mundane physics. There is a *shift from proper to improper*. In this case a shift from the lofty to the mundane.

Table 5.3: Reversal of Evaluation

While shooting the swimsuit issue of Sports Illustrated, a photographer and several models become hopelessly lost in a tropical rain forest. They make their way to an area with a waterfall and trees with plenty of fruit and shade. Thankful, they stop to rest, eat, and rehydrate.	Setting the scene.

---

11. Ibid, 24–25.

Noticing that the photographer has cigarettes and a lighter, one of the models said, "should we try to make a signal fire?"	Frame of reference established: hope of rescue
The photographer replies, "No! Someone might rescue us."	*Backtrack trigger*: Audience is forced to evaluate the scenario from a different perspective than the model hoping for rescue. The perspective of the male photographer is that rescue is undesirable compared to the prospect of being "stranded" with several attractive swimsuit models. There is a *reversal of evaluation*. Rescue, typically evaluated as desirable, is evaluated as undesirable in the second frame of reference.

Table 5.4: Absurd, Abnormal, and Quirky Logic

A man walks into a diner and orders an entire pie.	Setting the scene
The server asks if he wants that sliced into four pieces or eight pieces.	Ordinary logic: how many divisions of the same total quantity?
The man replies, "four pieces. I'm on a diet.[12]	*Backtrack trigger*: the man's statement must be evaluated from another type of logic. Absurd logic: Fewer slices mean fewer calories. Note: The logic of the second frame of reference is incongruent with the first *and* incongruent with real world logic because we know there is the same total amount of pie.

Note that in each of the above examples, the humor only works when the audience adopts a different perspective as a result of the backtrack trigger. The "punch line" only makes sense when this different perspective is

---

12. The above joke adapted from Partington, *Laughter*, 25.

adopted. In the last two examples the perspective of the character delivering the punch line must be adopted. This is a powerful rhetorical tool. In order to make sense of the joke, or humorous speech, one must accept the perspective of a particular character. Even if the perspective is to be ultimately rejected (no one can really get fewer calories out of the same amount of pie no matter how you slice it). Momentarily the audience shares the same perspective and at the same time shares the bond of an emotional release. This can be particularly effective in a narrative where the emotional release of humor comes at a time in the narrative where there is a high amount of dramatic tension. Not only does the audience share the perspective of a narrator delivering the punch line, but also they share a sense of relief from the tension of the narrative. They are therefore thankful for the perspective that brings the relief. Hence, comic relief can be a rhetorically effective tool.

Understanding of irony

What is Irony?

By its very nature irony tends to be subjective and therefore hard to define. The best definition I have found thus far remains that of Paul Duke,[13] who defines it as a *double layered* literary phenomenon in which two tiers of meaning stand in some *opposition* to each other and in which some degree of *unawareness* is expressed or implied. Let us look at each of the three elements within the definition.

Being *double layered* is not sufficient to create irony on its own. A literary device that presents two levels of meaning, a surface level and a deeper meaning, in and of itself is not irony. This could simply be a metaphor, simile, or symbolism.

There must be some sense of *opposition*. It is this sense of opposition that signals when irony is in use and that is distinctive to irony. Opposition occurs when there is a clash or incongruity in meaning. Often a statement will either say less or more than the underlying meaning and can be signaled by an opposition of tone and content. There is also often a strong sense of negation either lexically or within the deeper structure. If irony makes an *assertion* it is usually also *denying* an opposite.

---

13. This and following from Duke, *Irony*, 15–17.

Finally, irony often contains an element of *unawareness*. This unawareness can either be feigned (in the case of verbal irony, see below) or real (in the case of situational or dramatic irony, see below). It is an indirect communication that invites the audience to perceive the deeper meaning.

In elaborating this definition I will take the ironic statement of John 9:25 spoken by the healed man:

Table 5.5: Example of Irony using John 9:25

"Whether he is a sinner, I do not know.	*Unawareness* or feigned ignorance.
One thing I know;	Sense of *opposition* or incongruity: He does in fact know more and . . .
that being blind, now I see."	uses his healing as evidence that Jesus is "from God" in the following verses) and therefore not a sinner); but, it is argued indirectly here. Thus the communication is *double layered*: Surface meaning: I don't know; deeper meaning: I do know that he is not a sinner.

Finally, the whole sentence is both an *assertion* that Jesus is from God and more fundamentally a *denial* that Jesus is a sinner.

Wayne Booth presented a major work on irony.[14] In this work, he describes four marks of what he calls *stable irony*. It is *intended*: with indications from the text that the author intends the irony. It is *covert*: the statement is to be reconstructed with a meaning different from the surface meaning. It is *stable* or *fixed*: wherein once the audience has made an initial reconstruction, no further reconstructions are intended by the author. And, finally, it is applied in a *finite* way. Even though this application may be to a broadly sweeping subject such as sin or credibility, it is nevertheless finitely applied.[15] For irony to work, there are four steps (however he cautions against rigid sequential application) that the audience must manage. I will describe these in the table below using examples from the ironic statement by the healed man in 9:25.

14. Booth, *Irony*.
15. Ibid., 5–6.

Table 5.6: Steps for Irony with example from John 9:25

Steps the audience must manage:	Example from 9:25
1) a rejection of the literal meaning, which is usually signaled by an *incongruity* within the words or between the words and something else known by the audience;	*Incongruity 1*: the man knows Jesus is not a "sinner" having already declared him a prophet in 9:17, but here he says that he does not know whether Jesus is a sinner or not. *Incongruity 2*: The man says he just knows "one thing" that he was healed of blindness. In fact, the man knows more than just the "one thing" and will argue that the healing is itself evidence that Jesus is "from God" (9:33).
2) an *alternative interpretation is tried* in order to reconcile the incongruity;	*Alternative tried*: The man knows that Jesus is not a sinner.
3) a decision about the *ironist's knowledge or beliefs* is made in order to arrive at the correct alternative interpretation;	*Ironist's knowledge/beliefs*: The man thinks Jesus is a prophet; the man knows that he is no longer blind; and such miracles are not done by sinners (cf. 9:16b and 9:33)
4) a new *meaning is chosen* to correctly interpret the words spoken and resolve the incongruity. This final step can usually be restated with an assertion or a denial.	*Alternative* (deeper) meaning in the ironic statement: 1) I do know whether or not Jesus is a sinner: he is not. 2) I know more than just the fact of my healing. I know what my healing means, namely, that Jesus is from God. 3) You (Pharisees) don't know what my healing means.

When meaning is finally reconstructed in step 4, one sees how one ironic statement speaks volumes. Once 4 is arrived at, the audience is not invited by the author to further deconstruct and reconstruct the meaning of the original statement. Although the audience may do so, this is not intended by the implied author.[16]

16. Ibid., 10–12.

Since irony involves a reconstruction of meaning, it is an extremely powerful rhetorical device. It invites the audience to embark upon a mission of reconstruction that ultimately causes them to stand (at least temporarily) in the same place as the narrator. The rhetorical effect here is to create a community of insiders who "get it," who know what the ironist means. The audience becomes part of this community of people who "get it" along with the narrator. There is a shared communal bond between the audience and the narrator and also between the audience and those characters in the story who share the same values and beliefs contained in the reconstructed meaning of an ironic statement. Booth notes that often there is a sense of rejecting a whole set of meanings and values that may culminate in accepting or rejecting a whole way of life,[17] and that often the rejected meaning is a rival or a threat to the values of the reconstructed meaning.[18] It is this phenomenon that causes O'Day to describe the reconstructed deeper meaning as a form of "revelation."[19]

The phenomenon of *rejection, (re)construction,* and *acceptance of an opposite* meaning gives irony its rhetorical force. Even if only temporarily, in order to "get" (understand or comprehend) the irony, the audience must reconstruct and accept the deeper ironic, meaning. Again, in the above example of 9:25, the audience members who "get" the irony must mentally reconstruct that 1) the healed man knows whether or not Jesus is a sinner, and 2) he is asserting that Jesus is indeed not a sinner but rather the alternative, namely, that Jesus is from God. If these assertions are true, they challenge an entire value system represented in the narrative by the Pharisees.[20] At least for the moment it takes to reconstruct the meaning, the audience sees things the way the narrator and the healed man do.

It is important to note here that the real (as opposed to implied) audience need not already have a perspective similar or the same as the narrator as ironist in order to be rhetorically impacted by irony. Although they may already share the perspective of the ironist, it is not necessary for the irony to work. Everything necessary for the irony of the above example to work is already in the narrative. The real audience does not need to already have the belief that Jesus is "from God" and a "prophet"

---

17. Ibid, 36, 38.
18. Ibid, 40.
19. O'Day, *Revelation*, 8–9.

20. The danger, form the Pharisees' point of view, in the belief that Jesus is "from God," is noted when discussing conflict analysis in chapter 3 near the end of scene 6.

in order for the irony to work because those elements are communicated by the narrative itself. In other words, irony (and humor for that matter) can work to *create* insiders; it does not need them as a prerequisite. This is precisely why irony is such a powerful rhetorical tool. In order for an audience to make sense of the narrative or ironic discourse, one must at least temporarily adopt the viewpoint of the ironist. In a narrative where all the necessary elements for that perspective have been narrated one needs no additional knowledge beyond the narrative in order to adopt that viewpoint.

What kinds of irony are there?

While the types of irony that various authors may identify can be vast, Duke has identified three basic types which will be helpful for this paper: verbal irony, dramatic irony, and situational irony.

In *verbal irony*,[21] the implied meaning asserted by a speaker (surface meaning) differs from that which the speaker actually asserts (deeper or reconstructed meaning). In this type of irony, the intention of the speaker is assumed. In other words, the speaker both *knows and intends* to convey more than the surface level of the words. The speaker knows the deeper level and intends for the hearer to "get it" as well. In this type, the target of the irony is the person addressed. The speaker intends for the target of the irony to get the deeper meaning. Sarcasm is an example of this type, where the deeper meaning is barely covert. A simple example of verbal irony is when a person standing in the driving rain addresses another saying, "Lovely weather we are having."[22] This is such a simple form of verbal irony that it may be understood as sarcasm. A more subtle form may be when one is standing on a Chicago train platform in a wind chill of 15 degrees Fahrenheit and says to a bystander, "Would you be interested in attending a seminar on global warming with me? I think it is becoming a real problem." An example from our episode is John 9:27, "Do you also want to become..." Understatement or overstatement (John 9:30, "Here is and astonishing thing..."; and John 9:32, "Never since the world began...") are also ways of accomplishing verbal irony.

---

21. Duke, *Irony*, 21–23.
22. Ousby, *Cambridge Guide to Literature*, 475.

Dramatic irony[23] is achieved by a speaker or actor who *knows less* than is conveyed in the deeper meaning of the irony *and* whose speech or action is *unintentionally* ironic. The audience knows the deeper meaning that is unknown to the speaker. This is present in any irony where the author invites the audience to compare what the characters say and do with what the audience knows to be true.[24] In this type of irony, the aspect of *audience knowledge* is essential (either from the story to this point or current cultural knowledge). The omniscient prologue is one way in which the audience gains such knowledge; another is through a reliable narrator. There are essentially three ways this plays out: 1) Character/s act/s in a way totally inappropriate to the circumstances; 2) Character/s expect/s the opposite of what the narrative has in store; 3) Character/s say/s something that anticipates the outcome but not in the way intended.

An example of dramatic irony might be in the instance of a crime drama, in which the lead investigator of a murder is actually the murderer. It is ironic that the lead investigator is investigating the very crime he committed. If the audience has this information, this special knowledge, while some other characters do not, it is dramatic irony. In such an example, we see how each of the three ways listed in the above paragraph might work. 1) Character/s act/s in a way totally inappropriate to the circumstances by allowing the criminal to continue investigating; 2) Character/s expect/s the opposite of what the narrative has in store by trusting the criminal to solve the crime; 3) Character/s say/s something that anticipates the outcome but not in the way intended, such as, if the investigator's partner were to say to the investigator, "Don't worry, we will catch the person who did this." This special knowledge may already be held by the audience (the case of a well known real life crime being narrated). In this case the audience comes to the narrative with insider knowledge. But also this special knowledge may be presented in the narration itself. In this case insiders are *created* by the irony.

To extend this example let us say that later one other character, the lead investigator's partner, either suspects or learns the truth and is trying to prove it. This instance of dramatic irony serves to forge a bond of sympathy between the audience and the character who is "in the know." The audience can root for the character as she tries to prove that her partner is the murderer. In the case of the man born blind, the audience can root

---

23. Duke, *Irony*, 23–26.

24. Also, Booth, *Irony*, 61–63.

for the healed man as he tries to prove that Jesus is "from God," since the audience knows this already from the prologue.

Ironic situations which do not depend on the audience's superior knowledge are *situational irony*.[25] In such irony the situation present the reverse of an expectation or assertion. An example might be[26] Shelley's "Ozymandias" in which a traveler is describing the remains of an Egyptian statue:

> And on the pedestal these words appear:
> "My name is Ozymandias, king of kings;
> Look on my works, ye mighty, and despair?"
> Nothing beside remains. Round the decay
> Of that colossal wreck, boundless and bare
> The lone and level sands stretch far away.

This is ironic because the assertion of the king is inconsistent with the surroundings observed by the traveler. The boasts of the king that signs of his greatness are all around are contradicted by the decay of the monument itself and the desolation of the entire area around the monument. No special knowledge on the part of the audience is necessary.

A type of situational irony that Duke has identified is *irony of event* in which events or actions bring the unexpected. This is especially so when events bring that which they were intended to avoid. If, for example, a protagonist receives a prophecy about some terrible event, our protagonist may work to avoid the event; however, all the efforts designed to escape the fate, actually lead to its fulfillment. Special knowledge on the part of the audience is not required for the situation to be ironic.

Another type of irony Duke identifies is *irony of self-betrayal*.[27] This happens when the words or deeds of a character reveal a person to be different from what she or he claims or seems to be. For example, imagine a scene in a movie in which a rich philanthropist is on his way to be honored for his humanitarian efforts. On the way out of his building, he pushes away a homeless beggar, wipes his hands vigorously with his handkerchief, and under his breath mutters, "filthy." In John 9, it is an irony of self-betrayal when the Pharisees ask the healed man his opinion about Jesus, an apparent act of open-mindedness (John 9:17, ". . . what do you say?"). However, later in the story their own words and actions reveal

---

25. Duke, *Irony*, 26–27.
26. Beckson and Ganz, *Literary Terms*, 134.
27. Duke, *Irony*, 26–27, also Booth, *Irony*, 65.

them to be closed-minded (John 9:22, "... the Jews had *already agreed*[28] that anyone who confessed Jesus to be the Messiah would be put out of the synagogue." or John 9:34, "... you dare teach us!?").

Analysis by Scene

One will note that both humor and irony have similar elements. Both involve a shift in perspective at some point. Both involve a rejection of a particular perspective. Both involve an audience to adopt a different perspective in order to make sense of what is being said. Both involve a sense of oppositeness. Both can have the effect of dividing an audience into those who "get it" and those who do not. Both are tools that help an audience to see things from a particular perspective. Both cause an audience to bond with one another and also to the author, narrator and/or character/s who hold that perspective. The following will be an analysis, by scene, of how humor and irony function to these ends in John 9.

Scene 1: Jesus and the disciples (1–5)

In the very first scene, we are immediately signaled to the presence of irony when the disciples ask Jesus about the sin-related origins of the man born blind and Jesus rejects such an assumption. As an alternative he suggests that one who is blind will become a vehicle[29] for sight or revelation. This is not just any revelation, however, but rather a revelation of the "works of God." In the very first scene we have a dual pronged situational irony. The first prong of this irony is that through one who is blind[30] (physically and mentally) something will be seen[31] (revealed or understood). The second prong of the "ironic fork" is that what will be revealed is "the works of God;" however, it will be revealed by one culturally assumed to be associated with sin!

---

28. Italics mine.

29. "in order that" (ἵνα) "might be revealed" (φανερωθῇ) is a *hina* + subjunctive construction which indicates either purpose (most likely) or result (ἵνα, BDAG s.v. 1).

30. The word τυφλός can mean unable to see physically (BDAG s.v. 1) and unable to know or understand mentally (BDAG s.v. 2).

31. The word φανερόω can mean cause something to be seen physically (BDAG s.v. 1) and cause something to be revealed or understood mentally (BDAG s.v.2).

This interaction between Jesus and the disciples sets the tone for the rest of this episode. Upon hearing this initial interaction, an audience would be signaled that the rest of this episode, like many other portions of John's Gospel, will contain irony. Also, rhetorically speaking, this interaction sets up suspense. The tension between φανερωθῇ ("might be seen") and τυφλός ("blind") and between ἔργα τοῦ θεοῦ ("works of God") and ἁμαρτάνω ("to sin") acts to peak an audience's curiosity as to how precisely God's works might be seen in a blind (man who is assumed to be a) sinner.

Scene 2: Jesus and the man (6–7)

The healing itself is without irony as defined above; however, the attentive audience would take note at v. 7. The man is commanded by Jesus, who is working the works of the one who "sent" (πέμπω) him (vs. 4), to wash in the pool of Siloam. "Siloam is translated by a narrative aside as "sent" (ἀποστέλλω). As was discussed in the narrative and social-science chapters, πέμπω and ἀποστέλλω are virtually synonymous and used interchangeably throughout John. A careful hearer would take note that the one who sent the blind man to wash in the pool called "sent" was himself "sent" by God. This clever interplay, while not properly irony, humor, or sarcasm, deserves mention here for it would have the rhetorical effect of highlighting the fact that Jesus is indeed the one sent by the Father. Highlighting this fact now for the audience will serve as a reminder that Jesus is indeed "from God" (9:16, 32), a point that is discussed and argued later in the episode (9:29–30).

Scene 3: The man and the neighbors (8–12)

Again, while not properly irony, one must note the humor in the fact that the now sighted man does not know "where" (ποῦ, v. 12) Jesus is (nor what he looks like for that matter, cf. v. 36). Even though he cannot tell the neighbors and bystanders where Jesus is, those same onlookers take him to the Pharisees where he becomes a progressively courageous witness to "where he comes from" (πόθεν). Ironically, the one who does not know (οὐκ οἶδα) where Jesus is, knows, along with the audience, that Jesus is from God. This has the rhetorical effect of a shared bond of knowledge between the audience and the healed man, over against the Pharisees who do not know (οὐκ οἴδαμεν) where Jesus is from.

Scene 4: The man and the Pharisees: interview 1 (13–17)

The next scene is introduced by the neighbors and spectators of the previous scene, who bring the healed man to the Pharisees. It is at this point that the audience is given a crucial piece of information: It was a Sabbath when Jesus made the mud and healed the man (v. 14). After hearing the man's abbreviated version of the healing, the Pharisees return a split judgment. Some say that Jesus is not "from God" because he does not keep the Sabbath, while others wonder how a sinner can accomplish such a sign (v. 16).

A situational irony develops when the divided Pharisees must seek the counsel of the formerly blind man. The Pharisees, experts in the law, presume to act as judges in this episode. Ironically, their ability to judge fails them;[32] and they must seek the advice of the formerly blind man, culturally assumed to be both ignorant and associated with sin. His verdict is that Jesus is a "prophet."

This scene sets up a situational irony of self-betrayal that becomes clear later in the episode. The Pharisees are divided and cannot decide if Jesus is from God or a sinner. In the very next scene we are told, however, that they had already decided to expel anyone who confesses Jesus as messiah (v. 22). Furthermore, in the scene after that they assert, "We know this man is a sinner" (v. 24). Their split decision indicates a lack of knowledge, yet this lack of knowledge is inconsistent with their behavior of expulsion and their claim to "know" that Jesus is a sinner.

---

32. Ito, "Johannine Irony, part II," 373–74. Ito notes that the Pharisees unconsciously exhibit their ignorance about Jesus's origins while presuming to sit in judgment, presenting an irony of self betrayal.

Scene 5: The "Jews" and the man's parents (18–23)

In the questioning of the parents, it has already been noted that the Pharisees[33] have already made up their mind about Jesus, an irony of self betrayal. The fact that "the Jews had *already* (ἤδη) agreed together" (9:22, italics mine) to expel confessors of Jesus as Christ indicates that the series of questioning in 9:13ff. 18ff. and 24ff. are less an attempt to investigate and more of an attempt to condemn (cf. 5:18; 7:1, 19).

It is further ironic that "the Jews" not only ask the parents if their son was born blind but they also ask them *how* he now sees. The parents would have firsthand knowledge about his birth. However, they would only have second hand knowledge of the actual healing.[34]

The parents answer is interesting here. They say that they know that the man is their son, and they know that the man was born blind (v. 20). This answers the first part of the question of "the Jews." The second part, "how does he now see" is answered with more information than is necessary. In v. 21, the parents return a two-part answer, "We do not know how he now sees," and "We don't know who opened his eyes." The first part of the answer is wholly sufficient to answer the Pharisee's question. The second part of the answer is extraneous and telling. It answers not in regard to how (πῶς, which is what "the Jews asked in v. 19"); but instead it answers in regard to "who" (τίς). A denial of any knowledge about "who" healed their son preempts any questioning about Jesus as a healer.

As an indication of just how much the parents wished to avoid being questioned about who healed their son, the phrase "nor who opened his eyes we do not know" is constructed in the emphatic.[35] A translation such as, "We definitely don't know who opened his eyes!" This is a humorous *reversal of evaluation*. What should have been good news of their son's healing becomes a dangerous predicament for the parents.[36] The humor points out the Pharisee's true motives in the interrogation.

---

33. As noted on n33 of the narrative chapter, in this story I have concluded that the Pharisees and "the Jews" are the same character group.

34. Nothing in the episode indicates that the parents were present during the healing and, even if they were among the "neighbors and onlookers," they still did not witness the actual healing since the healed man had to describe the healing to the onlookers.

35. In the phrase ἡμεῖς οὐκ οἴδαμεν, the ἡμεῖς is redundant since the second person plural pronoun is already present in the pronominal ending of οἴδαμεν. Such a redundancy adds emphasis to the statement.

36. When this scene is performed for a modern audience, they typically laugh

Why might the parents so badly want to preempt any questioning about their son's healer? We are told in 9:22 what is at stake for those who confess Jesus to be Messiah. It would result in expulsion from the synagogue community. The parents no doubt wish to distance themselves from speaking about Jesus at all. The risk of seeming sympathetic is too great. Plus, their silence may suggest that they do know who Jesus is and believe, but out of fear they will not tell.

In this instance, the irony reveals something critical about the character of the Jewish authorities. Although they only ask "how" the man is healed, his parents understand they are really interested in condemning "who" healed him. The irony is that "the Jews" seem to be investigating the facts of the miracle but are revealed here to be interested in condemning the worker of the miracle, Jesus.

Scene 6: The man and the Pharisees: interview 2 (24–34)

In v. 24, we find situational irony on the lips of the Pharisees who compel the man to "give glory to God." This is specifically irony of event where the opposite of what is desired by the Pharisees is brought about by their command. The Pharisees are attempting to compel the man to agree with their dishonorable assessment of Jesus ("we know this man is a sinner"). Ironically, they are asking a sinner (born blind) about a sinner (Sabbath breaker). Their assumption is that the man born blind will "give glory to God" by agreeing with them. Knowledge of the patronage and brokerage system in antiquity enhances one's ability to understand this irony.[37] Such irony would not be lost on a first century audience, for what the Pharisees are essentially asking is that the man bear false witness against his very own patron (God) by "bad mouthing" his patron's broker, Jesus. It is ironic to think that God could be glorified by speaking badly about God's own agent. The answers of the man born blind bring glory to God, but the Pharisees do not.

While the Pharisees intended the man to agree with them, in (narrative) reality, he disagrees with the deeper intended meaning of the imperative while obeying the surface level of the statement with a result opposite of what they expect:

when the line, "we especially don't know who healed him" is delivered.

37. The primary duty of the client is to praise the patron and also the broker. See the section Patronage and Brokerage in the social-science chapter.

Table 5.7: Irony, Giving Glory to God

Pharisees' command: "give glory to God, We know this man is a sinner"	*Pharisees' intent*: condemn Jesus as a sinner for violating the sabbath.
Man's statement: ". . . one thing I know, I was blind but now I see"	*Result*: Man gives glory to God by stating what God's agent Jesus has done for him.

The man's statement fulfills the surface meaning of the Pharisees' command to glorify God, but it results in the opposite of what the Pharisees intended. Glory was indeed given[38] to God and to God's broker, as was the duty of a client. In this irony of event, the Pharisees intend one thing but an opposite thing happens because of their action.

The very next statement that the Pharisees make is both irony of self-betrayal and dramatic irony. "We know this man is a sinner," is inconsistent with the prior narrative statement "They were divided" and with their own question to the man, "What do you say about him?" Also, this is inconsistent with the knowledge of the audience who know Jesus's origins from the prologue. The dramatic irony works here because the audience knows, but the speaker, who is also the target of the irony, does not know. Rhetorically, this inside knowledge causes the Pharisees to appear foolish and binds the audience closer to the healed man and the narrator, who both also know Jesus is "from God."

The man's reply to the Pharisees' command is an example of verbal irony. The man answers, "whether or not he is a sinner I do not know" (9:25). The man *does know* Jesus is not a sinner based on his upcoming argument: "if he were not from God he could do nothing" (9:33). This is verbal irony since the man knows and intends the deeper level of his meaning to be realized by the Pharisees, even though the deeper meaning still remains covert. He does not say, "No you are wrong since he opened my eyes." He simply says, "All I know is I was blind and now I see." This is not yet sarcasm. The man has found a clever way of not overtly disagreeing with the Pharisees (his social superiors) while still maintaining the honor of his broker and giving glory to his patron.

A second instance of verbal irony is presented when he responds to the second set of questions which the Pharisees ask, "What did he do to you? How did he open your eyes?" The man's reply at this point becomes sarcastic: "Why again do you wish to hear? You don't wish to become his

---

38. Also, Moloney, *John*, 298.

disciples do you?" The deeper meaning here may be that they wish to hear more details so that they can condemn Jesus. This is especially true if the blind man's retelling of the sign to the Pharisees leaves out details of Sabbath violation.[39] The two things that the healed man omits in his report to the Pharisees during the first questioning are also those things which are forbidden on the Sabbath: "making" (ποιέω) and "anointing" (ἐπιχρίω). The irony is in the form of sarcasm here. They *do not* wish to become his disciples (surface meaning). They *do* wish to gather evidence to condemn him. This ironic statement sets up the Pharisees to be the victims of dramatic irony in their reply.

In their angry reply to the healed man the Pharisees unintentionally betray their own lack of insight and say of Jesus, "but this one, we do not know from where he comes." This is dramatic irony in that the audience has knowledge that some of the characters do not. The Pharisees do not know from where Jesus comes, but the audience does know. Thanks to the prologue, the audience knows that Jesus is from God. As explained earlier, characters who are victims of dramatic irony often act in ways that are inappropriate in light of the information that the audience possesses. The deeper meaning is that disciples of Moses do not know from where Jesus comes. From the audience's vantage point, they act inappropriately by attempting to condemn God's agent. From their vantage point, their actions are correct, because they don't know that Jesus is from God. The audience finds themselves on the side of the narrator and the man born blind because of this shared knowledge that the Pharisees do not possess. This scene also anticipates the final outcome of the episode, the Pharisees' own blindness.

Again, the healed man replies with verbal irony: "In this there is the wonder" or perhaps in keeping with the visual theme, "now here is a sight." The speaker signals his intention to speak ironically. If we understand "sight" or "marvel" (θαυμαστός) as another word for miracle or wonderful act of God,[40] the deeper or reconstructed meaning can be restated: "the real marvel or wonder here is not that a man blind from birth can see/understand but that the teachers of Israel cannot!" (Compare Nicodemus in 3:10.) He completes his argument with an appeal to Jesus's sign introduced by an overstatement which confirms the irony: "from the beginning of time it was not heard . . ."

39. Staley, "Stumbling," 67.
40. "θαυμαστός," in L&N, 1:311, §25.215.

Again the Pharisees are the victims of their own words in yet another example of dramatic irony, but this time with a double entendre: On one level the Pharisees attempt verbal irony: "born in sin . . . but you teach us." This instance of verbal irony displays a dramatic irony. The Pharisees act in a way inappropriate to the situation based on the knowledge that the audience possesses: Jesus is light of the world → light of the world kindled light within the man born blind → man born blind is in perfect position to teach ← man born blind is the one in whom "God's works are revealed." For this irony to work, it is important to remember the ancient understanding of how sight functions. Light moves from the heart out the eyes and falls upon that which is beheld. Since Jesus announced that he is the light of the world (9:5) and then restored the blind man's sight, an ancient Mediterranean audience would conclude that this light of the world has provided the new light with which the blind man now sees. In rejecting the healed man, the Pharisees are rejecting both the light which he possesses and God's broker who arranged for him to have it.

The Pharisees resort to expelling the healed man which introduces yet another situational irony. The phrase "They threw him out" is most likely indicative of expulsion, based on the foreshadowing of v. 22. The intention of the Pharisees was to isolate the man from community, a terrible fate for the dyadic personality. Cut off from a meaningful social group, a person would have no way in which to pursue the pivotal value of honor, a *socially* acknowledged claim to *worth*. Such isolation effectively makes one *worthless*. This would be worse than his condition prior to the healing, for at least then he had neighbors who could recognize him. This is a situational irony of event since the result was the opposite of the intended isolation: Jesus comes to the man and takes him into the community of believers.

If John has a socio-historical context of a community of Christians who are no longer welcome in the Jewish synagogues, then the promise of a social group where one is sought out and belongs is compelling. The rhetoric and message to the audience here works like this: It is alright to trust in Jesus, even if this means being cut off from synagogue life. You are welcome in the (Johannine) community of believers.

The audience has the opportunity to laugh *with* the healed man *at* the Pharisees on two occasions in this scene. The first occasion is in v. 27, "I told you already, and you did not listen. Why do you want to hear again? Surely you don't want to become his disciples?" This humor works on the level of absurd or quirky logic.

Table 5.8: Humor, Surely You Don't Want to Become His Disciples

"I told you already, and you did not listen.	Setting the scene.
"Why do you want to hear again?"	First frame of reference: investigation to gather information
"Surely you don't want to become his disciples?"	*Backtrack Trigger*: Alternative answer for why the Pharisees want to hear what happened again. Second frame of reference introduced: Absurd logic that the Pharisees wish to become Jesus's disciples. This is incongruent with the audience understanding of the Pharisees and the narrative depiction of the Pharisees.

The audience can laugh with the man at the Pharisees who have a clear agenda of judging Jesus as a sinner (v. 24). The humor also works on the level of *proper to improper shift*. The proper motive for the Pharisees is to investigate the truth of the event and arrive at an honest conclusion about Jesus's status as a sinner. The improper motive, which the Pharisees actually have, is trying to arrive at the conclusion they want, "this man is a sinner." Rhetorically, the Pharisees' hypocrisy is exposed and in laughing with the healed man, the audience's sympathetic bond with the man is strengthened.

The second instance is in v. 30, "Now here is a sight to see . . ." This is more a pun than the kind of humor one sees in a joke with a clear backtrack trigger. It can be analyzed as follows:

Table 5.9: Pun, Here is a Sight to See

Assumption: Pharisees *know and understand* the significance and meaning of miraculous signs.	First frame of reference: religious knowledge

"Now here is a sight to see, you don't know where he is from and yet he opened my eyes!"	Backtrack trigger: audience must evaluate what is truly shocking in the story based on the man's perspective.
Realization: Pharisees actually *don't* know and understand.	Second frame of reference: ignorance. Shift from the *proper to the improper*.

In this shift from proper to improper, the Pharisees properly should know what such a miracle indicates, that the one working the miracle is from God. The shift to the improper lies in the fact that they clearly are ignorant. It is improper for religious leaders to be ignorant about religious issues. Rhetorically the audience is made acutely aware of the man's superior insight and the Pharisees inferior knowledge.

Scene 7: Jesus and the healed man (35–38)

Upon being asked, "Do you trust in the son of man?" The man quite ironically replies, "And who is he . . . ?" The irony is situational. It serves to bind the audience with the healed man. The man, who has been defending the character of Jesus since his initial questioning, who has cleverly argued that his origins are "from God," and who was expelled from the synagogue for such argument, does not know that the very one he has been defending is speaking with him. The man was still blind when he left Jesus to wash in the pool of Siloam. This irony is delightful for the audience. They know who Jesus is before the man is told. In that moment of suspense, the audience can root for the man to find out and celebrate when he realizes and worships the one he has been defending. It is in this moment of realization, when the man worships, that the audience is carried along with the man as he confesses his trust and worships.

One must also note that "Son of Man" was never used by the man to describe Jesus. Jesus is offering yet another level of understanding of who he is.

Scene 8: Jesus and the Pharisees (39–41)

The final irony comes after the Pharisees reject the witness of the healed man and expel him. Verses 39 and 41 are not really ironic speech by themselves, but they do serve to explain or at least describe the irony of the entire chapter: Jesus said, "I came into this world for judgment, so that those who don't see might see, and those who see might become blind . . . If you were blind, you would have no sin. But now that you say, 'We see,' your sin remains." They also enclose a dramatic irony. The Pharisees ask a question expecting a negative answer, "surely we are not blind?" The characters are unaware of their own blindness but the audience is aware. The deeper or reconstructed meaning is that the Pharisees are "blind" but do not know it.

Irony with Respect to the Sabbath Day Violation

In addition to the specific scenes that were analyzed above, there are at least two ironies that can be framed in terms of a general reading of the episode. The first is irony with respect to the Sabbath day violation.

The Pharisees thought it their duty to protect the sanctity and holiness of the land and people. This was especially true in a post 70 CE era.[41] They wished all Jews to follow the regulations for priests so that all might be holy and therefore not jeopardize the presence of God among the people and in the land. This meant that they strove to protect purity with respect to people, places, and times as mentioned in the social-science chapter. A Sabbath day violation is a transgression of purity with respect to time. It is therefore ironic that the Pharisees would attempt to convict Jesus of a Sabbath day violation. Jesus as God's "sent" one is God's representative and symbolizes God's presence with the people and in the land (cf. use of ἐσκήνωσεν[42] in 1:14). For the Pharisees then to reject the symbol of God's presence in order to preserve God's presence is a dramatic irony (they do not know but the audience does) reflected in

---

41. On the story level this takes place prior to the Jewish war, but from the audience perspective it is heard after the destruction of the temple.

42. In the prologue, the word that has become flesh "tabernacles" or "pitches a tent" among his own people, who ironically reject him. The word σκηνόω is used only in 1:14 and is the verbal form of the noun (σκηνή, tabernacle, tent). In the LXX it depicts the way God's presence remains among the Israelites (cf. Exod 40:34).

the entire passage and ultimately in the whole Gospel as foreshadowed in the omniscient prologue (1:11).

This rejection does not result in the removal of God's presence from the land or people as one might expect. It does result in the judgment and condemnation of the Pharisees, i.e. the removal of God's presence from the Pharisees (9:39 and 41). Again, this is an irony of event in which the Pharisees own actions bring about the opposite of what they intend.

A further irony relating to Sabbath is the behavior of the Pharisees. As discussed previously, the setting in time for the episode is a Sabbath day. No other chronological references or markers are present in the episode to indicate a day has passed between the healing and the interrogations by the Pharisees. The irony of course is that they are trying Jesus for exactly the same thing that they are doing, work. While they are in the process of investigating a Sabbath violation—deliberating, calling witnesses, compelling testimony, and expelling from the synagogue community—they themselves are breaking the Sabbath!

Irony with respect to sin

The above discussion of the Sabbath violation in terms of purity is closely related to the issue of sin that weaves its way through the episode. The concept of sin in John has to do with both honor/shame from a social-science standpoint and also with trust in Jesus. Trust and faithfulness comprised the proper response of a client to a patron and also to the patron's broker. Early in the Gospel Jesus is characterized as the one who is sent from God to take away the sin of the world (John 1:29). For John, sin is associated with unbelief or failing to trust in the one whom God sent (8:21, 24; 15:22; 24; 16, 8–9).[43] With respect to sin in the episode of the man born blind, there is situational irony. Jesus comes to take away sin. On the one hand, this is accomplished in the blind man whose shame (cultural assumption that he or his parents sinned, v. 2) is removed and who comes to trust. On the other hand, sin is revealed in those who reject him. Those who were seeking to protect Israel from sin are themselves revealed to be sinners by the one sent to take away the sin of the world!

---

43. Peter Fiedler, "ἁμαρτία," in *EDNT*, 1:65.

Summary

From a rhetorical perspective, as the episode progresses, the audience is moved through the use of irony and wit closer to the man born blind and farther from the Pharisees. The Pharisees are the victims of several ironies of self-betrayal. They investigate the man twice and his parents as if to gather evidence to judge, but the audience sees that their minds have been made up (v. 22) and they will not listen (v. 27). Although they act in the role of judges claiming to know (v. 24), the audience sees that they are actually blind and ignorant (vs. 29–30, 40–41). These ironies of self-betrayal distance the audience from the Pharisees while sympathy grows for the man born blind.

Dramatic irony has a particularly powerful effect, for it depends on superior audience knowledge. Because the audience knows something that the other characters (who are usually the target of the irony) do not, they have a bond with the narrator and stand in a superior position over the target characters. The audience's knowledge of Jesus's origins (from hearing the prologue) equips them to judge the Pharisees in agreement with Jesus's final verdict, "Your sin (failure to trust in Jesus as the one God has sent) remains." When the Pharisees claim to "know" Jesus is a sinner, the audience already knows he is not because they are "in-on" the secret revealed in the prologue. When the healed man argues what the audience already knows, they are bonded together by that common knowledge and the Pharisees are excluded, even as they ironically sought to exclude the man (v. 34). In this way the narrative itself *creates* insiders.

Because the audience has already heard the prologue they can see how Jesus's action on the Sabbath trumps the law (also 5:18 cf. 8:21–24). While the law came through Moses (and the Pharisees are disciples of Moses), grace and truth came through Jesus Christ (1:14, 17). This means that Jesus actions to do the works of God transcend the law. Jesus can do this because he is the only one who has ever seen God (1:18).

6

Conclusions

Performance

As described in the introduction, it is likely that, like other first century literature, all of the New Testament writings were *composed for the purpose of a performance to a gathered audience* in some kind of setting. This must not be ignored in relation to how John 9 in particular, and the Fourth Gospel as a whole, impact an audience, drawing the audience toward trust in Jesus. In this concluding chapter I will synthesize the information and conclusions of the preceding chapters in order to discern how an ancient performance of John 9 may have looked and sounded. Understanding an ancient performance draws on the insights of various methodologies[1] so it is logical that this chapter come as a conclusion and synthesis of the prior chapters. As stated in the introduction, based on multiple disciplines (discourse, narrative, social science, and irony) I want to answer how John 9 would have been performed and how such a performance would lead an audience toward trust?

Overview

Shiner notes, "First-century literary works were almost always heard in a communal setting rather than read silently by individuals. This is generally accepted today . . ."[2] Shiner provides a long quote by Quintilian:

---

1. Rhoads, "Performance Part II," 165.
2. Shiner, *Proclaiming*, 1. This has been known in biblical scholarship at least since Achtemeier, "Omne Verbum Sonat."

> [16] But the advantages conferred by reading and listening are not identical. The speaker stimulates us by the *animation of his delivery*, and kindles the imagination, not by presenting us with an elaborate picture, but by *bringing us into actual touch with the things themselves*. Then all is life and movement, and we receive the new-born offspring of his imagination with enthusiastic approval. We are moved not merely by the actual issue of the trial, but by all that the orator himself has at stake. [17] Moreover his voice, the grace of his gestures, the adaptation of his delivery (which is of supreme importance in oratory), and, in a word, all his excellences in combination, have their educative effect. In reading, on the other hand, the critical faculty is a surer guide, inasmuch as the listener's judgment is often swept away by his preference for a particular speaker, or by the applause of an *enthusiastic audience*.[3] (Italics mine)

The above passage (where I have italicized) tells us three thing of importance for understanding ancient performance. *First*, the performance is "animated" (16) and the delivery involves the modulation of the voice and the use of body language and gestures (17). It is an audio-visual experience. How well something is said, according to Quintilian, is more important than what is being said. If the flair of delivery is not present, the effect of what is delivered falls flat.

> [2] But the thing itself has an extraordinarily powerful effect in oratory. For the nature of the speech that we have composed within our minds is not so important as the manner in which we produce it, since the emotion of each member of our audience will depend on the impression made upon his hearing. Consequently, no proof, at least if it be one devised by the orator himself, will ever be so secure as not to lose its force if the speaker fails to produce it in tones that drive it home.[4]

Second, the delivery carries the audience *into* the performance, into the oration or the story as the case may be. In doing so, they are in "actual touch with the things themselves" (16).

Third, there is an audience that reacts enthusiastically (17). This is not a passive constrained and silent spectating like one would watch a play or movie, careful not to interrupt the other audience members' experience. It is more like a sporting event where audience reaction to the

---

3. Quintilian, *Inst.* 10.1.16–17.
4. Quintilian, *Inst.* 11.6.2.

events on the field of play are not hidden or kept to oneself. Reactions of audiences were so commonplace that Plutarch provides instructions for the proper audience reaction to philosophical lectures, warning against overly bombastic reactions.[5] He cautions a hearer to not be "swept away by the current" of "clamor and shouting" of an audience.[6] Plutarch is of course arguing against being "swept away" by audience reaction, and arguing for a more contemplative hearing of an oration. Even so, the fact that he is making the argument indicates the phenomenon of an "enthusiastic audience" in Quintilian's words.

So an ancient performance involves the interplay of an *animated performer/orator* and an *enthusiastic audience* resulting in the audience being *drawn into* the oration/story. It is in the "drawing in" of the audience that performance has its particular rhetorical pull. This rhetorical effect is distinct from reading where "the critical faculty is a surer guide" (17). In the case of storytelling, an audience is drawn in when they experience the particular realities of the story world described by the unique (anti-)language of the narrative and when they sympathize with particularly noble and courageous characters and antipathize with cowardly, despicable or self-absorbed characters.

While we have no actual ancient performances (short of using a time machine) available for our study today, what we do have are extant manuscripts—namely, written remains of oral scripts. Holly Hearon writes, "It is appropriate to begin with the written remains because, in the end, that is all we have: written remains of ancient texts . . ." She goes on to discuss the fact that the structure of an ancient text is discernible through reading aloud or performing, *not* from the text itself.[7]

In other words, we find the structure of a text produced by an oral/aural culture in the reading aloud of the text. We find the structure of the text produced by a writing culture in the physical layout of the text. For example, in the second chapter I have laid out the translation of John 9 according to scenes that follow the dramatic rule of two. This is indicated by *physical divisions of the text* on the printed (or perhaps digital) page. Further, each *cola* is laid out in a *separate line* (with an indentation if the text wraps to the next line). This is clearly a visually oriented plan. An ancient text had no such frills!

---

5. Shiner, *Proclaiming*, 144.
6. Plut., *De recta ratione audiendi* 7 (Babbitt).
7. Hearon, "Implications of Orality," 15–16.

Compare:

Table 6.1: Formatted Modern-Style Text

John 9	NA27 John 9:
1 And passing by, He saw a man blind from birth.	1 Καὶ παράγων εἶδεν ἄνθρωπον τυφλὸν ἐκ γενετῆς.
2 And his disciples asked him, saying, "Teacher, who sinned, this one or his parents, that he was born blind?"	2 καὶ ἠρώτησαν αὐτὸν οἱ μαθηταὶ αὐτοῦ λέγοντες· ῥαββί, τίς ἥμαρτεν, οὗτος ἢ οἱ γονεῖς αὐτοῦ, ἵνα τυφλὸς γεννηθῇ;
3 Jesus answered, "Neither this one sinned nor his parents, but that the works of God might be revealed in him.	3 ἀπεκρίθη Ἰησοῦς· οὔτε οὗτος ἥμαρτεν οὔτε οἱ γονεῖς αὐτοῦ, ἀλλ' ἵνα φανερωθῇ τὰ ἔργα τοῦ θεοῦ ἐν αὐτῷ.
4 It is necessary for us to work the works of him who sent me while it is day. Night is coming when no one is able to work.	4 ἡμᾶς δεῖ ἐργάζεσθαι τὰ ἔργα τοῦ πέμψαντός με ἕως ἡμέρα ἐστίν· ἔρχεται νὺξ ὅτε οὐδεὶς δύναται ἐργάζεσθαι.
5 While I am in the world, I am *the* light of the world."	5 ὅταν ἐν τῷ κόσμῳ ὦ, φῶς εἰμι τοῦ κόσμου.

With the ancient layout:

Table 6.2: Unformatted, Ancient-Style Text

John 9	NA27 John 9:
andpassingbyhesawamanblindfrombirthandhisdisciplesaskedhimsayingteacherwhosinnedthisoneorhisparentsthathewasbornblindjesusansweredneitherthisonesinnednorhisparentsbutthattheworksofgodmightberevealedinhimitisnecessaryforustoworktheworksofhimwhosentmewhileitisdaynightiscomingwhennooneisabletoworkwhileiamintheworldiamthelightoftheworld	καὶπαράγωνεἶδενἄνθρωποντυφλὸνἐκγενετῆςκαὶἠρώτησαναὐτὸνοἱμαθηταὶαὐτοῦλέγοντες·ῥαββίτίςἤμαρτενοὗτοςἢοἱγονεῖςαὐτοῦἵνατυφλὸςγεννηθῇἀπεκρίθηἸησοῦςοὔτεοὗτοςἥμαρτενοὔτεοἱγονεῖςαὐτοῦἀλλ'ἵναφανερωθῇτὰἔργατοῦθεοῦἐναὐτῷἡμᾶςδεῖἐργάζεσθαιτὰἔργατοῦπέμψαντόςμεἕωςἡμέραἐστίνἔρχεταινὺξὅτεοὐδεὶςδύναταιἐργάζεσθαιὅτανἐντῷκόσμῳὦφῶςεἰμιτοῦκόσμου

The point here is, the internal logic, divisions, connections, and patterns of an ancient work are contained in the words themselves, not the layout. The second chapter of this dissertation was an attempt to discover that logic. Ancient authors relied on devices such as chiasms, alliteration, assonance, inclusio, parallelism, repetition of words and phrases and the like to structure their thought,[8] not space[9] on a page, extremely valuable real-estate in antiquity.

Specific Aspects of a Performance

Types of Performance and Setting

In antiquity, there were various types of performance. There were *public readings* that took place in large halls or outside to a gathered crowd. They could be featured at games or religious festivals. A reading could take place in a marketplace for example. Authors could perform such readings in order to "publish" their work or to generate interest. Public performances were common enough that members of the lower class had opportunity to hear a wide variety of performances such as speeches, drama, short stories, and epic stories. Public performances of *dramas* took place in theaters, and there was the public performance of *poetry*, often accompanied by the lyre and/or flute.

Guides at the temple in Delphi would often read aloud inscriptions for visitors and tell stories related to the god or the temple. Storytelling would often accompany rituals. Greek and Roman religions included the recitation of the exploits of their various gods as part of the religious services. Included with this sort of performance is a type of pantomime. As the exploits of the gods were recited another performer acted those out. It is interesting to speculate if this is how Christ was "portrayed as crucified" before the "eyes" of the Galatians (Gal 3:1).

Among the rich there were also *private readings* within one's house. For example Pliny the younger had a book read (aloud) every dinner, alone, with his wife, or with guests. Families enjoyed small intimate recitations of stories, fables and romantic novels. These could be read aloud in small gatherings in private homes.

---

8. Achtemeier, "Omne Verbum Sonat," 17, 23.

9. Space on a page is relatively unlimited in our modern print culture and even more so in digital text media.

The author of Revelation, Paul, and the author of Colossians (if not Paul) all expected their works to be read aloud (Rev. 1:3; 1 Thess 5:27; Col 4:16, each using ἀναγινώσκω *to read aloud* cf. Luke 4:16). It is difficult to say in exactly what setting a gospel might be performed. Shiner theorizes that of a house church.[10] This is entirely possible. Hypothetically it could be similar to a private reading with guests. A convened house church would meet in a house large enough to accommodate the members. Someone owning such a home would be wealthy. It is also possible that non-members, those curious, or potential initiates, could be invited to recitals of a gospel.

Emotion

The appeal to emotion, as seen in the above quote from Quintilian, was of great importance. Cicero speaks of how the instilling of emotion in the mind of the audience is the greatest tool of an orator.[11] There are various techniques aside from an emotionally charged dramatic presentation itself, which can help to convey emotion. A notable phrase or turn of words can signal emotion[12] such as, "Now here is a sight to see!" (John 9:30). Hyperbole may also signal emotion[13] such as, "never since the beginning of the world" (9:32). The swearing of an oath will signal heightened emotional content[14] such as, "Give glory to God" (9:24).[15] Of course in a narrative, the situation and the narration itself also dictate emotion, for example, the "fear" of "the Jews," the sympathy for the man as he is expelled, the anger toward the Pharisees as they persistently refuse to acknowledge Jesus is from God, the levity of the man's taunt, "you don't want to become his disciples do you?" and the venom in the Pharisee's response, "they reviled him . . ."

---

10. The preceding from Shiner, *Proclaiming*, 37–44, 51.
11. Cicero, *Brut.* 80.279 (Hendrickson, LCL), quoted by Shiner, *Proclaiming*, 64.
12. Shiner, *Proclaiming*, 61.
13. Ibid.
14. Ibid., 60.
15. For "give glory to God" as an oath formula see p. 101.

Delivery, Gesture, and Movement

Closely related to emotion is delivery. A line like "and they threw him out" (9:34) when delivered in a calm monotone falls flat, but when delivered with the emotional tension demanded by the scene's context has impact. Delivery depends on voice and body language, particularly gesture.[16] Cicero speaks of specific gestures such as stomping one's foot, slapping one's thigh, or striking one's brow as ways to convey emotion.[17] While such gestures would have been understood by an ancient audience the modern audience may recognize something more familiar such as shaking one's fist or throwing the arms up into the air. The important factor here is that the ability to convey emotion through voice and gesture are connected to the orator's ability to convince.

Audience Reaction

Just as performers and orators had specific stylized gestures and movements, so also the audience would react in predictable ways. They would shout approval or disapproval, applaud approvingly, cover their ears (cf. Acts 7:57) disapprovingly.[18] In terms of narrative, of interest are portions of the narrative where the audience is expected to applaud or voice approval (for a sympathetic character for example) or where the audience is expected to jeer, boo, or gesture disapproval (toward an antipathetic character for example). While we do not have an ancient audience at our disposal, we do have the remains of the performance, the text containing the narrative. From this we can extrapolate the expected audience reaction.

A striking statement or a well turned phrase in an oration or narration can be the onus for an audience reaction of applause. Audiences are likely to applaud when the protagonist defeats, or at least scores a win against the antagonist, especially if this is done in a catchy way, "... if he is a sinner I don't know, one thing I do know, I was blind, now I see" (9:25). The chiastic structure, the subtle way of disagreeing with the antagonists while not directly challenging them, all make for a well turned phrase that deserves applause (much like your team scoring a goal/basket/run).

---

16. Quintilian, *Inst.* 11.3 .14 (Butler, LCL) in Shiner, *Proclaiming*, 79.
17. Cicero, *Brut.* 80.278 in Shiner, *Proclaiming*, 83.
18. Shiner, *Proclaiming*, 146.

Conversely, the expulsion (9:34) of the man after a well argued position that Jesus is "from God" (9:30-33) would draw vocalizations and gestures of disapproval (much like a bad call from a referee).

Synthesis by Scene

Given the background of orality, performance, and audience response in the first century, it is likely that, as other literature of the time, a gospel such as John might well have been performed or at least read aloud dramatically. I will now examine by scene how such a performance may have looked and sounded. Insights from the analysis in each of the four prior chapters will be synthesized[19] here to inform that synopsis. Again, the penultimate goal is to discern the impact, logical and emotional, a performance of John, and particularly John 9, would have on an audience. The ultimate goal is to discern the rhetorical force or pull of the episode in relation to the expressed goal of the Fourth Gospel, "that you might [come to] trust[20] that Jesus is the Christ the Son of God, and that

---

19. A synthetic multidisciplinary approach is of course part of the discipline of performance criticism. Rhoads, "Performance Part II," 165.

20. Translated strictly, it is "come to trust" if the original is the aorist πιστεύςητε, "continue trusting" if it is the present πιστεύητε. The textual evidence is strong for both but slightly stronger for the present tense (Metzger, *Textual Commentary*, 219). Even so, the tenses may not be used strictly by John.

It seems clear from the use of the aorist subjunctive elsewhere in John that it is inceptive (John 6:30; 8:24; 9:36; 11:15, 40, 42; 20:25; perhaps 14:29 and 19:35 which has the same variant).

Excluding 19:35 and 20:31 we have the present subjunctive in John 6:29; 10:38; 17:21. It is hard to see the sense of 17:21 as "continue to trust," given the Johannine relationship with the "world." The idea of "come to trust" seems more likely from context. In 10:38 the negated subjunctive present seems to indicate a continued sense, they continue to not trust just as they were in the condition of not trusting prior to being addressed. In 6:29 Jesus is addressing those who do not yet trust and who ask for a sign (6:30) so that they "might come to trust" (aorist subj.). So "continue to trust" cannot be maintained for 6:29 or 17:21. Even if the autograph of John's Gospel contains the present subjunctive, the strict interpretation of "continue to trust" cannot be supported from John's use of the present subjunctive. Carson, "Purpose," 640, makes a similar point about 11:15; 1:7; 4:48.

It is also important to note that oral performances often tailor various words according to the audience. This may account for some textual variants among gospels. If a given manuscript is simply the snapshot of a particular performance event, variants may reflect, in some instances, differing performances. An audience of believers, or non-believers, or both, may well be addressed with the present subj. in a way that does not comment on the addressees' prior condition of faith.

trusting, you might have life in his name." In other words, when one puts it all together, how does this episode lead an audience toward trust?

Putting it all together (as mentioned in the introduction) can be likened to the days of transparencies and the overhead projector. As each transparency or layer is laid on top of another, a more complete image of the subject matter is projected.

Scene 1: Jesus and the Disciples, vv. 1–5

Contrast: Sin and Blindness vs. Revelation and God's Works, vv. 1–3

The linguistic patterns in this scene (p. 34) draw attention to at least two things of major importance. First, the man born "blind" (τυφλός) will serve as a means by which God's "works" will be "revealed" (φανερόω). This is an ironic pairing of concepts and would be performed in a way that draws audience attention to the mystery of how blindness can be a vehicle for revelation.

The irony is enhanced beyond that of simple lexical opposition, when one adds the social-science layer. Physiognomy (judging character based on physical characteristics) tells us the blind man would have been perceived as pitiable, shamefully associated with sin, ignorant, and, as a possessor of the evil eye, dangerous and unclean (pp. 122ff. and 125ff.). These presuppositions would inform the facial expressions, gestures, and tone of a performer as the man is introduced in v. 1.

Jesus is light of the world, vv. 4–5

Jesus as light of the world is the second issue of major importance to which the linguistic patterns draw attention (pp. 36ff.). Here we see Jesus as the light of the world, existing during the day when it is the appropriate time to do the "work" of God, the one who sent him. Characterizing Jesus as light is critical here and a performer would draw attention to it.

As we add layers from the narrative and social-science disciplines we find that by identifying Jesus as light, he is characterized as the one who brings *life*, who brings *insight, wisdom, and knowledge*, and who is the *presence of the divine* among people (pp. 82ff.).

Verses 1–5 would prime an audience to understand this episode in cosmic terms of light, life, darkness, and sin. As one blind, the man's heart/eyes or "lamp of the body" is filled with darkness. Jesus, the light of the world, will bring light/sight to the man as a revelation of God's work. Strikingly, God's very first work was to bring light out of darkness (Gen 1:1–5), and in this episode the Word through whom all things are created (John 1:3) brings light to the darkness (cf. John 1:4–5).

Scene 2: Jesus Heals the Man Born Blind, vv. 6–7

This scene describes the healing in a very stylized and balanced way. Jesus spits, makes, and rubs. Then he commands, "go and wash." In response the man went, washed and came back. The very last word of the scene, "βλέπων" is a circumstantial participle of manner[21] describing the way in which the man returned—seeing! This would be delivered in an emphatic way by the storyteller as the last thing the audience hears prior to the next scene, bringing that energy into the next scene.

Between Jesus's command and the man's response, is centered the narrative comment about Siloam being translated/interpreted "sent" (ἀποστέλλω). This centering brings attention to the word and a performer would highlight this.

From a narrative perspective this adds another nuance of Jesus's characterization as "sent" (πέμπω) from v. 4. It connects the episode with the rest of the gospel where Jesus is described as the one "sent" by the Father to do his work (5:36 and see note 10 on p. 41 and p. 84).

Adding a social-science layer, use of saliva for healing characterizes Jesus as one having great power and/or purity (pp. 137ff.). Tacitus tells the story of how Vespasian used saliva to heal a blind man and cited it as proof that he had the "favor of heaven and the partiality of the gods" (Tac., *Hist.* 4.81).[22] Of course the healed man will use the same reasoning to argue that Jesus is from God based on this healing (9:33).

Scene 3: Neighbors Question the Man, vv. 8–12

The energy of the healing, conveyed by a storyteller's emphatic "βλέπων" ("seeing!" or "able to see!") is perpetuated by the busyness of the repetition

21. Smyth, *Grammar*, §2062.
22. Church et. al., *Complete Works*.

of "ἔλεγον·" and "ἔλεγεν" ("were saying") five times in three verses (vv. 8–10). This scene gives rise to the first witness of the healed man, a simple account of what happened with a simple description of Jesus as "the man called Jesus." The neighbors serve two simple functions, they provide the backdrop of a public witness to the healing—the word is out, the people know what has happened. Also, they provide the mechanism by which the man is brought to the Pharisees.

Scene 4: Pharisees Question the Man, vv. 13–17

In this scene the narrator has waited until a more dramatic moment to give the audience crucial information about when the healing took place—a Sabbath day. This information is delayed until the Pharisees, for whom it is an important issue, come on the scene. A performer would draw great attention to v. 14. An audience would already know the issues of a sabbath day healing having encountered the aftermath of the lame man in chapter 5—"the Jews" were trying to kill Jesus (5:18 cf. 7:19–24). This announcement "now it was a sabbath . . ." would bring an ominous tone to the episode. An ideal audience might react with an "ooooh!"

A social-science perspective informs us that the issue at stake for the Pharisees is purity and defilement. A transgression of holy time has occurred (see discussion on p. 118). Even so, it would seem a holy man has performed the healing. Does this trump the Sabbath law? Not according to 5:18 and 7:19–24. Within this episode the Pharisees are divided, at least for this scene. The great irony here is that a full on investigation, no doubt involving work, ensues—an hypocrisy that would be noticed by the audience.

The rhetorical effect here is to begin to distance the audience from the Pharisees. The emotion of the audience will have suddenly shifted from the high energy of the healing and busy discussion of the neighbors to the ominous tone set by the Sabbath day announcement. This would not have been possible if the setting in time were announced initially. "While walking along on a Sabbath, they saw . . ." would not work here.

Scene 5: Pharisees Question the Man's Parents, vv. 18–23

In an attempt to verify, or perhaps undermine, the miracle, the Pharisees call the man's parents. They ask, "is this your son," "was he born blind," "how does he now see?" The parents react to the questioning in an interesting way. They answer the questions asked of them—he is our son, he was born blind, we don't know how he now sees—but they emphatically (p. 49) deny knowing *who* healed him. Social-science analysis tells us that illness and healing are both assumed to have a personal cause (p. 137ff.). It is understandable that the parents would offer the extra answer about not knowing who healed their son, but the emphatic aspect (again p. 49) of the answer is not necessary.

Before too much ill can be thought of the parents, the reason behind their response is disclosed to the audience in a narrative comment—the fear of the Jews, more specifically the threat of being expelled from the synagogue community (9:22 cf. 12:42; 16:2). Again, from a social-science perspective, expulsion from the community would be devastating, especially to a dyadic personality who see themselves as part of a group. This threat is enough to keep many from confessing their trust in Jesus (12:42).

The effect of this scene heightens the tension felt by the audience. The audience by this point in the story has begun to sympathize with Jesus and his actions, actions based on an intimate knowledge of God. This is the first time the audience has heard the decision about synagogue expulsion. This new information serves to further distance the audience from the Pharisees.

Scene 6: Pharisees Expel the Man, vv. 24–34

First conversation, the man "gives glory" to God, vv. 24–25

In an attempt to compel the man to bear (false, from his perspective) witness against Jesus the Pharisees invoke an oath formula "give glory to God." This indeed happens but not in the way the Pharisees want. The man shows increasing cleverness and wit throughout the episode but particularly in this scene. In terms of irony, the "joke is" continually "on" the Pharisees in this scene. They wish to compel one result, but in their attempt produce the opposite result (p. 170).

From an honor shame perspective, the man shows himself to be both honorable and clever. In v. 25 he manages to actually give glory to God by witnessing about what Jesus has done (". . . I was blind but now I see") while not directly challenging the Pharisees' domain of religious expertise, flawed as it was ("Whether he is a sinner, I do not know, one thing I know . . ."). Additionally the shame of dishonoring one's own patron, Jesus, is cleverly avoided.

A display of wit like this would win the man honor in the eyes of an audience, increasing their sympathy for him, while distancing them from the Pharisees. By this point in the story, a performer should be voicing the man with increasing courage and intelligence. In order to accomplish this perhaps a storyteller would need to exaggerate the meekness of the man in the earlier scenes to provide contrast.

Second conversation, Pharisees do not "hear," vv. 26–27

After not getting the result they wanted, the Pharisees persist in probing for specifics about the healing. In this sub-scene the man continues to be characterized with increasing wit and courage. The audience can laugh along with his sarcastic taunt in v. 27.

Third conversation, man demonstrates that Jesus is "from God," vv. 28–33

In the third conversation, the man reaches a crossroads. He is pushed by the Pharisees up to a point of no return. The Pharisees insist that they are disciples of Moses while at the same time unwittingly admitting their ignorance into Jesus's origins. They say they know that Jesus is not from God but admit not actually knowing where he is from. They are ironically correct. They think Jesus is from The Galilee (cf. 7:52, even though here they say they don't know his origins!). The audience knows from the prologue that Jesus is from the beginning, from above, and from God. In this episode, the Pharisees have hung themselves on their own words (from the perspective of the narrator at least) and as stated above, the "joke is" increasingly "on them." The rhetorical effect is that the audience is even further distanced from the Pharisees as their credibility as religious authorities is undermined.

At this point it is clear that the Pharisees will not relent. The man is forced to side with them or his patron, Jesus (whom he has yet to actually see!). The audience knows the consequences of siding with Jesus, expulsion (9:22). This does not prevent the man from making his choice. He produces a clear and logical argument (see p. 104) which on the one hand is a simple recounting of the facts, and on the other hand full of wit and wordplay. Translating the man's reply in v. 30 as "here is a sight to see" (ἐν τούτῳ γὰρ τὸ θαυμαστόν ἐστιν) the wordplay highlights the Pharisee's blindness to Jesus and recalls the man's experience of having been healed of blindness.

Verses 30–33 however clearly cross the line. The man has openly and sarcastically disagreed with authority in a public setting. This is what Scott calls a "rupture."[23] The Pharisee's response is not unexpected. The man is expelled from the synagogue community.

Again, social-science criticism tells us what a devastating thing expulsion would be for a dyadic personality. This is not a decision the man would have reached lightly. In narration a storyteller might demonstrate this by a long pause and a sigh of resignation prior to delivering vs. 30–33 with the passion and sarcasm they deserve.

The effect of the speech and expulsion is twofold. First, an audience would delight in the wit and wordplay—"sight to see" and placing the "we know" in (the ancient equivalent of) air quotes to mock the Pharisees instance that they "know" Jesus is a sinner.[24] Second, their sympathy for the man's predicament would be heightened. What will he do now that he has been expelled?

Scene 7: Jesus Receives the Man, vv. 35–38

In answer to the above question, which is in the mind of the audience, Jesus appears once again on the scene. He solicits the trust of the man. As the man places his trust in Jesus, the statement in v. 3 is completed. The works of God = trust in Jesus the sent one of God (6:29). As the man trusts in Jesus, the sent one, the works of God are "revealed in him" (9:3). The entire episode is a revelation of the works of God.

The impact on an audience is twofold. First, the audience, now sympathetic to the man's plight, sees that the man has a new in-group or fictive kin group. He is part of the family of God (cf. 1:12–13).[25] The threat of expulsion is effectively neutralized by availability of a new kin-group whose founder will never throw anyone out (6:37cf. 10:12, 28; 17:12, 15). This relieves the tension the audience feels with respect to the man's well

---

23. See chapter 4 and pp. 148–49.
24. See the discussion of ἡμεῖς οἴδαμεν chapter three's discussion of scene 6 and v. 31.
25. See the discussion of fictive kinship in chapter four's discussion of scene 7.

being. Second, the audience sees that entry into this new fictive kin group takes place specifically through trust in Jesus.

It is important to remember here that the man has yet to see Jesus. His vision was healed *after* he washed in the pool of Siloam. By then Jesus had disappeared from the scene. Up to this point the healed man had only heard Jesus's voice, like the sheep of chapter 10:3–5, 16. This is another bond shared between the healed man and the audience. The audience has also never seen (physically, literally) Jesus. They have only heard (or are hearing if for the first time) the Gospel story! Jesus seeks the audience out as well in this scene. A performer, speaking the role of Jesus, addresses the audience, and solicits trust. The audience experiences the portions of the scene where Jesus is speaking, as if they were the healed man receiving the invitation. A similar phenomenon happens with Thomas in 20:24–29. Jesus, speaking to Thomas in v. 29 says, "Because you have seen me have you trusted? Blessed are they who, not having seen, have come to trust." The risen Lord, in story form, pronounces a blessing on the (real) audience, who of course has never seen Jesus physically.

Scene 8: Jesus Passes Judgment upon the Pharisees, vv. 39–41

In this final scene, Jesus pronounces that the sin of the Pharisees remains. This pronouncement forms an *inclusio* with v. 2 framing the whole episode as an answer to "who sinned?" Neither of the two options suggested by the disciples were correct. The episode demonstrates that the Pharisees have sin that remains. From the perspective of the narrative, sin is essentially not trusting in the one whom God has sent (16:9; 8:24; 10:25, 37, 38). The final two scenes act as a double pronged fork to move an audience toward trust. Life and a caring family await those who trust in the one whom God has sent. Sin and death in one's sin (8:24), await those who reject the one whom God has sent.

It is the very presence of Jesus in the world, working the works of the one who sent him, that becomes the criteria for judgment. Those who accept and trust receive life and a new family (1:4, 12–13); those who reject and do not trust are condemned/judged (3:18) and die in their sins (8:24). Neutrality or not choosing is not an option. The audience, as they are presented with the episode of the man born blind, also must make a decision about Jesus. Trust like the healed man or reject and do not trust like the Pharisees. According to the tenants of Johannine worldview, one receives life as one trusts. As an audience is presented with the whole gospel story, they are continually presented with the opportunity to trust or reject Jesus. This episode is part of that ongoing presentation of possibility. If audience members choose to trust, at that moment they receive life.

Again, eternal life is defined in John as knowing both God and Jesus (17:3). This knowing is precisely the kind of intimate relationship expressed in 10:1–18 as Jesus the good shepherd cares for his sheep, those who have come to trust. Jesus knows his sheep and his sheep know him (10:14). Jesus knows God and God knows him (10:15). The sheep are cared for by the shepherd who loves them and lays down his life for them (10:11, 15 cf. 15:13). That same love exists within the community of believers (13:1, 34–35).

Rhetorical Implications

Rhetorically, the episode works to build distance between the audience and the disciples of Moses (the Pharisees). This is accomplished by progressively characterizing them as those who do not know and cannot see Jesus for who he is, God's sent one. On the other hand, sympathy is built between the healed man and the audience. This is done by depicting him as one who knows, who is clever, who is able to argue logically and with wit and humor; in short, as one who can truly see.

By the time an audience arrives at the episode of the man born blind there are a number of things they have already experienced from the story(telling). An audience enters the episode smarter than the Pharisees. Unlike the Pharisees, they know where Jesus is from. He was with God in the beginning (1:1–4) and has come down from heaven (1:14, 18; 3:13). He is not really from The Galilee! They have already been told that Jesus is the life that is the light of all (1:4) and is the light of the world (1:9) that brings life (8:12). They already know that "the Jews" are looking for a way to kill Jesus (5:18 7:1). The audience has gained all they need to know for the rhetoric of the story to work, from the story itself.

This superior knowledge on the part of the audience allows them to agree with the man born blind, as he progressively disagrees with the Pharisees. The audience can see things more easily from the perspective of the narrator and the blind man than from the perspective of the Pharisees. This is because the audience, by virtue of simply remaining engaged in the storytelling event, has been, to a degree, indoctrinated with the

Johannine world view. This indoctrination (once again, to a degree) is necessary when one follows any story. In order for the story to make sense one must engage in the ideas, concepts, values, and realities described in the story world. If not, one disengages from the story entirely.[26]

The knowledge that Jesus is from God is shared by the narrator, the healed man, and the audience. This shared knowledge creates an in-group bond. This is a bond that extends from the story world into the real world of the audience. This creates bonds between audience members also. The audience, in a way, begins to be the fictive kinship group actually described in the narrative. Furthermore, the audience begins to experience this bond as life.

If a telling of the Fourth Gospel was attended by those who already trust and have heard the story before (insiders), as well as those who do not yet trust and have not yet heard (outsiders), the latter would still have all the information they need from the narrative for the rhetoric to work. As that portion of the audience begins to root for the man born blind, for all the reasons described above, they find themselves rooting along with those who already believe. Outsider and insider are bonded together. This insider bond, even if for some only a product of the storytelling experience becomes a rhetorical pull into the Johannine fictive kinship group.

The audience is transformed as they begin to see Jesus in the way that the healed man sees him and as the narrator presents him. The story carries the audience to a tipping point, a point of decision. The audience is also confronted, via the story, with the light of the world. They too must decide to receive (1:12) or reject (1:1–11) the sent one of God. In deciding, they choose or reject life and light. The ah-ha moment comes in 9:41. Will the audience remain in the category of those who think they see and think they know, or will they accept that they are blind and receive the light that comes from the sent one? As the audience begins to see Jesus like the healed man sees him, they too experience life.

Furthermore, eternal life in John is knowing God and Jesus whom he sent (17:3). Just as the man born blind progressively comes to know Jesus more fully (man called Jesus → prophet → from God → Son of Man) and receives life, an audience, as they hear the gospel story, also comes to know Jesus (and therefore God) more fully. This coming to know and to trust is an experience of life in Johannine thought.

---

26. John 6:66ff. is perhaps a narrative ploy at preventing such disengagement—a narrator's version of "bear with me now while I explain this."

Jesus seeks out and includes the healed man in the fictive family of God, the flock of the good shepherd. This effectively nullifies the threat of expulsion from a synagogue community. If the real audience of John is actually experiencing threat of expulsion from the synagogues for confessing Jesus as Christ, or whether this is simply their perception, or whether it is simply a narrative ploy, continues to be debatable. However, one thing can be known from the narrative itself. Those who trust in Jesus as the Christ may experience a community of love under the care of the good shepherd.

Bibliography

Abbott, H. Porter. *The Cambridge Introduction to Narrative*. Cambridge: Cambridge University Press, 2008.

Achtemeier, Paul J. "Omne Verbum Sonat: The New Testament and the Oral Environment of Late Western Antiquity." *Journal of Biblical Literature* 109 (1990) 3–27.

Albl, M. C. "'Are Any Among You Sick?' The Health Care System in the Letter of James." *Journal of Biblical Literature* 121 (2002) 123–43.

Allison, Dale C. "The Eye Is the Lamp of the Body (Matthew 6:22–23 = Luke 11:34–36)." *New Testament Studies* 33 (1987) 61–83.

Ashton, John. *The Gospel of John and Christian Origins*. Minneapolis: Fortress, 2014.

———. *Understanding the Fourth Gospel*. 2nd ed. Oxford ; New York: Oxford University Press, 2007.

Attridge, Harold W. *Essays on John and Hebrews*. Grand Rapids: Baker Academic, 2012.

Avalos, Hector. *Illness and Health Care in the Ancient Near East: The Role of the Temple in Greece, Mesopotamia, and Israel*. Atlanta, Ga.: Scholars Press, 1995.

Bal, Mieke, and Christine van Boheemen. *Narratology: Introduction to the Theory of Narrative*. Toronto: University of Toronto Press, 2009. Online: http://site.ebrary.com/id/10383413.

Ball, David Mark. *"I Am" in John's Gospel: Literary Function, Background and Theological Implications*. Sheffield Academic, 1996.

Balz, Horst, and Gerhard Schneider eds. *Exegetical Dictionary of the New Testament*. 3 vols. Grand Rapids, Michigan: Eerdmans, 1993.

Barrett, C. K. *The Gospel according to St. John: An Introduction With Commentary and Notes on the Greek Text*. Philadelphia: Westminster, 1978.

Bauckham, Richard. *The Gospels for All Christians: Rethinking the Gospel Audiences*. Grand Rapids: Eerdmans, 1998.

———. *The Testimony of the Beloved Disciple: Narrative, History, and Theology in the Gospel of John*. Grand Rapids: Baker, 2007.

Bauer, W., F. W. Danker, W. F. Arndt, and F. W. Gingrich. *A Greek-English Lexicon of the New Testament and Other Early Christian Literature*. 3rd ed. Logos Bible Software version 4. 2000–2010. Print ed.: Chicago: University of Chicago Press, 2000.

Beasley-Murray, G. R. *John*. Word Biblical Commentary 36. Waco, TX: Word, 1987.

Beckson, Karl E. *Literary Terms: A Dictionary*. Rev. ed. New York: Farrar, Straus & Giroux, 1975.

Berger, Allan S. "The Evil Eye—an Ancient Superstition." *Journal of Religion and Health* 51 (2012) 1098–103.

Bernidaki-Aldous, Eleftheria A. *Blindness in a Culture of Light: Especially the Case of Oedipus at Colonus of Sophocles.* American University Studies Series XVII. Classical Languages and Literature 8. New York: Lang, 1990.

Betz, Hans Dieter. "Matthew 6:22f and Ancient Greek Theories of Vision." In *Text and Interpretation: Studies in the New Testament Presented to Matthew Black,* edited by Ernest Best and R. McL. Wilson, 43–56. Cambridge: Cambridge University Press, 1979.

Black, David Alan. *Learn to Read New Testament Greek.* Nashville: Broadman & Holman, 2009.

———. *Linguistics for Students of New Testament Greek: A Survey of Basic Concepts and Applications.* Grand Rapids: Baker, 1988.

Boomershine, Thomas E. *Story Journey: An Invitation to the Gospel as Storytelling.* Nashville: Abingdon, 1988.

———. "The Structure of Narrative Rhetoric in Genesis 2–3." *Semeia* 18 (1980) 113–29.

Booth, Wayne C. *The Rhetoric of Fiction.* Chicago: University of Chicago Press, 1961.

———. *A Rhetoric of Irony.* Chicago: University of Chicago Press, 1975.

Bowe, B. E. "Reading the Bible through Filipino Eyes." *Missiology* 36 (1998) 345–60.

Boyarin, Daniel. "Justin Martyr Invents Judaism." *Church History* 70 (2001) 427–61.

Brant, Jo-Ann A. *John.* Grand Rapids: Baker Academic, 2011.

Bridges, Carl B., and Ronald E. Wheeler. "The Evil Eye in the Sermon on the Mount." *Stone-Campbell Journal* 4 (2001) 69–79.

Brown, Colin, ed. *The New International Dictionary of New Testament Theology.* 4 vols. Grand Rapids: Zondervan. 1975–1985.

Brown, Raymond Edward. *An Introduction to the Gospel of John.* Anchor Bible Reference Library. New York: Doubleday, 2003.

———. *The Community of the Beloved Disciple.* New York: Paulist 1979.

———. *The Epistles of John.* Anchor Bible 30. Doubleday, 1982.

———. *The Gospel according to John.* Anchor Bible 29, 29A. Garden City, NY: Doubleday, 1966, 1970.

Bruns, J. Edgar. "Prologue and Gospel: The Theology of the Fourth Evangelist." *Catholic Biblical Quarterly* 57 (1995) 812–13.

Burkett, Delbert. *The Son of The Man in the Gospel of John.* Journal for the Study of the New Testament Supplements 56. Sheffield: JSOT Press, 1991.

Carroll, J. T. "Sickness and Healing in the New Testament Gospels." *Interpretation* 49 (1995) 130–42.

Carson, D. A. "The Purpose of the Fourth Gospel: John 20:31 Reconsidered." *Journal of Biblical Literature* 106 (1987) 639–51.

———. "Syntactical and Text-Critical Observations on John 20:30–31: One More Round on the Purpose of the Fourth Gospel." *Journal of Biblical Literature* 124 (2005) 693–714.

Carter, Warren. *John and Empire: Initial Explorations.* New York: T. & T. Clark, 2008.

Cassidy, Richard J. *John's Gospel in New Perspective: Christology and the Realities of Roman Power.* Maryknoll, NY: Orbis, 1992.

Cho, Sukmin. *Jesus as Prophet in the Fourth Gospel.* New Testament Monographs 15. Sheffield: Sheffield Phoenix, 2006.

Cohen, Shaye J. D. *The Beginnings of Jewishness: Boundaries, Varieties, Uncertainties.* Berkeley: University of California Press, 1999.

Craffert, Pieter F. "Medical Anthropology as an Antidote for Ethnocentrism in Jesus Research? Putting the Illness-Disease Distinction into Perspective." *HTS Teologiese Studies/Theological Studies* 67/1 (2011) 970.

Crook, Zeba A. *Reconceptualising Conversion: Patronage, Loyalty, and Conversion in the Religions of the Ancient Mediterranean.* Beihefte zur Zeitschrift für die neutestamentliche Wissenschaft 130. Berlin: de Gruyter, 2004.

———. "Honor, Shame, and Social Status Revisited." *Journal of Biblical Literature* 128 (2009) 591–611.

———. "Structure versus Agency in Studies of the Biblical Social World: Engaging with Louise Lawrence." *Journal for the Study of the New Testament* 29 (2007) 251–75.

Cullmann, Oscar. *The Johannine Circle.* Philadelphia: Westminster, 1975.

Culpepper, R. Alan. *Anatomy of the Fourth Gospel: A Study in Literary Design.* Foundations and Facets. Philadelphia: Fortress, 1983.

———. *The Gospel and Letters of John.* Interpreting Biblical Texts. Nashville: Abingdon, 1998.

———. "Humor and Wit (New Testament)." In *ABD* 3:333.

Culpepper, R. Alan, and Fernando F. Segovia. *The Fourth Gospel from a Literary Perspective.* Semeia 53. Atlanta: Scholars, 1991.

Culpeper, R. Alan, Barnabas Lindars, Ruth Edwards, and John M. Court. *Johannine Literature: With an Introduction by R. A. Culpepper.* Sheffield: Sheffield Academic, 2000.

Dawson, Audrey. *Healing, Weakness and Power: Perspectives on Healing in the Writings of Mark, Luke and Paul.* Paternoster Biblical Monographs. Milton Keynes, UK: Paternoster, 2008.

deSilva, David A. *An Introduction to the New Testament: Contexts, Methods & Ministry Formation.* Downers Grove, IL: InterVarsity, 2004.

———. *Honor, Patronage, Kinship & Purity: Unlocking New Testament Culture.* Downers Grove, IL: InterVarsity, 2000.

Doležel, Lubomír. *Heterocosmica: Fiction and Possible Worlds.* Baltimore: Johns Hopkins University Press, 1998.

Douglas, Mary. *Purity and Danger: An Analysis of Concept[s] of Pollution and Taboo.* London: Routledge, 2002.

Duke, Paul D. *Irony in the Fourth Gospel.* Atlanta: John Knox, 1985.

Dunn, James D. G. "John 6: A Eucharistic Discourse?" *New Testament Studies* 17 (1971) 328–38.

Eastman, Susan Grove. "The Evil Eye and the Curse of the Law: Galatians 3.1 Revisited." *Journal for the Study of the New Testament* 83 (2001) 69–87.

Eck, E. van, and A. G. van Aarde. "Sickness and Healing in Mark: A Social Scientific Interpretation." *Neotestamentica* 27/1 (1993) 27–54.

Ellens, J. Harold. *The Son of Man in the Gospel of John.* New Testament Monographs 28. Sheffield: Sheffield Phoenix, 2010.

Elliott, John H. "The Evil Eye and the Sermon on the Mount: Contours of a Pervasive Belief in Social Scientific Perspective." *Biblical Interpretation* 2 (1994) 51–84.

———. "The Evil Eye in the First Testament: The Ecology and Culture of a Pervasive Belief." In *Bible and the Politics of Exegesis: Essays in Honor of Norman K. Gottwald on His Sixty-Fifth Birthday*, edited by David Jobling et al., 147–59. Cleveland: Pilgrim, 1991.

———. "The Fear of the Leer: The Evil Eye from the Bible to Li'l Abner." *Forum* 4/4 (1988) 42–71.

———. "Paul, Galatians, and the Evil Eye." *Currents in Theology and Mission* 17 (1990) 262–73.

Esler, Philip F. "The Mediterranean Context of Early Christianity." In *The Early Christian World*, 3–25. London: Routledge, 2000.

Euripides. *Iphigenia in Tauris*. Translated by Robert Potter. New York: Random House, 1938.

Fludernik, Monika. *An Introduction to Narratology*. London: Routledge, 2009.

Freedman, David Noel, ed. *The Anchor Bible Dictionary*. 6 vols. New York: Doubleday, 1992.

Fuglseth, Kåre. *Johannine Sectarianism in Perspective: A Sociological, Historical, and Comparative Analysis of Temple and Social Relationships in the Gospel of John, Philo and Qumran*. Supplements to Novum Testamentum 119. Leiden: Brill, 2005.

Gemeren, Willem A. Van, ed. *New International Dictionary of Old Testament Theology & Exegesis*. 5 vols. Pradis version 6.01. Zondervan, 2006. No pages. Online: Print Ed.: Gemeren, Willem A. Van. *New International Dictionary of Old Testament Theology and Exegesis*. 5 vols. Grand Rapids: Zondervan, 1997.

Gilmore, David D. "Anthropology of the Mediterranean Area." *Annual Review of Anthropology* 11 (1982) 175–205.

Gowler, David B. "Characterization in Luke: A Socio-Narratological Approach." *Biblical Theology Bulletin* 19 (1989) 54–62.

Guijarro, Santiago. "Healing Stories and Medical Anthropology: A Reading of Mark 10:46–52." *Biblical Theology Bulletin* 30 (2000) 102–12.

Hahn, Robert A. *Sickness and Healing: An Anthropological Perspective*. New Haven: Yale University Press, 1995.

Ham, Clay. "The Title 'Son of Man' in the Gospel of John." *Stone-Campbell Journal* 1 (1998) 67–84.

Harris, Elizabeth. *Prologue and Gospel: The Theology of the Fourth Evangelist*. Journal for the Study of the New Testament Supplements 107. Sheffield Academic, 1994.

Hartsock, Chad. *Sight and Blindness in Luke-Acts: The Use of Physical Features in Characterization*. Biblical Interpretation Series 94. Leiden: Brill, 2008.

Hatfield, Chad. "Sin, Sickness, and Salvation." *Christian Bioethics* 12 (2006) 199–211.

Hearon, Holly E. "The Implications of Orality for Studies of the Biblical Text." In *Performing the Gospel: Orality, Memory, and Mark: Essays Dedicated to Werner Kelber*, 3–20. Minneapolis: Fortress, 2006.

Herzog, William R., II. "Dissembling, a Weapon of the Weak: The Case of Christ and Caesar in Mark 12:13–17 and Romans 13:1–7." *Perspectives in Religious Studies* 2 (1994) 339–60.

Hoffman, Joy J. "Unmasking the Drama: The Rhetoric of John 9." In *Church Divinity, 1984*, 113–29. Bristol, IN: Wyndham Hall, 1984.

Holleran, J. W. "Seeing the Light: A Narrative Reading of John 9." *Ephemerides Theologicae Lovanienses* 69 (1993) 5–26, 354–82.

Horsley, Richard A, ed. *Hidden Transcripts and the Arts of Resistance: Applying the Work of James C. Scott to Jesus and Paul*. Semeia Studies 48. Leiden: Brill, 2004.

Horsley, Richard A., Jonathan A. Draper, and John Miles Foley, eds. *Performing the Gospel: Orality, Memory, and Mark: Essays Dedicated to Werner Kelber*. Minneapolis: Fortress, 2006.

Howard, John M. "The Significance of Minor Characters in the Gospel of John." *Bibliotheca Sacra* 163 (2006) 63–78.

Ito, Hisayasu. "Johannine Irony Demonstrated in John 9. Part I." *Neotestamentica* 34 (2000) 361–71.

———. "Johannine Irony Demonstrated in John 9. Part II." *Neotestamentica* 34 (2000) 373–87.

Jobling, David et al., eds. *The Bible and the Politics of Exegesis: Essays in Honor of Norman K. Gottwald on His Sixty-Fifth Birthday*. Cleveland: Pilgrim, 1991.

Joubert, Stefan J. "No Culture Shock? Addressing the Achilles Heel of Modern Bible Translations." *Verbum et Ecclesia* 22/2 (2001). Online: http://www.ve.org.za/index.php/VE/article/view/650.

Kalmin, Richard. "The Evil Eye in Rabbinic Literature of Late Antiquity." In *Judaea-Palaestina, Babylon and Rome: Jews in Antiquity*, edited by Benjamin Isaac and Yuval Shahar, 111–38. Texte und Studien zum antiken Judentum 147. Tübingen: Mohr Siebeck, 2012.

Keener, Craig S. *The Gospel of John: A Commentary*. Grand Rapids: Baker Academic, 2012.

Kern-Ulmer, Brigitte. "The Power of the Evil Eye and the Good Eye in Midrashic Literature." *Judaism* 40 (1991) 344–53.

Kim, Stephen S. "The Significance of Jesus' Healing the Blind Man in John 9." *Bibliotheca Sacra* 167 (2010) 307–18.

Kimelman, Reuven. "Birkat Ha-Minim and the Lack of Evidence for an Anti-Christian Jewish Prayer in Late Antiquity." In *Jewish and Christian Self-Definition*, 2:226–44. Philadelphia: Fortress, 1981.

Kittel, Gerhard, and Gerhard Friedrich, eds. *Theological Dictionary of the New Testament*. 10 vols. Logos Bible Software version 4. 2000–2010. Print ed.: Kittel, Gerhard, and Gerhard Friedrich, eds. Theological Dictionary of the New Testament. 10 vols. Translated by G. W. Bromiley. Grand Rapids: Erdmans, 1964–1976.

———, eds.*Theological Dictionary of the New Testament: Abridged in One Volume*. Translated by G. W. Bromiley. Logos Bible Software version 4. 2000–2010. Print ed.: *Theological Dictionary of the New Testament: Abridged in One Volume*. Translated by G. W. Bromiley. Grand Rapids: Eerdmans, 1985.

Kleinman, Arthur. *Patients and Healers in the Context of Culture: An Exploration of the Borderland between Anthropology, Medicine, and Psychiatry*. Comparative Studies in Health Systems and Medical Care 3. Berkeley: University of California Press, 1980.

Klingbeil, Gerald A. "Entre Individualismo y Colectivismo: Hacia Una Perspectiva Biblica de La Naturaleza de La Iglesia." In *Pensar La Iglesia Hoy*, 3–23. Libertador San Martín, Argentina: Editorial Universidad Adventista del Plata, 2002.

Klink, Edward W., III. *The Sheep of the Fold: The Audience and Origin of the Gospel of John*. Society for New Testament Studies Monograph Series 141. Cambridge: Cambridge University Press, 2007.

Köstenberger, Andreas J. *The Missions of Jesus and the Disciples according to the Fourth Gospel: With Implications for the Fourth Gospel's Purpose and the Mission of the Contemporary Church*. Grand Rapids: Eerdmans, 1998.

Kruse, Colin G. *The Gospel according to John: An Introduction and Commentary*. Tyndale New Testament Commentaries 4. Downers Grove, IL: Intervarsity, 2008.

Kysar, Robert. "The Whence and Whither of the Johannine Community." In *Life in Abundance: Studies of John's Gospel in Tribute to Raymond E. Brown, S.S.*, edited by John R. Donahue, 65–81. Collegeville, MN: Liturgical, 2005.

Langbrandtner, Wolfgang. *Weltferner Gott oder Gott der Liebe: Der Ketzerstreit in der johanneischen Kirche: Eine exegetisch-religionsgeschichtliche Untersuchung mit Berücksichtigung der koptisch-gnostischen Texte aus Nag-Hammadi*. Beiträge zur biblischen Exegese und Theologie 6. Frankfurt: Lang, 1977.

Lawrence, Louise Joy. "Structure, Agency and Ideology: A Response to Zeba Crook." *Journal for the Study of the New Testament* 29 (2007) 277–86.

Lee, Margaret Ellen, and Bernard Brandon Scott. *Sound Mapping the New Testament*. Salem, OR: Polebridge, 2009.

Lewis, Karoline M. *Rereading the Shepherd Discourse: Restoring the Integrity of John 9:39—10:21*. Studies in Biblical Literature 113. New York: Lang, 2008.

Liddell, H. G., and R. Scott. *A Lexicon: Abridged from Liddell and Scott's Greek-English Lexicon*. Logos Bible Software version 4. 2000–2010. Print ed.: H. G. Liddell, R. Scott. *An Intermediate Greek-English Lexicon*. Oxford: Clarendon, 1889.

Liddell, H. G., R. Scott, H. S. Jones. *A Greek-English Lexicon*. Oxford: Clarendon, 1940. Online: http://www.perseus.tufts.edu/hopper/text?doc=Perseus:text:1999.04.0057.

Lieu, Judith. "Blindness in the Johannine Tradition." *New Testament Studies* 34 (1988) 83–95.

Lilly, Joseph L. "Eucharistic Discourse of John 6." *Catholic Biblical Quarterly* 12 (1950) 48–51.

Lincoln, Andrew T. "The Fourth Gospel under Modern and Postmodern Interrogation." *Reading the Gospels Today*, edited by Stanley E. Porter, 127–49. Grand Rapids: Eerdmans, 2004.

———. *The Gospel According to Saint John*. Black's New Testament Commentaries 4. Peabody, MA: Hendrickson, 2005.

———. "Trials, Plots and the Narrative of the Fourth Gospel." *Journal for the Study of the New Testament* 56 (1994) 3–30.

———. *Truth on Trial: The Lawsuit Motif in the Fourth Gospel*. Peabody, MA: Hendrickson, 2000.

Ling, Timothy J. M. *The Judean Poor and the Fourth Gospel*. Society for New Testament Studies Monograph Series 136. Cambridge: Cambridge University Press, 2006.

Louw, J. P., and Eugene A. Nida, eds. *Greek-English Lexicon of the New Testament: Based on Semantic Domains*. 1st ed. Logos Bible Software version 4. 2000–2010. Print ed.: Louw, J. P. and Eugene A. Nida, ed. *Greek-English Lexicon of the New Testament Based on Semantic Domains*. New York: United Bible Societies, 1988.

Malatesta, Edward. *Interiority and Covenant: A Study of Einai En and Menein En in the First Letter of Saint John*. Analecta biblica 69. Rome: Biblical Institute Press, 1978.

Malina, Bruce J. "John's: The Maverick Christian Group: The Evidence of Sociolinguistics." *Biblical Theology Bulletin* 24 (1994) 167–82.

———. "The Individual and the Community: Personality in the Social World of Early Christianity." *Biblical Theology Bulletin* 9 (1979) 126–38.

———. *The New Testament World: Insights from Cultural Anthropology*. 3rd ed. Louisville: Westminster John Knox Press, 2001.

Malina, Bruce J., and Jerome H. Neyrey. *Portraits of Paul: An Archaeology of Ancient Personality*. Louisville: Westminster John Knox, 1996.

Malina, Bruce J., and Jerome H. Neyrey. "First-Century Personality: Dyadic, Not Individualistic." In *The Social World of Luke-Acts: Models for Interpretation*, edited by Jerome H. Neyrey, 67–96. Peabody, MA: Hendrickson, 1991.

Malina, Bruce J., and Richard L. Rohrbaugh. *Social-Science Commentary on the Gospel of John*. Minneapolis: Fortress, 1998.

———. *Social-Science Commentary on the Synoptic Gospels*. 2nd ed. Minneapolis: Fortress, 2003.

Maloney, Clarence, ed. *The Evil Eye*. New York: Columbia University Press, 1976.

Marguerat, Daniel, Yvan Bourquin, and Marcel Durrer. *How to Read Bible Stories: An Introduction to Narrative Criticism*. London: SCM, 1999.

Martyn, J. Louis. *History & Theology in the Fourth Gospel*. 2nd ed. Nashville: Abingdon, 1979.

———. *History and Theology in the Fourth Gospel*. 3rd ed. New Testament Library. Louisville: Westminster John Knox, 2003.

McAllister, Ray. "Theology of Blindness in the Hebrew Scriptures." PhD diss., Andrews University, Seventh-day Adventist Theological Seminary, 2010.

McCready, Wayne O. "Johannine Self-Understanding and the Synagogue Episode of John 9." In *Self-Definition and Self-Discovery in Early Christianity: A Study in Changing Horizons: Essays in Appreciation of Ben F. Meyer from Former Students*, edited by David J. Hawkin and Tom Robinson, 147–66. Lewiston, NY: Mellen, 1990.

Meeks, Wayne A. "Breaking Away: Three New Testament Pictures of Christianity's Separation from the Jewish Communities." In *To See Ourselves as Others See Us: Christians, Jews, "Others" in Late Antiquity*, edited by Jacob Neusner and Ernest S. Frerichs, 93–115. Scholars Press Studies in the Humanities Series. Chico, CA: Scholars, 1985.

———. "The Man from Heaven in Johannine Sectarianism." *Journal of Biblical Literature* 91 (1972) 44–72.

Metzger, Bruce M. *A Textual Commentary on the Greek New Testament*. Stuttgart: Deutsche Biblegesellschaft, 2002.

Michaels, J. Ramsey. *The Gospel of John*. New International Commentary on the New Testament. Grand Rapids: Eerdmans, 2010.

Moloney, Francis J. *Belief in the Word: Reading the Fourth Gospel, John 1–4*. Minneapolis: Fortress, 1993.

———. *Glory Not Dishonor: Reading John 13–21*. Minneapolis: Fortress, 1998.

———. *The Gospel of John*. Sacra Pagina 4. Collegeville, MN: Liturgical, 1998.

———. *The Gospel Of John: Text and Context*. Boston: Brill, 2005.

———. *The Johannine Son of Man*. Biblioteca di scienze religiose 14. Roma: LAS, 1976.

———. *Love in the Gospel of John: An Exegetical, Theological, and Literary Study*. Grand Rapids: Baker Academic, 2013.

———. *Signs and Shadows: Reading John 5–12*. Minneapolis: Fortress, 1996.

Moss, Candida R. "Blurred Vision and Ethical Confusion: The Rhetorical Function of Matthew 6:22–23." *Catholic Biblical Quarterly* 73 (2011) 757–76.

Moss, Candida R., and Jeffrey Stackert. "The Devastation of Darkness: Disability in Exodus 10:21–23, 27, and Intensification in the Plagues." *Journal of Religion* 92 (2012) 362–72.

Myers, Alicia D. *Characterizing Jesus: A Rhetorical Analysis on the Fourth Gospel's Use of Scripture in Its Presentation of Jesus*. Library of New Testament Studies 458. London: T. & T. Clark, 2012.

Nelson, Richard D. *Raising up a Faithful Priest: Community and Priesthood in Biblical Theology*. Louisville: Westminster John Knox, 1993.

Nestle, Eberhard, Erwin Nestle, Barbara Aland, and Kurt Aland. *Novum Testamentum Graece*. 27th ed. Stuttgart: Deutsche Bibelgesellschaft, 2007.

Neufeld, Dietmar, ed. *The Social Sciences and Biblical Translation*. SBL Symposium Series 41. Atlanta: Society of Biblical Literature, 2008.

Neyrey, Jerome H. *The Gospel of John*. New Cambridge Bible Commentary. New York: Cambridge University Press, 2007.

———. *The Gospel of John in Cultural and Rhetorical Perspective*. Grand Rapids: Eerdmans, 2009.

———. "The Idea of Purity in Mark's Gospel." *Semeia* 35 (1986) 91–128.

———. *An Ideology of Revolt: John's Christology in Social-Science Perspective*. 1988. Reprinted, Eugene, OR: Wipf & Stock, 2007.

Nuño, Antón Alvar. "Ocular Pathologies and the Evil Eye in the Early Roman Principate." *Numen* 59 (2012) 295–321.

O'Brien, Kelli S. "Written That You May Believe: John 20 and Narrative Rhetoric." *Catholic Biblical Quarterly* 67 (2005) 284–302.

O'Day, Gail R. *Revelation in the Fourth Gospel: Narrative Mode and Theological Claim*. Philadelphia: Fortress, 1986.

———. "The Gospel of John." In *The New Interpreter's Bible, Luke–John*, edited by Leander E. Keck, 9:491–865. Nashville: Abingdon, 1996.

Olyan, Saul M. "'Anyone Blind or Lame Shall Not Enter the House': On the Interpretation of Second Samuel 5:8b." *Catholic Biblical Quarterly* 60 (1998) 218–27.

Opatrny, Dominik. "The Figure of a Blind Man in the Light of the Papyrological Evidence." *Biblica* 91 (2010) 583–94.

Osiek, Carolyn, and David L Balch. *Families in the New Testament World: Households and House Churches*. The Family, Religion, and Culture. Louisville: Westminster John Knox, 1997.

Ousby, Ian. *The Cambridge Guide to Literature in English*. New ed. Cambridge: Cambridge University Press, 1993.

Owen, Paul, and David Shepherd. "Speaking up for Qumran, Dalman and the Son of Man: Was *Bar Enasha* a Common Term for 'Man' in the Time of Jesus?" *Journal for the Study of the New Testament* 81 (2001) 81–122.

Oxford University Press. *The Holy Bible: Containing the Old and New Testaments with the Apocryphal/Deuterocanonical Books: New Revised Standard Version*. New York: Oxford University Press, 1989.

Painter, John, R. Alan Culpepper, and Fernando F. Segovia. *Word, Theology, and Community in John*. St. Louis: Chalice, 2002.

Partington, Alan. *The Linguistics of Laughter: A Corpus-Assisted Study of Laughter-Talk*. Routledge Studies in Linguistics 5. London: Routledge, 2006.

Perkins, Pheme. "Crisis in Jerusalem: Narrative Criticism in New Testament Studies." *Theological Studies* 50 (1989) 296–313.

Petersen, Norman R. *The Gospel of John and the Sociology of Light: Language and Characterization in the Fourth Gospel*. 1993. Reprinted, Eugene, OR: Wipf & Stock, 2008.

Philo of Alexandria. *The Works of Philo: Complete and Unabridged.* Translated by C. D. Yonge. Peabody, MA: Hendrickson, 1995.
Pilch, John J. "Biblical Leprosy and Body Symbolism." *Biblical Theology Bulletin* 11 (1981) 108–13.
———. "Blindness." In *NIBD* 1:477–81.
———. *The Cultural Dictionary of the Bible.* Collegeville, MN: Liturgical, 1999.
———. "Healing in Mark: A Social Science Analysis." *Biblical Theology Bulletin* 15 (1985) 142–50.
———. *Healing in the New Testament: Insights from Medical and Mediterranean Anthropology.* Minneapolis: Fortress, 2000.
———. "Improving Bible Translations: The Example of Sickness and Healing." *Biblical Theology Bulletin* 30 (2000) 129–34.
———. "Understanding Healing in the Social World of Early Christianity." *Biblical Theology Bulletin* 22 (1992) 26–33.
Pilch, John J., and Bruce J. Malina, eds. *Biblical Social Values and Their Meaning: A Handbook.* Peabody, MA: Hendrickson, 1993.
Plato, *Timaeus.*
Plutarch. *Plutarch's Morals.* Translated by William Watson Goodwin. Medford, MA: Little, Brown, 1874.
Plutarch. *Moralia.* Translation by Frank Cole Babbitt. Loeb Classical Library. Cambridge. Harvard University Press, 1927.
Porter, Stanley E. "Prominence: An Overview." In *Linguist as Pedagogue*, 45–74. Sheffield: Sheffield Phoenix, 2009.
Porter, Stanley E., and Matthew Brook O'Donnell, eds. *The Linguist as Pedagogue: Trends in the Teaching and Linguistic Analysis of the Greek New Testament.* New Testament Monographs 11. Sheffield: Sheffield Phoenix, 2009.
Powell, Mark Allan. *What Is Narrative Criticism?* Guides to Biblical Scholarship. Minneapolis: Fortress, 1990.
Quintilian. *With an English Translation.* Harold Edgeworth Butler. Cambridge: Harvard University Press, 1920.
Reinhartz, Adele. "'And the Word Was Begotten': Divine Epigenesis in the Gospel of John." *Semeia* 85 (1999) 83–103.
———. "Jesus as Prophet: Predictive Prolepses in the Fourth Gospel." *Journal for the Study of the New Testament* 36 (1989) 3–16.
Resseguie, James L. *Narrative Criticism of the New Testament: An Introduction.* Grand Rapids: Baker Academic, 2005.
Reynolds, Benjamin E. *The Apocalyptic Son of Man in the Gospel of John.* Wissenschaftliche Untersuchungen zum Neuen Testament 249. Tübingen: Mohr Siebeck, 2008.
———. "The Use of the Son of Man Idiom in the Gospel of John." In *"Who Is This Son of Man?: The Latest Scholarship on a Puzzling Expression of the Historical Jesus,"* edited by Larry W. Hurtado and Paul L. Owen, 101–29. Library of New Testament Studies 390. London: T. & T. Clark, 2011.
Rhoads, David M,. "Performance Criticism: An Emerging Methodology in Second Testament Studies—Part I." *Biblical Theology Bulletin* 36 (2006) 118–33.
———. "Performance Criticism: An Emerging Methodology in Second Testament Studies–Part II." *Biblical Theology Bulletin* 36 (2006) 164–84.
———. *Reading Mark: Engaging the Gospel.* Minneapolis: Fortress, 2004.

Rhoads, David M., and Kari Syreeni. *Characterization in the Gospels: Reconceiving Narrative Criticism*. Journal for the Study of the New Testament Supplements 184. Sheffield: Sheffield Academic, 1999.

Rhoads, David M., Joanna Dewey, and Donald Michie. *Mark as Story: An Introduction to the Narrative of a Gospel*. 2nd ed. Minneapolis: Fortress, 1999.

Richter, Georg. "Präsentische und Futurische Eschatologie im 4ten Evangelium." Pages In *Gegenwart und Kommendes Reich: Schülergabe Anton Vögtle zum 65. Geburtstag*, edited by Peter Fiedler and Dieter Zeller, 117–52. Stuttgarter biblische Beiträge. Stuttgart: Katholisches Bibelwerk, 1975.

Ricœur, Paul. *Time and Narrative*. 3 vols. Chicago: University of Chicago Press, 1984, 1986, 1988.

Rohrbaugh, Richard L. "The Gospel of John in the Twenty-First Century." In *What Is John? II, Literary and Social Readings of the Fourth Gospel*, edited by Fernando F. Segovia, 257–63. SBL Symposium Series 7. Atlanta: Scholars, 1998.

Russell, Walter. *Intertestamental and New Testament Periods from a Missiological Perspective*. La Mirada, CA: Talbot School of Theology.

Russell, Walter B. "Getting Fitted with Mediterranean Glasses" (n.d.). Cited 31 March 2014. Online: http://www.wciu.edu/docs/resources/course5_readerGC2_C5F.pdf.

Sakenfeld, Katharine Doob, ed. *The New Interpreter's Dictionary of the Bible*. 5 vols. Nashville: Abingdon, 2006–2009.

Schipper, Jeremy. "Reconsidering the Imagery of Disability in 2 Samuel 5:8b." *Catholic Biblical Quarterly* 67 (2005) 422–34.

Schneiders, Sandra Marie. *Written That You May Believe: Encountering Jesus in the Fourth Gospel*. New York: Crossroad, 1999.

Scott, James C. *Domination and the Arts of Resistance: Hidden Transcripts*. New Haven: Yale University Press, 1990.

———. *Weapons of the Weak: Everyday Forms of Peasant Resistance*. New Haven: Yale University Press, 1985.

Seybold, Klaus, and Ulrich B Müller. *Sickness and Healing*. Translated by Douglas W. Stott. Biblical Encounter Series. Nashville: Abingdon, 1981.

Shiner, Whitney Taylor. *Proclaiming the Gospel: First-Century Performance of Mark*. Harrisburg, PA: Trinity, 2003.

Simundson, Daniel J. "Health and Healing in the Bible." *Word & World* 2, no. 4 (1982) 330–39.

Skinner, Christopher W., Kelly R. Iverson, and Frank J. Matera, eds. *Unity and Diversity in the Gospels and Paul: Essays in Honor of Frank J. Matera*. Early Christianity and its literature number 7. Atlanta: Society of Biblical Literature, 2012.

Smith, David. "Jesus and the Pharisees in Socio-Anthropological Perspective." *Trinity Journal* 6.2 (1985) 151–56.

Smyth, Herbert Weir. *Greek Grammar*. Rev. ed. Cambridge: Harvard University Press, 1956. Online: http://www.perseus.tufts.edu/hopper/text?doc=Perseus:text:1999.04.0007.

Snyman, A. H. "Hebrews 6:4–6: from a Semiotic Discourse Perspective." In *Discourse Analysis and the New Testament*, 354–68. Sheffield: Sheffield Academic, 1999.

Sophocles. *The Oedipus at Colonus of Sophocles*. Edited With Introduction and Notes by Sir Richard Jebb. Edited by Sir Richard Jebb. Medford, MA: Cambridge University Press, 1889.

Staley, Jeffrey Lloyd. *The Print's First Kiss: A Rhetorical Investigation of The Implied Reader in the Fourth Gospel*. SBL Dissertation Series 82. Atlanta: Scholars, 1988.

———. "Stumbling In The Dark, Reaching for the Light: Reading Character in John 5 and 9." *Semeia* 53 (1991) 55–80.

Steegen, Martijn. "To Worship the Johannine 'Son of Man': John 9,38 as Refocusing on the Father." *Biblica* 91 (2010) 534–54.

Stibbe, Mark W. G. *The Gospel of John as Literature: An Anthology of Twentieth-Century Perspectives*. New Testament Tools and Studies 17. Leiden: Brill, 1993.

———. *John*. Readings. Sheffield: JSOT Press, 1993.

———. *John as Storyteller: Narrative Criticism and the Fourth Gospel*. Society for New Testament Studies Monograph Series 73. Cambridge: Cambridge University Press, 1992.

———. *John's Gospel*. New York: Routledge, 1994.

Streeter, Burnett Hillman. *The Four Gospels: A Study of Origins*. New York: Macmillan, 1925.

Tacitus, Cornelius. *The Complete Works of Tacitus*. Translated by Alfred John Church, William Jackson Brodribb, and Moses Hadas. New York: Modern Library, 1942.

———. *Complete Works of Tacitus*. Alfred John Church. William Jackson Brodribb. Sara Bryant. New York: Random House, 1873, reprinted 1942. Edited for Perseus.

Thatcher, Tom, and Catrin H Williams, eds. *Engaging with C. H. Dodd on the Gospel of John: Sixty Years of Tradition and Interpretation*. New York: Cambridge University Press, 2013.

———. *Greater than Caesar: Christology and Empire in the Fourth Gospel*. Minneapolis: Fortress, 2009.

———. "The Sabbath Trick: Unstable Irony in the Fourth Gospel." *Journal for the Study of the New Testament* 76 (1999) 53–77.

Thatcher, Tom, and Stephen D Moore. *Anatomies of Narrative Criticism: The Past, Present, and Futures of the Fourth Gospel as Literature*. SBL Resources for Biblical Study 55. Atlanta: Society of Biblical Literature, 2008.

Thompson, Marianne Meye. "'God's Voice You Have Never Heard, God's Form You Have Never Seen': The Characterization of God in the Gospel of John." *Semeia* 63 (1993) 177–204.

Thomsen, Marie Louise. "The Evil Eye in Mesopotamia." *Journal of Near Eastern Studies* 51 (1992) 19–32.

Van der Watt, Jan G. *Family of the King: Dynamics of Metaphor in the Gospel according to John*. Biblical Interpretation Series 47. Leiden: Brill, 2000.

Verbrugge, Verlyn D. *New International Dictionary of New Testament Theology*. Pradis version 6.01. Zondervan, 2002. No pages. Online: Print Ed: Verbrugge, Verlyn D. *New International Dictionary of New Testament Theology: Abridged Edition*. Grand Rapids: Zondervan, 2000.

Voelz, J. W. "The Discourse on the Bread of Life in John 6: Is It Eucharistic?" *Concordia Journal* 15 (1989) 29–37.

Von Wahlde, Urban C. *The Gospel and Letters of John*. Eerdmans Critical Commentary. Grand Rapids: Eerdmans, 2010.

———. "The Johannine 'Jews': A Critical Survey." *New Testament Studies* 28 (1982) 33–60.

Walker, William O. "John 1:43–51 and 'The Son of Man' in the Fourth Gospel." *Journal for the Study of the New Testament* 56 (1994) 31–42.

Wazana, Nili. "A Case of the Evil Eye: Qohelet 4:4–8." *Journal of Biblical Literature* 126 (2007) 685–702.

Wead, David W. *The Literary Devices in John's Gospel*. Theologische Dissertationen 4. Basel: Reinhardt, 1970.

Westfall, Cynthia Long. "A Method for the Analysis of Prominence in Hellenistic Greek." In *Linguist as Pedagogue: Trends in the Teaching and Linguistic Analysis of the Greek New Testament*, edited by Stanley E. Porter and Matthew Brook O'Donnell, 75–94. New Testament Monographs 11. Sheffield: Sheffield Phoenix, 2009.

www.ingramcontent.com/pod-product-compliance
Lightning Source LLC
Chambersburg PA
CBHW070256230426
43664CB00014B/2550